The Six Day War

THE SIX DAY WAR

RANDOLPH S. CHURCHILL
AND
WINSTON S. CHURCHILL

ISBN-13: 9781782924364
ISBN-10: 1782924361

This book was organized and written by Randolph and Winston Churchill, son and grandson respectively of the late Sir Winston Churchill. Winston was in Israel (briefly also in Jordan and Lebanon) for three weeks before the war, writing articles for the *News of the World*; and he covered the week of the war for the *News of the World* and the *Evening News*. When the war ended he spent another three weeks studying the battlefields on the spot, talking to all ranks of the Israeli armed forces including all the senior commanders and meeting most of the political leaders. Randolph stayed at home following the war avidly in the press and on television; and organized the many lines of enquiry available to him at home. Thus in the main the story of the fighting has been written by the son and the father has been mainly responsible for the political and diplomatic side. But this has been very much a joint effort and both authors accept responsibility for the whole book.

It would be difficult for the authors to thank all the numerous people in various countries who helped them in their work. It is, therefore, hoped that this blanket expression of gratitude will be acceptable to the scores of military and air commanders, soldiers, journalists, diplomats and politicians who helped to make this work possible.

Contents

N
CYPRUS
SYRIA
LEBANON
Beirut
Damascus
IRAQ
MEDITERRANEAN SEA
ISRAEL
Jordan
Tel Aviv
Amman
JERUSALEM
JORDAN
Alexandria
Port Said
Suez Canal
Cairo
SINAI
EGYPT
Gulf of Suez
Sharm el Sheikh
Gulf of Aqaba
SAUDI ARABIA
Strait of Tiran
Nile
RED SEA
0 100
Miles
ARTHUR BANKS

Chapter One
The Past

According to a tradition accepted both by the Arabs and the Jews, the two peoples are sprung respectively from Ishmael and Isaac, who were both sons of Abraham. Ishmael, because his mother was an Egyptian slave, was forced to leave his father's land and became an exile in the wilderness. He was believed to be the progenitor of twelve bedouin tribes, from whom the Arab nations of today claim their descent. Ishmael's brother, Isaac, became the ancestor of the twelve tribes of the Jews, of which two were lost. Many people, including Admiral Fisher, have claimed that the British are one of the lost tribes. The rivalry of Jew and Arab is the rivalry of brothers; they both belong to the Semitic race and their languages echo each other. They both claim Palestine as their home.

Three thousand five hundred years ago, Moses led the Jewish people back from captivity in Egypt, through the wilderness of Sinai, to Canaan, where the patriarch Abraham was believed to have settled after his migration from Mesopotamia. The Jews, inspired by their warlike God, conquered and subdued the tribes who lived in Canaan; and despite every tribulation – the Babylonian captivity, the marauding of Alexander the Great, the victories of the

Roman Legions – the Jewish people remained there until 70 AD, when the destruction of Jerusalem by Titus began the *diaspora,* the dispersion of the Jews over the continents of the world. Though a small number of Jews always remained in Palestine, a new religion springing from deep in Arabia, Islam, won supremacy in the Promised Land, and held it until General Allenby's victories led to the establishment of the British mandate in 1920.

While in the desert Moses introduced a moral and ethical system which the Jews have preserved to this day and promulgated a code of laws on which Jewish civil and religious practice was to be based. When they reached the valley of the River Jordan the Jews recognized their Promised Land and after successfully defeating the Egyptian garrison at Jericho settled and defended themselves against the attacks of neighbouring tribes.

Beset by enemies, struggling to build up an agricultural community in a land not entirely 'flowing with milk and honey', and falling for a while into the terrors of civil war, the twelve tribes of Israel lived in Palestine for a thousand years, until over-run by the Babylonians and taken captive to Babylon. But the first exile lasted only fifty years and in 538 BC the first of forty thousand Jews returned to Jerusalem, rebuilt the Temple and set up a second Jewish commonwealth. For five hundred years they remained the rulers of Palestine until in 63 B C the Roman forces led by Pompey entered the Holy of Holies in Jerusalem and brought Palestine under their rule as a Roman tributary. The Jews remained in their Promised Land, bound in a tight religious and social community but no longer masters of their political destiny.

In 70 A D the Jews revolted against the Romans but in vain. The Roman forces sacked Jerusalem and burnt the

Temple. Masada, the last stronghold of the heroic Jews, was captured three years later. The sacrifice of Masada is one of the most sacred stories of Jewish resistance in their long history. When the commander realized that the capitulation of the stronghold was inevitable he urged his comrades to kill themselves rather than fall into captivity. Each man slew his wife and children and ten men were chosen by lot to kill the rest. One man then slew the remaining nine and fell upon his sword. When the garrison was stormed, only two old women and five children, who had hidden themselves in caves, remained alive. Jewish independence was at an end and in the Roman Forum a commemorative arch depicted the Jewish captives and the Temple spoils. Sixty years later the desperate revolt of Barkochba was suppressed with Roman ruthlessness; Jerusalem was finally reduced to rubble and the harrow drawn across its former glories. In the new Roman city of Jerusalem no Jew was allowed to set foot more than once a year. The practice of Judaism was forbidden and even circumcision proscribed. Although the Jews remained in Palestine, there could be no further hope of a Jewish Kingdom.

During the period of Roman rule in Palestine Jewish settlements had spread throughout Asia Minor into Southern Spain, the Rhône Valley, Italy and Greece, and there were also settlements along the Red Sea coast and in Persia. With the close of the dark ages and the moving of the centres of European civilization northwards, the Jews followed, settling throughout Europe and in particular in Russia, Germany and England. Despite the continued existence of Jewish settlements throughout the East, the Jews ceased to be Orientals and became Europeans. The majority of the Jews were scattered in exile throughout the Roman Empire and Christianity became the dominant religious faith of the West. Everywhere in Europe and Asia the Jews were isolated, both in religious and social customs. They resisted assimilation, and by means of a devoted and at times rigid adherence to the law of Moses preserved their identity as a people. It was the Book that they treasured which prevented their assimilation and guaranteed their survival. It was in Europe that they made their greatest contribution to the advance of civilization. It was in medieval Europe that they developed their laws and literature, elaborated on their religious customs and intensified their social life; it was in Europe that they played the role of money-lenders forbidden to Christians; and it was in Europe that they absorbed and added to the intellectual achievements of those with whom they settled, while preserving their religious framework and national and racial identity.

Meanwhile in the East a new religion had been born. Islam (the word itself means submission to the will of God) is based on the teachings of the prophet Mohammed who was born in Mecca in 570 A D. It is a religion of conquest which led to the unification of the Near East and bound together the Arabs and their subject peoples in a common culture. In the year 632 Mohammed died. During the next century the creed of Islam swept from Mecca to the west and was not halted until Charles Martel defeated Abdul Rahman at the battle of Tours in 732, exactly one hundred years later.

Jerusalem, which had long been the focal point both of Christianity and of Judaism, became a centre of major importance for the Muslims as well. In the Middle Ages in particular, a time of great religious fervency, the word Jerusalem assumed a deep significance to the followers of all three religions. For more than two hundred years the crusaders tried to regain Jerusalem for Christianity and in the same period it became for the Arabs a symbol of resistance to intrusion from the West. For the Jews it remained a city to which they hoped one day to return.

The history of European Jewry from the year 1000 to 1900 is one of continual violence, humiliation, and segregation into ghettoes. First the crusaders in their zeal to spread Christianity, and then the Inquisition in its desire to chastise the heathen, kept alight the flames of intolerance and murder. The 17th Earl of Derby once asked the British historian Namier why it was that, although he was a Jew, he wrote about British history and not about Jewish history. Namier replied: 'Derby! There is no Jewish history, only a Jewish martyrology, and that is not amusing enough for me.' Yet the story of the dispersion was not entirely black. Jews played an important role in many countries in art, literature, science and medicine. They found havens such as England, at the time of Cromwell and after, where, there was no religious persecution. Indeed the early nineteenth century seemed to find the Jew emancipated in all Europe except Russia, and eminent Jews respected and honoured by the non-Jewish communities with which they were now so closely linked. Total assimilation was not unknown, as religious practice declined, and the division between Jew and non-Jew became less marked. With the establishment of religious liberty and the disappearance of specific barriers to Jewish participation in national life, emancipation appeared complete and the Holy Land a distant memory from an oriental, almost alien, past.

In the early 1870s the spirit of medieval intolerance returned. In Germany lews were accused of dominating the national life and of being aliens. In 1881 an 'Anti-Semitic League' asked Bismarck to disfranchise the Jews and to bar their further immigration into Germany. In 1882 an

Anti-Semitic Congress was held in Dresden. When, in 1894, the French officer Alfred Dreyfus was accused of selling military secrets to Germany, anti-Semitism broke out in France. In Russia pogroms against the Jews increased in intensity during the 1890s, when the Jews were deported from Moscow and Kiev and refused the right to resettle in these cities. The only Jewish women allowed to live in Moscow were those who held the 'yellow ticket of prostitution'.

The revival of persecution towards the end of the nineteenth century led to a new development in Jewish thought. In 1882 a Jewish physician from Odessa published a brochure in which he asserted that the Jews were deluding themselves if they thought they could ever identify with the people amongst whom they lived. He suggested that the only way to restore their dignity was to re-create the Palestine national home. A few Russian Jews actually went to the Holy Land, then under Turkish rule, and formed small agricultural colonies which were given financial aid by the Paris banker, Baron Edmund de Rothschild. In 1894, a Viennese Jewish writer, Theodor Herzl, attended Dreyfus' court martial as a correspondent of *Neue Freie Presse*, the Viennese newspaper. He had been a staunch protagonist of assimilation; but the Dreyfus case convinced Herzl and many other European Jews of the need for a permanent national home in Palestine. Under Herzl the first Zionist conference was held in Basle in 1897 and defined as its object 'the securing for the Jewish people of a home in Palestine guided by public law'. Many Jews were hostile to Zionism. They feared that it would draw undue attention to them as a group and in turn encourage anti-Semitism. But it held powerful attraction to an increasingly harassed and isolated people. The British Government was impressed by Herzl and offered him a tract of land in Sinai. But when difficulties arose

Joseph Chamberlain, the Colonial Secretary, proposed instead some territory in Uganda. Herzl decided that they could never arouse national enthusiasm in an area outside Palestine, the Holy Land, and declined the offer. He died, aged forty-four, in 1904 but the Zionist movement flourished and the Jewish National Fund began collecting money to purchase small pieces of land in Palestine. By 1914 this Turkish territory was dotted with Jewish agricultural settlements and the first kibbutz was established at Deganiah in 1909. The Jews even founded a new town, Tel Aviv, or 'hill of spring', in the sandhills near the Arab town of Jaffa, and by 1914 a Jewish centre of arts and crafts was established in Jerusalem.

⚜ ⚜ ⚜

Before the outbreak of the First World War the idea of a Jewish National Home in Palestine was a dream of idealists and a fond child of philanthropists and the persecuted. But the War turned it into a political issue capable of realization.

During the second half of the nineteenth century as the Turkish empire crumbled and the European powers stumbled over each other in a scramble for territory in Africa, British statesmen had found themselves increasingly involved in the affairs of Egypt. It was the christianized Jewish Prime Minister, Benjamin Disraeli, who purchased the controlling shares in the Suez Canal in 1875. Henceforth the Canal region was to be a vital British strategic and economic interest.

In its chequered past Egypt had been for almost nine hundred years (640–1517) under the rule of Arabs, first as part of the Caliphate, and later under its own Sultans. In 1517 this uncongenial land, mostly desert and administered from an enervating but fertile delta which afforded the sole wealth, was conquered by the Ottoman Turks. It remained a province of Constantinople until, in the nineteenth century, Mohamed Ali and his successors won for Cairo a growing measure of autonomy, recognized by the Turks in 1867 when the title of Khedive was formally granted to the Governor, Ismail.

When the Turks proved incapable of supporting the Cairo administration, as it declined into prodigality and bankruptcy, so Britain was drawn in, at first as a protecting power operating under Turkish licence.

In 1882, as a result of Arabi Pasha's rebellion against the Khedive, Mr Gladstone intervened in order to protect the rights of the foreign bond-holders. The Royal Navy bombarded Alexandria and started an occupation of Egypt which was to last until 1954. Mr Gladstone's behaviour called forth one of the liveliest of Lord Randolph Churchill's attacks upon the Liberal leader. Speaking in Edinburgh in December 1883 he said:

> The other day the poor Egyptians were very near effecting a successful revolution; they were very near throwing off their suffocating bonds; but, unfortunately for us, Mr Gladstone, the Prime Minister of Great Britain – Mr Gladstone, the leader, the idol, the demigod of the Liberal party – Mr Gladstone, the member for Midlothian, came upon them with his armies and his fleets, destroyed their towns, devastated their country, slaughtered their thousands, and flung back these struggling wretches into the morass of oppression, back into the toils of their taskmasters.

In fact, Gladstone had intervened reluctantly, intending to withdraw as soon as possible. But forty years later, when another Liberal government was confronted with a European war crisis, the British remained in Egypt.

When, at the end of October 1914, the Cabinet met to consider not only powerful Turkish hostility to Britain but actual war, it was Lloyd George, the Chancellor of the Exchequer, who urged his colleagues to consider 'the ultimate destiny of Palestine' and Herbert Samuel, the only Jewish Cabinet Minister, immediately approached Sir Edward Grey, the Foreign Secretary, for 'a possible formation of a Jewish State in Palestine which, because of its proximity to the Suez Canal would render its goodwill a matter of importance to the British Empire'. But the first immediate British reaction was in Egypt, over which the British Protectorate was declared on 18 December 1914. Henceforth Britain was to rule even more directly in Egypt than before, and thereby provoke Egyptian national aspirations to the full.

The Jews were not slow in seeing where their advantage lay. By the end of 1915 Jewish refugees who had fled from the Turks in Palestine to the British in Egypt formed a Zion Mule Corps and 650 of its members fought with the British at the Dardanelles. In March 1916 Sir Edward Grey took the initiative in approaching the French and Russian Governments about the possibility of offering the Jews 'an arrangement in regard to Palestine'. The British Government began its discussion with Chaim Weizmann and other Jewish leaders. Weizmann, in succession to Herzl, was becoming the torch-bearer of the Zionist cause. But in the same month the British sought an agreement with France about the Near East. This was the famous Sykes-Picot Agreement, which provided for the ultimate independence of an Arab Federation and sought for it an entirely Arab settlement. Britain was to receive a small enclave which included Haifa. Palestine was to have an international administration 'the form of which is to be decided upon after consultations with Russia'. To gain support in their fight against the Central Powers (the German and Austro-Hungarian empires), Britain sought to arouse World Jewry, and in particular Russian and American Jewry. In the pursuit of the latter, the 'Balfour Declaration' had been drawn up and was made public on 7 November 1917.

It took the form of a letter from the Foreign Secretary to Lord Rothschild :

> I have much pleasure in conveying to you, on behalf of His Majesty's Government, the following declaration of sympathy with Jewish Zionist aspirations which has been submitted to, and approved by, the Cabinet:—'His Majesty's Government view with favour the establishment in Palestine of a national home for the Jewish people, and will use their best endeavours to facilitate the achievement of this object, it being clearly understood that nothing shall be done which may prejudice the civil and religious rights of existing non-Jewish communities in Palestine, or the rights and political status enjoyed by Jews in any other country.' I should be grateful if you would bring this declaration to the knowledge of the Zionist Federation.

The rider safeguarding the rights of other communities was to cause much misunderstanding and difficulty. Hence the cry that Palestine was a 'twice-promised' land. Of course different things were promised to different people through different channels and at different times. All the goodwill in the world could not reconcile these promises. And there was to be very little goodwill. Meanwhile, the Arabists of the British Army and the Foreign Office, which latter group of men never fully reconciled themselves to the Balfour Declaration, were encouraging T. E. Lawrence in the military and political work which he contributed to the Arab revolt. And, of course, it was easier for the Arabs to help their race than it was for the Jews; the Jewish population at that time was negligible. But their propaganda served greatly to influence the policy of President Woodrow Wilson.

Many rich Jews still failed to respond to the cause of Zionism. The English Rothschilds did not join the cause until after the rise of Hitler. And, in America, Mr Bernard Baruch was opposed to Zionism all his life. Right up to the time when the state of Israel was proclaimed, he opposed Zionism, saying that when there was a Jewish state they would say to him: 'Baruch, you go there.' 'But,' he said, 'I'm an American first and I want to stay here in these United States.'

After the war the British sought to implement the Balfour Declaration. At the San Remo Conference in April 1920 the Palestine Mandate was awarded to the British Government. Strange though it seems Balfour himself commented without enthusiasm, 'I should prefer somewhere else', and Lord Robert Cecil described the mandate as 'no great catch'. But the greatest hostility came from the Arabs and the first of a series of almost annual anti-Jewish riots took place in Jaffa in 1921. Nor was the British rule in Egypt any more serene. Although in 1922 it became 'an independent sovereign state', the British influence was still paramount in matters of foreign policy and imperial communications, with the result that Egyptian nationalism continued to grow under Zaglul Pasha. In 1924 Egyptian nationalists murdered the British Governor General in the Sudan, Sir Lee Stack, in a main street in Cairo.

⚜ ⚜ ⚜

When Haz Amin el-Husseini was appointed Mufti (Muslim High Priest) of Jerusalem in 1921 the British Government and the Jews had to contend with a formidable opponent. The new Mufti turned his energies to anti-Zionist agitation and to sabotaging the policy of the Mandate. His argument was that the Jews were attemping to take away Palestine and the Holy Places from the Arabs and that the creation of the British Mandate was the first move in implementing the scheme. He was believed to be behind the riots that erupted annually from 1921 onwards and in March 1933 he supported the Arab Executive Committee's Manifesto protesting against Jewish immigration and the Jewish purchase of land. Later, in April 1936, he headed the Arab movement which proclaimed a general strike throughout the country and formulated three demands. These were the stoppage of Jewish immigration, the prohibition of the sale of land to Jews and the creation of a 'National Representative Government', When these demands were rejected by the Government he led a campaign of terrorism which included not only the destruction of Jewish life, but also an organized revolt against the Government. It was officially admitted that the terrorists were not only assisted by mercenaries from over the border (especially from Iraq and Syria) but also by funds and arms from foreign countries. The two countries primarily implicated, though not mentioned at the time, were Nazi Germany and Fascist Italy. In June 1937 the campaign of terrorism became so effective that the Palestine Government was at last impelled, as it announced officially on 1 October 1937, to 'institute action against certain persons whose activities have been prejudicial to the maintenance of public security in Palestine, and who must thus be regarded as morally responsible for these events'. The Mufti of Jerusalem was deprived of his office as President of the Supreme Moslem Council and a fortnight later he escaped in disguise to Beirut.

After the war, attempts were made by Jews and many Englishmen to get the Grand Mufti tried as a war criminal. These attempts, however, failed and the Mufti withdrew to Egypt where he was officially received by King Farouk and given a palace. He now lives in the Lebanon and is still politically active. He styles himself 'Chairman of the Arab Higher Committee' – one of the positions he was deprived of in 1937 – and recently he went over to meet King Hussein and even succeeded in getting a number of his supporters elected to the Jordanian Parliament.

The pressure of Jewish immigration into Palestine grew in 1924 when the United States immigration laws closed the previously unrestricted 'melting pot' of America to all but a limited number of nationals from all groups and countries on a quota system. Within five years, in 1929, 'A Jewish Agency for Palestine' was set up which represented World Jewry in its relations with the British Mandate. Thus a quota came to be established against the Jews no less in the United States than in Palestine. The Jews assumed that as their numbers increased in Palestine they would come to form a majority over the Arabs already living there, and that in due course the mandate would be given up and the Government transferred to the Jewish majority. In 1930 the British Government, influenced by the riots which had gone on since 1924, told the Permanent Mandates Commission of the League of Nations that it considered self-government impossible for Palestine as Jewish and Arab interests could never be sufficiently reconciled to enable a working Government to be set up. In 1936 following the outbreak of a third Arab rebellion the Peel Commission was set up and recommended as a solution to the problem of Arab and Jewish hostility the partition of Palestine into two separate states.

From 1933 the pressure of Jewish immigration into Palestine rose sharply. As a result of Hitler's persecution of the Jews the British Government raised the quota of Jews allowed to enter Palestine. Whereas the Jews had formed only 11% of the total population in 1921 this rose by 1939 to 29%. The Arabs realized that if this rate of growth were maintained the Jews would overtake them numerically by 1962 and that indeed Palestine would thereafter be dominated politically by the Jews. It is interesting to note that during the three years of the Arab rebellion, from 1936 to 1939, some forty thousand Arabs left Palestine as refugees. They returned when peace was restored. Christopher Sykes, son of Sir Frederick Sykes of the Sykes-Picot Agreement, has commented on this exodus of the Arabs in *Crossroads to Israel* (London: 1965): 'To flee the wrath to come is an Arab way. In the chaotic conditions of the failing administration the numbers of those who now went was inevitably much larger than on any previous occasion. There is a certain feudal dependence in Arab life, and more than in any Western society men tend to follow the example of the mayor and the notable and the local clergy. When these local leaders sought safety outside the country, many humble people had a scared longing to do the same, and the local leaders were not encouraged to stay when they found that a large proportion of the professional classes, the rich, the municipal authorities and the members of the Arab Higher Committee itself were intent on flight. Arab commanders were known to take flight when the battle turned against their side and this happened even in large-scale actions such as those fought at Tiberias, Acre, Haifa and Jaffa later on in the war.'

On 17 May 1939 the British Government published its Palestine White Paper. The White Paper fixed at 75,000 the number of Jewish immigrants who could enter in the next five years, meaning that all immigration would cease in 1944. This was to prove one of the turning-points in the relations between the Jewish Age/icy and the British Mandated Power. Any further increase beyond that number was to be subject to Arab approval. Although the White Paper thereby ensured that there could never be a Jewish numerical majority over the Arabs it was at once rejected by the Arabs no less than by the Jews 'as only half a loaf', an indication of the mounting Arab refusal to contemplate a Jewish state or Jewish participation in an Arab state.

There is no need here to tell again the ghastly story of the fate of the Jews under Hitler. As a result of the Palestine White Paper, refugees fleeing from persecution were, forbidden to land in Palestine. It became the distasteful duty of the British Government to intercept those Jews who were seeking illegal entry. When the old and badly leaking vessel *Struma* reached the Eastern Mediterranean with 769 Jewish refugees seeking entry to the Promised Land the British Government and then the Turkish Government refused to allow them to land, and all but one of the passengers were drowned when the ship sank in the Black Sea.

When war came in September 1939 the Jews in Palestine found themselves in a difficult position. It was obviously in their interest to support Britain in its war effort against Nazi Germany. But it was equally in their interest to challenge the principles on which the White Paper was based, and the stringent quota which the White Paper imposed.

The British, who had many Arabs enlisted in their forces, and many Moslems in the Indian Army, were hostile to the expedient of having a separate Jewish Army which they and many Arabs thought could be used to impose a settlement at the end of the war. Thus, though many Palestinian Jews fought in British units, only one Jewish brigade was permitted. Although the Jews in general supported allied aims and fought in the allied armies, there grew up also a Jewish terrorist movement dedicated to anti-British activities of the most violent sort. In March 1943 the House of Lords debated the proposal to open British immigration restrictions to any Jews fleeing from Nazi-occupied Germany. For the Government, Lord Plymouth declared that there could be absolutely no letting-up of the existing restrictions.

In Palestine the Stern Gang, around which the Jewish terrorism was organized, was responsible for the murder of Lord Moyne, the British Minister of State in Cairo, and began to foster on an ever-increasing scale illegal immigration, gun-running, thefts of British arms and the murder of British police.

Anglo-Jewish tension reached a climax on 22 July 1946 when Jewish extremists, angered by the continued immigration restrictions and by the detention of Jews from Europe in Cyprus, dynamited, in a daring exploit, the British military quarters in the King David Hotel in Jerusalem, destroying one wing and killing eight Englishmen. In retaliation for this act of terrorism Lieutenant-General Sir Evelyn Barker issued a military order forbidding troops to buy from Jewish shops and announced publicly that the boycott would punish the Jews 'where it will hurt them most, by striking at their pockets and showing our contempt for them'.

With the end of the war in 1945, the British attitude towards Palestine changed. The Egyptians demanded the evacuation of British forces, without conditions from their country, and rejected an agreement made with Ernest Bevin for a conditional withdrawal in 1949. Britain therefore turned to Palestine as a strategic substitute for Egypt and the Canal Zone. At the end of 1946 and in early 1947 the British began moving 'square miles of war stores' from Egypt to Palestine.

Tension rose swiftly in 1947. President Truman disagreed with British policy and there was Anglo-American friction over the future of Palestine as an asylum for European Jewry. On 1 August 1947 the murder of two British sergeants by Jewish extremists created a sense of revulsion in England and led even to a series of anti-Semitic outbursts.

This crisis also accentuated anti-American feeling in Britain, as American Jews had subscribed to Zionist funds and to anti-British advertisements. The mounting anti-Jewish hostility led to many cruel incidents. Three Jews were killed when the ship *Exodus* was rammed by a British destroyer in Haifa harbour as it tried to break the blockade and land Jewish refugees from German camps. Ernest Bevin ordered all the refugees on the *Exodus* to be returned to Displaced Persons Camps in Germany.

On 25 February 1947 the British Government announced that it would submit the Palestine problem to the United Nations. The United Nations Special Committee on Palestine (U.N.S.C.O.P.) was set up on 15 May 1947 and instantly recommended the termination of the Mandate while advising the partition of Palestine into an Arab state, a Jewish state, and a special international régime for Jerusalem. On 29 November 1947 the United Nations General Assembly adopted a partition plan by a vote of 33 to 13, with 10 abstentions. Russia, America and France voted for partition. The Jews accepted the partition plan, but the Palestine Arabs and the Arab states denounced the handing over even of the small areas concerned to the Jews. The British Government declared that until the Mandate ended on 15 May 1948 they would remain in full control and that the Palestine Commission set up by the United Nations was not to enter Palestine until two weeks before the end of the Mandate. Bevin explained the position on 23 March 1948 in the House of Commons: 'We have to get in a position to enable us to get out of Palestine.'

From the beginning of 1948 fighting between Jew and Arab became fiercer. Arab armed bands infiltrated from Syria and Trans-Jordan. Christopher Sykes has described in detail the way in which Arab-Jewish feelings mounted. Reprisals and counter-reprisals led on 8 April 1948 to the massacre by Jewish terrorists of 254 men, women and children in the village of Bir Yassin. Ben-Gurion immediately telegraphed his full apologies to King Abdullah of Trans-Jordan and sought to dissociate himself from the terrorist activities but it was hard to do so. And on 12 April 1948 an Arab retaliation killed 77 Jewish doctors, nurses, teachers and students, travelling under Red Cross bands to an isolated Jewish hospital. These atrocities accelerated' the Arab exodus which had already begun. Of this period Sykes wrote:

> The readiness to take to flight (which, easy to see both then and now, the Arab authorities should have been at the utmost pains to prevent) became greater every day after the news of Bir Yassin had been first broadcast. The news was repeated with inflated figures and invented vileness in excess of the vileness of the deed itself. Coming at a moment of growing Jewish armed success throughout Palestine, the terror-effect turned the already large exodus of the Arabs into a mass-migration. The thousands turned into tens of thousands. The Zionists believed on rough calculation that by the last week of April the Arab refugees from Palestine numbered 150,000.

By the end of the Arab exodus the Arab population had fallen from an estimated 700,000 to under 170,000.

The creation of the state of Israel on 14 May 1948 was followed immediately by a general Arab attack. It was not until 18 November 1948 that Israel accepted the United Nations armistice resolution and there was a further ten days fighting in the Negev against Egypt in February 1949. As a result of the Israeli-Arab war the Jews defeated the Arab attempt to drive them out of Palestine entirely. They also increased the area under their control beyond that of the partition plan. But the lines of the armistice were not conducive to security. During the war the forces in Jerusalem were commanded by Lieutenant-Colonel Dayan. The balance of forces is thought to have been some 20,000 Jews (including women) against 35,000 combat and irregular troops belonging to the seven Arab states. Outside military supplies for Israel came by airlift from Czechoslovakia: 77mm field guns, small tanks, Bren automatic rifles and machine-guns. Jerusalem was besieged by the Arabs from 18 May 1948 until 11 June when the first convoy carrying food and medical supplies reached the city from Tel Aviv.

The United States had recognized the state of Israel on a *de facto* basis within an hour or so of its declaration as a state on 14 May 1948, and the Russians, ironically, gave their recognition three days later. South Africa, at that time still a member of the Commonwealth, followed on, May 24 and Canada at the end of the year. Britain was to lag ten months after the United States. During thestf'morrths Mr Winston Churchill, as he then was, repeatedly girded the Attlee Government and its Foreign Secretary, Mr Ernest Bevin, to take a more realistic view of the situation. In December 1948 he argued that the issue was causing a deep divergence between Britain and the United States:

> For every reason, therefore, it is to our interest to be represented àt Tel Aviv as we are at Amman.

Attacking the Foreign Secretary in a speech of 26 January 1949, he repeated the point:

> I am quite sure that the right honourable Gentleman will have to recognize the Israeli Government, and that cannot be long delayed. I regret that he has not had the manliness to tell us in plain terms tonight, and that he preferred to retire under a cloud of inky water and vapour, like a cuttlefish. . .

Recognition, four days later, was followed swiftly by France, Belgium, Holland, Italy, Switzerland, Australia, New Zealand, Denmark, Norway and the Latin American countries.

The Arab countries all refused and have since persisted in their refusal to recognize the state of Israel. Every traveller to the Near East knows if he wants to visit Israel as well as some Arab country, that he should equip himself with two passports. Moreover the Arab countries have persisted in the perverse assertion that they are in a permanent state of war with a nation which they do not recognize. Hence the denial since 1948 to Israel of right to use the Suez Canal. Scarcely less absurd were the frontiers resulting from the armistice following the 1948 war. The old city of Jerusalem bisected from the new: a strategically indefensible frontier with Syria: the narrow waist between Jordan and the sea: and Sharm el-Sheikh in Egyptian hands, commanding the Straits of Tiran and denying to Israel the opportunity of creating a port at Eilat; finally, the nonsense of the Gaza Strip and its festering slum of Arab refugees maintained at the cost of the United Nations, since none of the Arab nations have been prepared to make a wnip-round for their brothers. Surrounded by friends, such frontiers would have been inconvenient. Surrounded by enemies who preached war and extermination it was not likely that such a situation could be indefinitely maintained. It is a measure of the incapacity of the United Nations that they have never had the collective will-power to seek a better solution.

In July 1952, Israel's major antagonist in the Arab world, Egypt, staged a nationalist revival which led to the abdication of King Farouk after an army coup led by General Neguib. Neguib was President of the Cairo Officers' Club, commander of an infantry division and a veteran of the 1948 war, in which he was three times wounded. One of the charges levelled against the old régime was that:

> People who received bribes contributed to our defeat in the Palestine war. Traitors plotted against the army after the Palestine war, but now we have purged 'ourselves'.

In February 1954, Neguib's position was challenged by Colonel Nasser. For an uneasy period Nasser and Neguib were rivals for power but in November 1954 Nasser successfully placed Neguib under arrest, where, so far as is known, he remains.

Successive Egyptian Governments began from 1951 to stage acts of sabotage in order to drive the British out of the Canal Zone before 1956 when the 1936 Treaty was due to expire. On 21 November 1952 the *New York Herald-Tribune* reported the views of Colonel Nasser, when he was asked how Egypt would act towards the British Forces:

> Not formal war. That would be suicidal. It will be a guerrilla war. Grenades will be thrown in the night. British soldiers will

be stabbed stealthily. There will be such terror, we hope, it will become far too expensive for the British to maintain their citizens in occupation of our country.

During 1952 Egyptian labour was withdrawn from work in the British Canal Zone and the 80,000 British troops stationed there were in constant danger worn Egyptian terrorism. On one occasion, to preserve the Canal Zone water supply from sabotage, British soldiers burnt down part of an Egyptian village. In April 1954 an Anglo-Egyptian agreement was signed whereby Britain agreed to leave the Canal Zone without conditions in 1956. It was noted that Nasser, who had negotiated the agreement, felt that his position was precarious. It did not satisfy the inflamed nationalist aspirations of the Egyptian people. Nasser therefore cast about for a policy which would rally Egyptian opinion behind him and perhaps show the other Arab leaders, who had not approved of his *coup d'état*, that he was the true leader of Arab nationalism. Nasser chose Israel as the object of his hostile attention. On 28 February 1955, in retaliation against repeated Egyptian armed raids across the Israeli border, Ben-Gurion, Israel's new Defence Minister, staged a military attack on Gaza and Egyptian military installations were destroyed.

During his early years in power, Nasser was much encouraged by the United States, where policy-makers considered him to be a moderate, and a potential friend of the West. When Nasser succeeded Neguib, Kermit Roosevelt of the CIA installed for the Egyptian premier a permanent consultant, Miles Copeland, in the next office.

Even after Nasser made his arms deal with Russia in 1955, the Arabists in the US State Department and in the CIA still had hopes of his remaining essentially pro-Western.

In fact, Kermit Roosevelt told Stephen Barber of the *Sunday Telegraph* that, looking back, he felt Nasser had 'begun to go wrong' at the time of the Russian arms deal. When corrected that it was a Czech arms deal, he replied: 'No, it never was a Czech arms deal. I invented that myself. You see, I was sitting in Nasser's office one morning when an orderly came in and said Sir Humphrey Trevelyan, the British Ambassador and now High Commissioner in Aden, was downstairs asking to see Nasser. Nasser asked me what I thought Sir Humphrey wanted. I said it was surely about the rumours that were already buzzing about the Russian deal. "What shall I tell him?" said Nasser. 'Oh, tell him it isn't a Russian arms deal but a Czech one – if won't sound so bad." '

American policy towards the Middle East has been curiously self-contradictory, possibly as the result of the split in policy-making between the State Department and the CIA.

When the British left the Canal Zone Egypt sought financial aid from Britain, America and the World Bank to build the Aswan High Dam on the Nile. On 19 July 1956 Britain and the United States announced that they would not continue with the financing of the High Dam. A week later Nasser announced that he was nationalizing the Suez Canal. This at once produced startled reactions in Paris and London. And for the rest of the summer attempts were made through the United States and the United Nations to find some way of circumventing what had been done.

Israel had, meanwhile, wearied of the terrorist raids by which she was harassed, not only from Egypt but also from Syria and Jordan. Through the good offices of the French, Britain and Israel, by a series of collusive plans, were drawn into an attack upon Port Said. The Israelis themselves struck against Egyptian positions in the Sinai desert. A lightning campaign beginning at the end of October and lasting five days brought them within 50 miles of the Canal and enabled them to seize Sharm el-Sheikh and to reopen the Gulf of Aqaba which had been closed to their shipping by the Egyptian blockade of the Straits of Tiran.

In this brilliant campaign the Israelis did achieve temporary security along their southern border and freedom of passage to and from the Port of Eilat. Britain and France, however, were deprived of the fruits of victory by an urgent demand for a cease-fire by the General Assembly of the United Nations, passed by 64 votes to 5 with 6 abstentions. And after many weeks of negotiations they withdrew their forces, which were replaced on the Egyptian side by the United Nations Expeditionary Force.

The steadily mounting number of refugees on Israel's borders were increasingly being formed into military units ready to carry out *fedayeen* raids across the border. The position became more and more intolerable to the Israelis who between 1957 and 1962 complained to the United Nations of no fewer than 422 raids and breaches of the truce by the Syrians. From time to time the Israelis mounted considerable reprisal raids notably on the Jordanian village of Samu in November 1966, and in defence of an Israeli farm which was shelled from the Syrian Heights across the border on 7 April 1967. On this occasion the Israeli Air Force shot down 6 MiGs. It became apparent that, heavily though Syria was equipped with Russian aircraft and tanks, its Air Force and Army lacked the trained personnel which were necessary to operate such sophisticated weapons.

⚜ ⚜ ⚜

It has always been a grievance of the Arab countries that their brothers who had been driven out in 1948 and are still living in refugee camps along the borders had been deprived of their natural land. There was a good deal of force behind these grievances, which were aired with growing violence by Cairo radio. And Nasser, capitalizing on the embarrassment of Britain and France after Suez, exploited the situation to claim with some credence the leadership of the Arab world.

Israel represents but .2% of the lands to which the Arabs lay claim. The forces of World Jewry have combined to raise hundreds of millions of pounds, most of it by subscription in Britain and still more in the United States, to settle the European Jews either in Israel or in the countries of the West. No attempt was made by the oil-rich states of the Persian Gulf, notably Kuwait and Saudi Arabia, to provide food and shelter for those whom they proudly saluted as their brothers. Instead, they were content that they should live on near starvation rations provided by the United Nations. The Egyptians found it convenient to tolerate these refugee camps, which festered like an angry boil on Israel's borders. Here was a situation waiting to be exploited by the Egyptians at any moment which seemed desirable to Nasser.

After Suez, although the Israelis completed the withdrawal from the Sinai Peninsula which was demanded of them early in 1957, it was not until March that they were prepared to withdraw from the two areas which they considered most vital to their national interests – the Gaza Strip and Sharm el-Sheikh, commanding the Straits of Tiran. This reflected Israel's anxiety that her security had not yet been guaranteed by the Great Powers. Indeed, when Israel continued to refuse to hand over Gaza and Sharm el-Sheikh to the United Nations peace-keeping force, John Foster Dulles went so far as to threaten the use of economic sanctions against Israel if the United Nations called for them in order to implement its resolutions.

That was on 5 February 1957. Four weeks later, on 6 March 1957, the Israelis had withdrawn from Gaza and from the Straits. In the meantime, President Eisenhower had said on February 20 that if the Egyptians did violate the armistice agreement or other obligations 'this should be dealt with firmly by the society of nations'. And on March 1 Sir Alan Noble, the British Minister of State and delegate to the General Assembly, declared: 'Her Majesty's Government will assert its right of free passage through the Gulf on behalf of all British shipping and is prepared to join with others to secure general recognition of its right.'

But David Ben-Gurion pointed out that, while the President of the United States had personally assumed a moral responsibility and the maritime nations had recognized Israel's rights in the Straits, Israel had still not received any specific guarantees concerning her rights in the Gaza Strip or the Straits of Tiran.

The ensuing decade saw a steady growth in the purchase of armaments by both sides. The Egyptians after acquiring three Soviet submarines in July 1957, quickly stepped up their purchases from Russia and other Eastern bloc countries to include MiG jets, TU-16 jet bombers and, more recently, a variety of missiles. Britain and America showed at least some moderation but Russia positively thrust the most expensive toys upon Egypt and Syria. The United States for its part decided to counterbalance this large purchase by the Egyptians with a sale of their ground-to-air missiles to Israel. But while the armaments flowed in to Egypt, Nasser was engaged in a struggle to establish and maintain his own position as leader of the Arab world. In the wake of the Suez 'victory', Nasser used his immense prestige to bring about an alliance with Syria, thus creating the United Arab Republic in February 1958. Those who did not wish to be tied to Nasser and his new empire were now subjected to systematic attack by Cairo radio and other means of propaganda from without and to subversion from within.

At first Nasser's efforts went unrewarded. In Iraq there was indeed a bloody revolution. King Feisal and his Prime Minister Nuri-es-Said were butchered in the coup of 14 luly 1958. But Kassem, who took over, soon showed himself to be as hostile to Nasser as the rest.

Immediately after the Iraqi coup US Marines had landed in the Lebanon on July 15, and British paratroops were airlifted into Jordan two days later, thereby preserving these two countries from subversion.

Nasser was rapidly losing ground as leader of the Arab world. Though he tried to sustain his position by instituting increasingly Socialist policies in the UAR, some 90% of Egypt's industrial and commercial assets having been nationalized by decree in July 1961, he could not prevent the most humiliating setback to his personal prestige – the break up of the UAR by the secession of Syria. The emergence of an anti-Nasser party in Syria was a serious embarrassment to him; but looking back on it, it was probably not as embarrassing as the re-emergence of the extremist doctrinaire pan-Arab Ba'ath party which took over Syria in 1963 and challenged Nasser's leadership of the Arab world. He was never able to control the Syrian revolutionaries who made their own arrangements with the Soviet Union for credits and arms. In spite of this, the Russians themselves had no greater restraining influence in Damascus.

Nasser had his own good reasons for increasing the pressure on Israel. Instead of using the vast amounts of aid which poured into Egypt from both East and West after

FRANCE
Marseilles
SPAIN
Barcelona
BALEARIC IS.
CORSICA
SARDINIA
ITALY
Naples
YUGOSLAVIA
RUMANIA
Danube
BULGARIA
ALBANIA
GREECE
Athens
SICILY
MALTA
Mediterranean
Algiers
Tunis
TUNISIA
Tripoli
Benghazi
ALGERIA
LIBYA
SAHARA
MALI
NIGER
CHAD
NIGERIA
THE MEDITERRANEAN
AND
THE MIDDLE EAST
MARTIN GILBERT

U. S. S. R.
Caspian Sea
ISRAEL
0 500
Miles
AFGHANISTAN
Sea
KEY
SYRIA
Aleppo
Tigris
Euphrates
Baghdad
IRAN (PERSIA)
LEB.
Amman
JORDAN
IRAQ
KUWAIT
NEUTRAL TERRITORIES
Gulf of Aqaba
Persian Gulf
BAHRAIN
QATAR
Gulf of Oman
SAUDI
Riyadh
TRUCIAL OMAN
MUSCAT and OMAN
Red Sea
ARABIA
Mecca
Port Sudan
YEMEN
San'a
SOUTH ARABIAN FED.
Aden Protectorate
ERITREA
Aden
PERIM
Gulf of Aden
SOCOTRA
FRENCH SOMALILAND
N
SOMALIA
Addis Ababa
ETHIOPIA
ARTHUR BANKS

Suez for the betterment of his people, Nasser squandered the greater part of it on massive military expenditure. For several years afterwards Nasser who claimed, not without a certain plausibility, to be the victor of Suez rode high on the crest of a popularity wave that rolled throughout the Arab world. The high point of this popularity came in 1958 with the creation of the United Arab Republic with Syria. When this experiment in Arab unity proved a failure he sought to re-establish his standing at home and regain his leadership abroad by embarking on a foreign war in the Yemen.

The overthrow by revolutionary army officers in September 1962 of the most reactionary ruler in the world, the Imam of Yemen, at first seemed to promise well for Nasser. But it gradually became clear that the Yemenis did not like being ruled by Egyptians. For nearly five years these tough, primitive mountain people have held their own against Nasser's 60,000 strong army of occupation and, in spite of daily bombing and strafing of their defenceless villages by Egypt's Russian jets, in spite of Nasser's poisoned gas attacks and in spite of the indifference of world opinion to their plight, the Yemenis have continued their struggle, backed only by money and arms from Saudi Arabia. What should have been a quick victory for the Egyptians turned instead into a prolonged and expensive campaign.

Nasser's involvement in the Yemen is based on both political and geographical considerations. Politically it is not only a part of his struggle for the leadership of the Arab World but is also represented as a fight between the forces of progress and reaction. Geographically the southern entrance to the Red Sea presents a springboard from which it would be possible to dominate the oil fields of the Persian Gulf. However, in spite of Egypt's claim that she is bringing progress to the Yemen, traditional pre-republican Yemenite methods of subjugation such as public executions, mass arrests and the confiscation of property are still used, no less by the Egyptians than by the adherents of the Imam.

From the beginning of 1967 it was in Nasser's power to provoke an attack on whatever date best suited his own military preparedness. Meanwhile, the Israelis had not been idle. They had equipped themselves with some 240 fighter aircraft, for the most part French Mirages and Mystères, and with 800 tanks, mainly Centurions.

In the last days of peace a bizarre diversion occurred in Egypt when Field Marshal Viscount Montgomery visited the country for a week, from May 3 to May 10. In the autumn of 1942, Montgomery had fought at el Alamein one of the decisive battles in world history, and Egyptian officers were keen to hear him talk about the strategy and tactics of desert warfare. The visit was arranged by General Mortagi, the Sinai commander of land forces, who accompanied 'Monty' in Cairo and Alexandria on the first two days of his visit. A special correspondent of *The Times* commented on the welcome he received: 'experienced observers here affirm that they have never known a visitor afforded such meticulous care and attention'. (*The Times,* May 4.)

Montgomery caused a stir in the British press when he visited the site of his victory, on May 7, and in praising the Egyptian Government and people, condemned the 1956 attack on Egypt as morally wrong. And at the end of the week, just before leaving, he lectured to Egyptian officers at the Higher Military Academy, described the battle of Alamein and answered a barrage of questions, from the men who were soon to be so disastrously trapped in Sinai. He does not seem to have given them the right answers. Perhaps they did not ask the right questions.

Chapter Two
Closing the Straits

It all started with a lie – a Russian lie. In early May the Soviet Government passed to Cairo the story of a large Israeli troop concentration on the Syrian border. Over the following two weeks Cairo received further and more detailed information indicating that an Israeli force of up to 11 brigades was involved. However, at the time the Israelis had no more than a company (120 men) in this particular area, waiting in ambush for Syrian saboteurs. The United Nations, which had observation posts along the Israeli–Syrian border, confirmed, on May 19, that they had no evidence of these alleged troop movements.* It seems that the Russians, alarmed by the possibility that Israel might carry out a punitive raid on Syria, wanted Nasser to commit his forces in Sinai in order to deter the Israelis from attacking. The allegations were in fact completely fabricated.

In his bogus resignation speech of June 9, President Nasser said :

---

* See : Secretary General's report to the Security Council, May 19, S7879, para. 9: 'Reports from UNTSO observers have confirmed the absence of troop concentrations and significant troop movements on both sides of the line.'

We all know how the crisis began in the first half of last May. There was an enemy plan to invade Syria, and the statements by his politicians and all his military commanders declared that frankly. The evidence was ample.

The sources of our Syrian brothers and our own reliable information were categorical on this.

Even our friends in the Soviet Union told the parliamentary delegation which was visiting Moscow early last month that there was a calculated intention. It was our duty not to accept this in silence.

The crisis which was to lead to war had already been building up for six months. In October and November of 1966 there had been an intensification of Arab terrorist activities against Israel by the El Fatah terrorist organization. On November 4, Syria and Egypt signed a defence agreement. There followed two incidents in which the Israelis undertook major punitive action. On November 13 a large Israeli force including tanks and armoured cars rolled over the Jordanian border and attacked Samu, a village of 4,000 people. According to U Thant the Israelis destroyed 125 houses, a school and a clinic. Israel felt no great hostility towards Jordan but carried out the raid in order to show that she was not prepared to tolerate the use of Jordanian territory by the El Fatah organization. At the beginning of April 1967, the Israelis decided to knock out Syrian artillery which was bombarding Israeli farm workers who were ploughing land in a demilitarized zone near the Sea of Galilee. In the resulting air battle of April 7 the Syrians lost 6 MiG fighters, a significant proportion of their total air strength. When, despite this action, Syrian terrorism continued unabated, Israeli leaders gave warnings that they might strike again. On May 10 the Chief of Staff, General Rabin, antagonized the

Syrians by suggesting that his forces might attack Damascus and topple the régime of Nureddin Atassi. Speaking on May 14 at the Yhdar Club in Tel Aviv, the Prime Minister, Levi Eshkol, said, 'In view of the 14 incidents in the past month alone, we may have to adopt measures no less drastic than those of April 7.'

The situation was clearly becoming increasingly embarrassing for President Nasser. In particular the presence of the United Nations Emergency Force on Egyptian territory was a subject of scandal and scorn among his Arab rivals. Why, it was asked, was there so little terrorist activity against Israel from bases in Egypt? Nasser, believing that a confrontation was imminent between Israel and Syria, wanted to silence his critics and reassert his flagging leadership of the Arab world. He felt bound to demonstrate the reality of his defence pact with Syria by some evidence of military zeal.

On May 15 large bodies of Egyptian troops were seen moving through Cairo on their way to the Suez Canal. They were accorded the maximum publicity by the Government-controlled press, radio and television. When on the same day the Israelis held their annual Independence Day Parade in Jerusalem, more fuel was heaped on the crisis. The Israeli sector of Jerusalem was a demilitarized zone. Observing the regulations, the Israelis included no heavy armour or artillery in the parade, and kept the number of troops to a minimum. The Arabs, ignoring this explanation, alleged that Israeli forces were clearly deployed elsewhere.

At 10 pm on May 16 the Egyptian Chief of Staff, General Fawzy, sent a telegram to General Rikhye: 'To your information, I gave my instructions to all UAR armed forces to be ready for action against Israel the moment it might carry out any aggressive action against any Arab country. Due to these instructions our troops are already concentrated in Sinai on our eastern borders. For the sake of complete secure [*sic*] of all UN troops which install O.P's along our borders, I request that you issue orders to withdraw all these troops immediately. I have given my instructions to our Commander of the Eastern Zone concerning this subject. Inform back the fulfilment of this request.'* The demand was reported by Cairo Radio the following day.

General Rikhye at once communicated the Egyptian request to U Thant and retired to bed. The broadcasts of Cairo radio on May 17 made it clear that the Egyptian intention was to remove the United Nations force from the probable field of battle so that they would 'not be harmed if hostilities break out'. It was added that General Rikhye had been asked to withdraw his men from the border and concentrate them inside the Gaza Strip. No mention was made of the UN forces at Sharm el-Sheikh. However, after receiving from Rikhye the text of Fawzy's telegram, U Thant sent for Mr El Kony, the Egyptian representative at the United Nations, and informed him that a partial withdrawal of the force was impossible. The United Nations could not be asked 'to stand aside in order to enable the * The translation was provided by the Egyptians. two sides to resume fighting'. Nasser was therefore informed that he must either request the complete withdrawal of the Emergency Force from Egyptian territory or else allow it to remain in its existing positions.

UNEF was the peacekeeping force which had policed the Egypt–Israel border since the time of Suez. It had originally been established there under an agreement concluded between President Nasser and the UN Secretary-General, Dag Hammarskjöld, in November 1956.* The

* The UN Force comprised 978 Indians, 795 Canadians, 579 Yugoslavs, 530 Swedes, 430 Brazilians, 61 Norwegians and 2 Danes.

public conditions governing its presence were ambiguous. In an *aide-mémoire* presented to the UN by Hammarskjöld at the time of the agreement, the Egyptian Government was said to have accepted that it would be guided 'in good faith, by its acceptance of the General Assembly resolution of November 5, 1956'. As will be seen, it was alleged after UNEF's withdrawal that U Thant should have been bound by a more specific but unpublished compact between Hammarskjöld and Nasser. However, there was little doubt of the practical position of the Force when it was originally established. The Egyptian Director-General of Information, Colonel Hatem, said on 12 November 1956 that it had been agreed that UNEF should be *immediately withdrawn from Egypt whenever the Egyptian Government requested its withdrawal.*

Now that the situation had at last been put to the test how should U Thant have reacted? Dag Hammarskjöld, the previous UN Secretary-General, had given a great deal of thought to such a possibility. Indeed, it was the main topic of discussion between him and Nasser during a seven-hour conference on 17 November 1956.

Hammarskjöld wrote a confidential *aide-mémoire* on 5 August 1957 stating that he and President Nasser had reached an agreement about the circumstances under which the Emergency Force might be withdrawn. He claimed that Nasser had accepted the arrangement after a heated argument in which Hammarskjöld threatened on three occasions to withdraw the Force at once unless Nasser consented.

Egypt and the UN made a compact that no withdrawal should take place before the 'task' was accomplished. In the event of an Egyptian request for the UN troops to leave, Hammarskjöld recorded: 'The matter would at once be brought before the General Assembly. If the General

Assembly found that its task was completed, everything would be all right. If they found that the task was not completed, and Egypt, all the same, maintained its stand and enforced the withdrawal, Egypt would break the agreement with the United Nations.' Though U Thant has pointed out that the Hammarskjöld memorandum was not an official UN document, it was soon to become apparent how far he would deoart from his predecessor's code of action.

On the Wednesday morning of the war, after accepting a golden lifetime-pass to National Football League games, Johnson spent an hour with the National Security Council, and officially announced that McGeorge Bundy would work with a special committee of the NSC, which would include Richard Helms, Head of the Central Intelligence Agency. The function of McGeorge Bundy's new committee of the NSC would be to co-ordinate efforts to end the war and work out a long-term US policy for the Middle East, establishing firm relations with both Israel and the Arabs. Bundy had been the late President Kennedy's chief adviser at the White House during the Cuban missiles crisis. When he retired from the political scene in 1966 his place as Special Assistant to the President on international security affairs was taken by Walt Rostow. Rostow was widely regarded as an incurable optimist about Vietnam, and was also one of the leading 'hawks', having openly talked about the advisability of bombing Hanoi even before Johnson sent US combat forces to the war in 1965. His interest, and indeed, that of the State Department itself in Vietnam, had been such as to preclude his paying appropriate attention to other world trouble-spots.

Rostow's brother, Eugene, number two to Dean Rusk at the State Department, had been only slightly less of an optimist. It was his serious belief right up to the moment the war started that the problem posed by President Nasser's seizing Sharm el-Sheikh at the mouth of the Gulf of Aqaba, could be solved by lashing together a multi-lateral decla ration of maritime powers.

Like other presidential advisers, the Rostows had been loth to contemplate a new military commitment. When the war began many junior officials of the State Department felt bitter that none of their earlier warnings had been heeded. Those who had foreseen the crisis did not hesitate to say so. Not least among them was Mr David Nes, then deputy Chief of the US mission in Cairo. He was convinced that as early as January Nasser was planning a showdown with Israel and the West. He even wrote to Senator Fulbright, Chairman of the Senate Foreign Relations Committee, urgently asking for the appointment of a US Ambassador to Cairo. But the ambassadorship remained vacant for a full three months before the crisis. As Chargé d'Affaires, David Nes was so convinced of the danger that he began to draw up a plan for the evacuation of American citizens. Eventually Richard Nolte was appointed Ambassador. He had arrived in Cairo on May 21, exclaiming to reporters: 'What crisis?' Nes thought that Nolte was the wrong man for the job. Events were to prove that the Johnson administration required better machinery in Washington as well as in Cairo for coping with the problems of the Jews and Arabs.

Johnson's statements that the Americans would work both inside and outside the United Nations was taken to mean that an attempt would be made to work directly with Russia.

But Bundy, however, had quite an augean stable to clean up. There is no question but that US policy towards Nasser had long been inconsistent. The irony is that back in the early days, after Nasser and his military junta of Free

Officers, with General Neguib as their figurehead, ousted King Farouk, it was the Central Intelligence Agency that befriended Nasser.

The man who did more than any other American to build up Nasser was Kermit Roosevelt, vice-president of Gulf Oil and ex-CIA agent. He was also the man who helped unhorse Moussadeq of Iraq in 1952. Roosevelt installed Miles Copeland, euphemistically referred to on the BBC programme *24 Hours* on June 7 as 'the former American diplomat in the Middle East and intimate of President Nasser'. He worked in the next office to Nasser as a 'consultant' during the days when Nasser, having ousted Neguib, was running Egypt at the head of the Revolutionary Command Council on Gezira Island from the Palace alongside the mooring of Farouk's yacht.

Long before the Suez debacle the Americans had been unhelpful to British interests in the Middle East. They seemed to feel the necessity for working out a policy that was different from that of Britain. And after Suez, of course, Britain's repute in the Middle East had greatly fallen and America had some reason for distrusting the British expertise. If Britain and America had been able to work jointly together many misfortunes might have been averted. But it was to a large extent the unhelpful American attitude in Egypt and the Middle East which led Sir Anthony Eden to strike out so vehemently on his own. Much of the trouble seems to have been due to the fact that to a large extent the CIA operated on its own without any very close liaison with the State Department. When two separate departments of Government start playing in the same field without any clear overriding directive from the President American foreign policy is always apt to be disconcerting.

Nasser eventually broke with the US when John Foster Dulles, Eisenhower's Foreign Secretary, dashed Nasser's hope of US help in constructing the Aswan Dam in 1956. This had the fatal consequence of goading Nasser into nationalizing the Suez Canal – a move which led inexorably to the Anglo-French-Israeli attack in November of that year. The US disapproved of the Suez intervention and thereafter she switched once more to the wooing of Nasser. American stock rose to a high point around 1963, while that of the Russians gradually declined, in spite of the latter having stepped in to build the Aswan High Dam. During the Kennedy era, Nasser and the US President were engaged in warm personal correspondence. Nasser was regarded as a force to be reckoned with and therefore propitiated.

With Johnson's accession to power, relations once more grew cooler. The new notion had grown up with the policy men that the people to back were the Arabian oil monarchs who were represented as 'moderates'. This led to the State visit of Saudi Arabia's King Feisal to the US in June 1966. During that visit Feisal warned President Johnson that the Arabs were confused by American policy in the Middle East. He was particularly concerned about what he regarded, according to his staff, as the incredible lack of interest Washington seemed to take in the probable course of events that would flow from Britain's announcement of her intention to withdraw from Aden by 1969. He told Johnson that Nasser had become so deeply beholden to the Russians for his military equipment and had fallen so far behind in his barter payments for it due to the cost of the war against the Royalists in the Yemen and the cotton crop failures owing to the boll weevil plague, that he was no longer a free agent.

After this visit the final break with Nasser came when Washington put off wheat shipments to Egypt in 1966.

The Egyptians had not waited for any formal response from U Thant. By 8 am (GMT) on May 17 they were already taking over Yugoslav observation posts along the border. It was becoming too late for U Thant to preserve the integrity of the force. In Cairo, Mahmoud Riad called in the envoys of each of the seven nations contributing to UNEF and demanded the withdrawal of their contingents, receiving immediate assent from the Yugoslavs and Indians.

That same day in New York the permanent representatives to the UN of India and Yugoslavia made it plain to U Thant that they would withdraw their contingents as and when this was demanded by Nasser, whose sovereignty they were unwilling to infringe. Though U Thant spent many hours with representatives of the UNEF nations, he could not overcome this difficulty. Meanwhile, in Egypt, the force was crumbling away.

Shortly after midday (GMT) on May 18 the Egyptians ordered the force of 32 UN soldiers who were manning observation posts at Sharm el-Sheikh to withdraw in 15 minutes. It was only later that day at 4 pm (GMT) that the official Egyptian request for the withdrawal of the force reached U Thant:

'The Government of the United Arab Republic has the honour to inform your Excellency that it has decided to terminate the presence of the United Nations Emergency Force from the territory of the United Arab Republic and Gaza Strip. Therefore, I request that the necessary steps be taken for the withdrawal of the force as soon as possible.'

It seemed to U Thant that there was little to do but to draft a formal note to Riad which simply said he was giving the necessary orders for UNEF to make 'without delay an orderly withdrawal with its vehicles and equipment and for the disposal of all properties pertaining to it'. However he added a warning that: 'Irrespective of the reasons for the action you have taken, in all frankness may I advise you that I have serious misgivings about it for as I have said in my annual reports to the General Assembly on UNEF, I believe this force has been an important factor in maintaining peace.'

On May 19 U Thant announced to the General Assembly that he had received this request and that the force was being withdrawn immediately. At a brief ceremony in Gaza that day the blue and white flag of the United Nations was lowered and UNEF ceased to exist – an ignominious and abrupt demise.

The Canadians, who had contributed 800 men to the UN Force, showed themselves extremely displeased that U Thant had acted so precipitately. It is strange too that neither Britain nor the United States called for a meeting of the Security Council. Finally it fell to the Canadians and the Danes to raise the matter.

Though U Thant had from the outset claimed an absolutely clean bill of health for the righteousness of what he did, American charges that he could have done more to prevent the dissolution of UNEF had evidently weighed him down. And on June 26, a full month after the whole episode, he thought it necessary to issue a 32-page memorandum justifying his conduct. His main point was that UNEF had been effectively destroyed by the Egyptians before their formal request for its withdrawal. He also explained why there had been so little consultation. He had not called the Security Council because its members were already divided, and he had not called the General Assembly because it would have been unable to act 'expeditiously'.

On the evening of May 19, an Israeli official in Tel Aviv said that 'Israel might put the issue before the General Assembly as the Emergency Force's presence in the area was based on a General Assembly resolution and it cannot be nullified by a unilateral announcement'.

At a forty-five-minute meeting with U Thant in New York Mr Goldberg, the United States' representative, pledged full support 'for any United Nations' action required to keep the peace'. Later he publicly expressed 'deep concern' over the rising tension in the area.

Perhaps no one was more surprised than Nasser when U Thant acceded to his demands so promptly, without even consulting the Security Council or the General Assembly.

The attitude of the Russians to UNEF may also have influenced U Thant's decision. They have consistently refused to pay a rouble towards its upkeep and have never missed an opportunity to represent it as a cover for America's Central Intelligence Agency.

On Friday May 19 Mr Brown postponed at half an hour's notice his long-planned visit to Russia. His decision led to a savage attack on him in Mr Cecil Harmsworth-King's *Sunday Mirror.* The *Mirror* revived the *Sunday Telegraph's* story of a few weeks before of the Foreign Secretary's gaffes at social gatherings and concluded by asking three questions:

1. On what possible grounds does the Foreign Secretary consider that the tiny contribution he can personally offer to easing the tensions on the border between Israel and Egypt is more important than urgent talking – or perhaps, for a change, urgent listening – about Vietnam with Mr Kosygin in Moscow?
2. Has Mr Brown's visit to the USSR been crudely postponed – or cancelled?
3. When is the Foreign Office, or Mr Brown himself, planning to issue a full and coherent public statement on his curious change of plan?

On Saturday May 20 Israel completed a partial mobilization of her reservists, and in Cairo Field-Marshal Amer, the Deputy Commander of the Egyptian Armed Forces, after touring the area where Egyptian and Palestine Liberation Army troops were replacing those of the retiring UNEF, issued an order calling up Egyptian reservists.

The Indian Government responded warmly to Nasser's measures. The Prime Minister, Mrs Indira Gandhi, was reported in the *Deccan Herald* on May 21 to have expressed India's support for President Nasser, and the Arabs generally, in their preparations to aid Syria.

On Monday May 22 Egypt declared the Straits of Tiran closed to Israeli ships. President Nasser said that the UAR had closed the Gulf of Aqaba to Israeli shipping and also to strategic materials being shipped to Israel on board non-Israeli vessels. 'The Israeli flag will no longer pass the Gulf of Aqaba; our sovereignty over the Gulf is indisputable. If Israel threatens us with war, we will reply thus: Go ahead, then.'

On Tuesday May 23 Mr Eshkol, speaking in the Knesset in Jerusalem, said that interference with Israeli shipping in the Straits of Tiran would be regarded as an act of war.

On the same day President Johnson declared that the blockade of Israeli shipping by Egypt was illegal and that the United States was firmly committed to support the integrity of all the nations of the Middle East. He went on to say, 'We are dismayed at the hurried withdrawal without action by either the General Assembly or the Security Council.' He is reported to have sent a personal message to Mr Kosygin the previous weekend urging him to act in concert with the United States to get the Arabs and Israelis to exercise restraint and Arthur Goldberg was instructed to impress upon Mr Federenko, the Russian delegate at the UN, that

America was anxious to avoid a head-on collision with the Russians.

Having announced on the Sunday that he would fly to Cairo, U Thant arrived on the Tuesday and had dinner with the Foreign Minister. It was not until Wednesday that he was received by Nasser.

British warships in the Mediterranean were placed on the alert and the Cabinet decided that Mr George Thomson, Minister of State for the Foreign Office, should fly at once to Washington and New York. Mr Brown after again delaying his departure a few hours to attend a special Cabinet, finally took off for Moscow.

He left accompanied by a reasoned defence of his delay in *The Guardian* :

> Having lost his buffer force, U Thant is right to go to Cairo as the point where he might most effectively restrain events in the Middle East. By the same token, Mr Brown now stands the best chance of influencing events by talking to the Russians, who have been largely responsible for the military build-up both in Egypt and in Syria. Had he gone to the Soviet Union before the weekend, he would have been isolated from events, a tourist well away from Moscow. Now he is to stay in the capital throughout a shorter and more businesslike visit.

Meanwhile on Tuesday May 23 the Tory leader Mr Edward Heath, speaking in Hastings, urged that the British Government must give a clear lead and must try to get an effective United Nations presence re-established along the frontier between Israel and Egypt. He went on to say: 'The United Nations seems to have agreed without discussion that the relative peacekeeping force should be withdrawn.... The United Arab Republic's request should never have been accepted without reference to the Security Council and, if necessary, to the Assembly.' He concluded: 'Now the British Government must act quickly in demanding an immediate meeting of the Security Council.' The same evening Heath and Sir Alec Douglas-Home called on the Prime Minister at Downing Street and asked him what the Government were going to do about asserting their rights through the Gulf and what the position was about British shipping. The same night Heath spoke again at Dorking where he said it was not enough for the Government to say they were asserting their rights. The Prime Minister must go on and show that he had got the wherewithal to assert British rights and that was his responsibility.

Sir Alec Douglas-Home also spoke out that night at Beckenham. 'Meanwhile, the United States have declared that the Gulf of Aqaba must be kept an international waterway. They are right. In 1956 the Americans did not then understand the urgency of curtailing Egypt's expansionist activities. They do now, and they should be fully supported in their determination to see that international law prevails.'

The following day. May 24, the Prime Minister paid a hurried helicopter visit to the Annual Conference of the Electrical Trades Union in Margate and seized the opportunity to assert the right of all British shipping to use the Straits of Tiran as an international waterway. He added that Britain was prepared 'to join with others to secure general recognition of this right'. More importantly the Prime Minister based his view on the statement made by Sir Alan Noble as British delegate of the Tory government to the General Assembly of the United Nations on 1 March 1957 after the collapse of the Suez enterprise. The crucial words of Noble's declaration had been 'Her Majesty's Government will assert this right on behalf of all British shipping, and is prepared to join with others to secure general recognition of this right'. To this the Prime Minister added, 'His words were echoed by other delegates representing substantial maritime nations. The declaration then made [by Noble] remains the view and the policy of Her Majesty's Government and we shall promote and support international action to uphold this right of free passage.'

Public opinion in England rallied strongly to the cause of Israel and on May 27 most educated opinion was well summed up in *The Times* leader *Law and the Gulf*:

> Egypt's claim to control shipping passing through the Strait of Tiran touches one of Israel's most sensitive nerves as an established nation state. At the northernmost point of the Gulf of Aqaba is Eilat, Israel's only point of access to the east and thus to her main sources of oil. The gulf itself is bordered by Egyptian territory on the west and Saudi Arabian on the east, save for the northern shores, where both Jordan and Israel have access. A hundred miles long, it varies in width from seventeen to twenty miles. The narrow Strait of Tiran, further blocked by islands, allows Egypt to control shipping by asserting rights over territorial waters at the entrance to the gulf.
>
> Such control exerted over the vital lifeline of another state has long been an issue secured by international law. Its best known and geographically most classic case is the access to the Black Sea through the Dardanelles and the Bosporus. These famous straits fell under sole Turkish control with the capture of Constantinople in 1453, but it was not until 1774, when Catherine the Great brought the northern shores of the Black Sea under Russian rule, that an agreement was reached giving free use of the straits to Russian ships. Thereafter, the debate went on over the conditions of such use, notably in the question of warships. A succession of treaties all through the

nineteenth century, coloured by the interests of the major signatories, broadened the principles of free navigation and ended any possibility that one state should ever be allowed to dominate another purely by such accidents of geography. With the fall of the Ottoman Empire, an international commission took charge, to be followed by the Lausanne Treaty of 1923 and the Montreux Convention of 1936, which still holds.

The Strait of Tiran and the Gulf of Aqaba fall precisely into this pattern and call forth the same cause of international freedom in navigation. That this freedom is and should be internationally acknowledged was the purpose of the Convention of the Territorial Sea and the Contiguous Zone reached at Geneva in 1958 after discussion among all interested powers. One article in that convention declares that there shall be 'no suspension of the innocent passage of foreign ships through the straits which are used for international navigation between one point of the high seas and another point of the high seas or the territorial sea of a sovereign state'.

The Egyptians contest this provision in several ways. Another article in the convention defines innocent passage as 'not prejudicial to the peace, good order, or security of the coastal state', which the Egyptians might argue is the case with Israel's traffic up this waterway in strategic goods. Alternatively there is the argument that albeit a participant at Geneva, Egypt has not ratified the agreement. A third argument claims that the gulf itself – given the now accepted limit of twelve miles for territorial waters – falls wholly into this category and cannot be regarded as the high seas for the purpose of the 1958 convention. Finally there is the argument to embrace all others that Egypt is at war with Israel and is no longer bound by any such agreements over rights of passage.

Some of these arguments are untenable in law: all of them run against the accepted international principle of rights of access which needs to be upheld whatever other opinions may be held of the crisis. The argument over the gulf as itself territorial waters is not accepted in international law where several littoral states exist – what applies to the Jordanian port of Aqaba must apply equally to its neighbour Eilat. Egypt's claim to be at war runs against the Security Council resolution recording the progress of the Israel-Egypt armistice and establishing its permanence as an end to the war even if no settlement were possible. Egypt is not attempting to maintain belligerent rights at any other port or in any other way. Finally the case for the agreed convention has the ratification of twenty-two interested countries, among them the United States, Russia and Britain, as well as the force of two centuries of international evolution.

To allow Egypt's rights in the Tiran strait would depart from this accepted principle. There is not only the example of Turkey and access to the Mediterranean by Russia, Rumania and Bulgaria. The Baltic is a sea that could be closed if Sweden and Denmark chose to apply the geographical arguments that Egypt uses at Tiran. In asserting the freedom of navigation of the gulf Israel, and Britain and the United States, have the merit of international law behind them.

It is idle, however, to deny that the Egyptians had a strong juridical case in the matter of the Straits of Tiran. It is unfortunate that no impartial international tribunal existed before whom the matter could be settled.

The Egyptian case was well put by Mr Talib El-Shibib, the representative of the League of Arab States, in a letter to *The Times* on May 29, in which he set out four points which certainly have a plausible ring about them:

1. The existence of an Israeli coast line on the Gulf of Aqaba is a direct result of an act of force by Israel contrary to the

1947 UN Partition Plan of Palestine. Israel's occupation of the Port of Eilat and that part of the coast line are an example of Israeli military expansionist policy in defiance of the UN rule.
2. The entrance of the Gulf of Aqaba is less than nine miles wide and it is therefore within the 12 mile limit legally allowed for territorial waters. Due to the state of war between Israel and Egypt the passage of Israeli ships through the Tiran Straits was denied until 1956 on legally accepted grounds. Their passage since 1956 was a result of the Suez aggression against Egypt which was resoundingly condemned by the UN and whose final traces had to be liquidated. Surely it is not the rule of law to allow an aggressor to retain the fruits of his aggression.
3. Israel has continuously flouted UN resolutions and hindered UN peacekeeping efforts. It has refused to accept UN troops on its side of the border in 1957 and had since boycotted the UN mixed armistice commission with the UAR.
4. The military attacks by Israel against a number of neighbouring Arab countries for which Israel was six times condemned by the Security Council are examples of the rule of the jungle which Israel pursues. Its claim for sympathy on the basis of legality and international law are manifestations of extreme cynicism.

On Wednesday May 24 Britain and the United States agreed that the Gulf of Aqaba should be reopened to international shipping. It was said that, 'military action was not to be excluded' and the United States 6th Fleet took up positions at the eastern end of the Mediterranean in support of diplomatic efforts to open the Gulf. Egypt announced that the blockade had begun, that mines had been laid and that air and naval forces had been alerted. The shore batteries were stated to be in position and manned. At the request of Denmark and Canada the Security Council had an urgent meeting 'to consider the extremely grave situation in the Middle East which is threatening international peace and security'. At this meeting Russia demanded that the United States and British fleets should leave the Mediterranean. The Jordanian Government stated in Amman that permission had been given to Saudi Arabian and Iraqi forces to enter Jordan 'for the defence of the nation'. The aircraft carrier HMS *Victorious,* on its way back from the Far East through the Mediterranean, was ordered to stand by in Malta.

Meanwhile, on Thursday May 25, there were signs of mounting pressure on the Israeli Prime Minister, Mr Eshkol, for Israel to 'go it alone'. President Johnson flew to Canada for the inside of a day to discuss the crisis with Mr Lester Pearson. The same day the Egyptian Defence Minister, accompanied by a ten-man delegation, arrived in Moscow to seek Russian support and material and was received by the Soviet Defence Minister, Marshal Grechko.

On the day before the Israeli Foreign Minister, Mr Eban, left for Washington, via Paris and London, to see President Johnson and later to address the United Nations Security Council. In Paris General de Gaulle spoke of a Four-Power summit meeting and the American Government supported the idea; but the next day it was learnt that the Russians had ruled out the possibility. Eban arrived in Washington on May 25 for talks with Dean Rusk, the United States Secretary of State. Before leaving London he had told reporters that the object of his journey was 'to bring back a clear picture of whether those powers who have undertaken solemnly to exercise their right of free passage in the Straits of Tiran intend to carry out that undertaking or not'. The Gulf of

Aqaba, he declared, was the most vital of Israel's interests, and he pointed out that Eilat handled all of Israel's oil imports.

On May 26, after keeping Eban waiting for most of the day, Johnson at last called him in for a talk. The President was disconcerted when Eban produced from his briefcase a file of documents which the Israelis considered to be evidence of a firm American commitment to uphold the principle of 'free and innocent passage' through the Gulf of Aqaba. Among these papers was the draft of a speech made by Eban's immediate predecessor, Mrs Golda Meir, to the United Nations General Assembly on 1 March 1957. The speech set forth the terms upon which Israel agreed to quit Sharm el-Sheikh. They made it clear that Israel would regard interference with her shipping in the Straits of Tiran 'as entitling her to exercise her inherent rights of self-defence'. The text had been prepared jointly by Eban, at that time Israeli Ambassador in Washington, and John Foster Dulles, and amended by Dulles in his own hand. Furthermore, after Mrs Meir had delivered the speech, it had been welcomed by Cabot Lodge, then America's chief UN delegate.

Eban was also able to remind Johnson, during their 85-minute encounter, of the President's own record on the issue. When Johnson was Senate Democratic leader in 1956/7 he had been strongly pro-Israel. He had hotly criticized Dulles for even considering applying economic sanctions against Israel to force her withdrawal from the crucial area.

In his talk with Eban, Johnson was full of friendly bluster – 'I want to see that little blue and white Israeli flag sailing down those Straits' – but would make no firm commitment. His domestic political situation was difficult. So far, he had confined himself to a statement on May 23 reaffirming that the Straits of Tiran were an international waterway. If he failed to act positively over the blockade, he was bound to come under fire from both pro-Israeli liberals and conservatives. On the other hand Congress was giving little support to any idea of unilateral action by the United States: one war seemed to be enough for the time being. Johnson told Eban that an enabling resolution would have to go through Congress before the Americans could possibly go to the help of Israel; and Eban, having been ambassador in Washington for years, was well aware that this could only be done after a protracted struggle during which the military situation would become increasingly less favourable to Israel.

For Johnson, the tactic seemed to be to stay cool and above all avoid a head-on collision with the Soviet Union. The Russian response, relayed by his UN ambassador Arthur Goldberg from the Russian delegate Federenko, and by the American ambassador in Moscow, Llewellyn Thompson, was reasonably encouraging. But there was no chance of devising with the Russians a common solution. So the policy of Lyndon Johnson and Harold Wilson was to concoct a declaration by the maritime powers affirming the right of free passage through the Straits.

Eban was asked to procrastinate and give Washington ten days or a fortnight to complete this task. But the project was in trouble from the start. Hardly any of the maritime nations displayed the least eagerness to court trouble with the Arabs.

For his part, Eban genuinely believed that something might be achieved through negotiations; he has argued in private since the war that for the sake of Israel's international reputation it was essential that the diplomatic method be tested, even though it might be found wanting. He maintained that Israel might have been accused of indecent haste had she struck the moment the Straits were closed.

On May 27 Mr Eban returned to Israel from Washington. Speaking to press correspondents in Paris on his return journey, he said: 'I have made an exploratory trip to be informed of the viewpoint of the three friendly governments about the illegal measures taken by Egypt in the Straits of Tiran.... It is self evident that peace cannot co-exist with an illegal blockade. I have explained this thesis to the eminent French, British and American leaders. They represent the three governments which ten years ago pledged solemnly to insist on the international character of this waterway and to practise there their right of free and innocent passage.'

The proposal under discussion was for a flotilla, preferably under the auspices of the UN, or failing that of such maritime powers as would participate, to break the Egyptian blockade of the Straits. There were various plans under consideration. One was for an oil tanker flying a non-Israeli flag (but carrying what Egypt classed as strategic freight), another for a merchant ship flying the Israeli flag, to pass through the Straits. The flotilla, which would no doubt be composed largely of US and conceivably of British vessels, would escort the ships bound for Eilat through the Straits of Tiran. It was hoped that the demonstration of force made by the presence of this great armada would dissuade the Egyptians from opening fire. However, if they did so, the flotilla would make what was termed a 'controlled response' to this action. This can be taken as meaning the taking out of the batteries at Sharm el-Sheikh.

In the period between Johnson's meeting with Eban and the arrival of Wilson, the situation in the Middle East took a decisive turn. On May 26 President Nasser, addressing the leaders of the Pan-Arab Federation of Trade Unions, said that if war came 'it will be total and the objective will be to destroy Israel. We feel confident that we can win and are ready now for a war with Israel. . . . This time it will not be like 1956 because we were not fighting Israel at that time, but Britain and France'. He called the United States 'the main enemy' and described Britain as 'a lackey of America'. He said that 'Wilson cannot move without taking orders from Johnson'. Earlier the Egyptian Ministry of Religious Affairs had ordered all preachers to make 'Jihad' (Holy War) the subject of their sermons in the mosques. The preachers were told that they must stress to their congregations that it was an honour to die as a martyr in a holy battle. This was all that was needed to whip up the war fever in the capital. Even Pope Kyrillos VI, head of the Coptic Orthodox Church in Egypt, joined in. He supported all steps taken by Egypt to 'regain Palestine from those who crucified Christ'. The message from now on was more than ever one of hate. Israel was constantly referred to as 'the enemy' and Egypt was eager to fight.

The great powers were alarmed by Nasser's recklessness. He appeared to be losing his balance. On the day of this latest pugnacious declaration, President Johnson sent a note to the Egyptian ambassador in Washington requesting the Egyptians to exercise restraint, and *not* to open fire first. That night Nasser was called out of bed at 3.30 am to hear an urgent message from the Soviet ambassador in Cairo. He told Nasser that Egypt was strongly advised not to initiate the fighting.

According to the *Washington Post* of June 15 the Russians had a substantial ground for concern. While wishing to avoid a confrontation, they were also informed of the inadequate condition of Egyptian military preparations. A team of Soviet inspectors, checking Egyptian airfields, found pilots who had not been airborne for days. Egypt's dummy planes were unconvincing; and their real ones were massed together where they would be easy targets.

Informed naval opinion now expressed doubts as to whether Egypt was indeed capable of mining the Straits of Tiran owing to the complications raised by the width and depth of the waterway; and the inward passage of a German cargo ship to the Jordanian port of Aqaba on May 25 indicated that there was indeed an open channel.

In Israel the feeling that she was not prepared to wait indefinitely for an end to the blockade gained further strength when high-ranking Israeli officials in Jerusalem warned that Israel would be entirely within her rights in ending the blockade as an act of self-defence if the United Nations or the maritime powers did not do so.

Only two hours after Mr Brown had flown back to London from Moscow a Soviet statement was issued attacking Israel 'for pursuing a hostile policy against the Arab States'. Brown himself came under further attack in the press in a leader in the *Daily Telegraph* on Saturday May 27: 'Nothing of any value seems to have been achieved by Mr Brown's twice postponed visit to Moscow, even though it appears to have been largely devoted to discussions of the Middle East crisis. . . . The clear meaning of what was said to Mr Brown and at a subsequent press conference in Moscow yesterday is that the Russians believe that they have little to lose and all to gain from a serious weakening, if not total defeat, of the most Western-orientated nation in the Middle East – short of escalation into a major war.'

On Saturday May 27, U Thant, who had flown back to Washington on the Thursday night without issuing any statement, made his report to the Security Council. He said that President Nasser and Dr Riad had assured him that

Egypt would not 'initiate offensive action against Israel'. The Egyptians' general aim was for 'a return to the conditions prior to 1956 and to full observance by both parties of the provisions of the general armistice agreement between Israel and Egypt'.

From Paris it was reported that General de Gaulle had sent a message to President Nasser urging moderation in the crisis. Previously Nasser had praised de Gaulle for not having 'followed the Anglo-American line'. General de Gaulle's intervention, however, can have had little effect for on Sunday May 28, at a press conference in Cairo, Nasser threatened to close the Suez Canal if war broke out between Egypt and Israel and any other nation interfered. He said: 'The Tiran Straits are Egyptian territorial waters over which we exercise our sovereign rights. No power however strong it may be can touch Egypt's sovereign rights or skirt them. Any such attempt will be aggression on the Egyptian people and all Arabs and will bring unimaginable harm to the aggressors. ... If war breaks out with Israel, conditions in the Suez Canal will remain unchanged, but in the event of intervention by other countries there will be no Suez Canal.'

The same day, the Egyptian Defence Minister, Mr Badran, ended a four-day visit to Moscow, during which he had consulted Kosygin, Gromyko, and the Soviet Defence Minister, Marshal Grechko.

Nasser's judgment was distorted by the enormous failure of his sycophantic intelligence service, which underestimated the enemy's strength. There is little reason to believe that Nasser was bent on a military show-down with Israel from the outset. However, as Eban put it 'Nasser was like a man who had gone to Monte Carlo with £100 and staked it at the roulette wheel. Each time his number came up he became more courageous – he felt that Fortune was smiling on him.'

The atmosphere in Cairo during the ten days before the war was tense but optimistic. There were no signs of apprehension among civilians as there were in Israel. Although the army had taken up forward positions in Sinai the crisis still had the appearance of a war of words, and attention was focused on Britain and America rather than on Israel. Even the appointment of General Dayan as Defence Minister was not regarded as a final danger signal.

Mr Eban's tour of the Western capitals was reported fully and reasonably by the Cairo press. It was judged that Britain and America had given some guarantee that they would reopen the Straits of Tiran and therefore were the real enemies. The proposed declaration by the maritime powers was watched at first with concern but later with derision. Intelligent Egyptian observers felt that Nasser had won a major political victory over his primary enemies, Britain and the United States. The announcement on June 4 that Zakaria Mohieddin would be welcome to visit Washington was interpreted as a sign of American appeasement.

Reaction to the crisis came from other countries in the Arab world in the form of threats to British and American oil supplies, which were reported over the weekend. According to Baghdad radio the Iraqi Cabinet decided to deny oil to any country supporting aggression against an Arab state. Kuwait also threatened to freeze the Anglo-American oil concession in the event of Western support for Israel. Britain and Western Europe are still heavily dependent upon supplies from Arab countries. Though there has been a rapid exploitation of African resources the major new producers, Algeria and Libya, are Arab nations aligned with Nasser against the West. However, the new geography of oil did reduce the effectiveness of Nasser's threat to the Suez Canal. Eleven years ago more than 80% of Western Europe's oil supplies came through the Suez Canal. The figure is now under 60%.

On Monday night, May 29, at an emergency session of the Security Council in New York, the United States proposed that Egypt should allow freedom of navigation through the Straits of Tiran during a 'breathing spell' which the United Nations should use to resolve the crisis. The Egyptian delegate, however, retorted that control of the Straits was historically the right of the Arabs. The proposal never came to a vote and collapsed through lack of support.

In Jerusalem Mr Eshkol said that he expected the United States, Britain and other countries to take action shortly to end the blockade. The US and Britain, among others, had undertaken to ensure the freedom of shipping in the Straits of Tiran and 'it is our duty to put the pledges to the test. Very shortly it will be clear if this prospect materializes.' Since the withdrawal of UNEF ten days before, the Israeli Army had, for the first time since 1956, patrolled the border of the Gaza Strip. Eshkol was speaking not long after an outbreak of firing on the Gaza Strip between Arabs and Israelis – the first outbreak of this kind for nearly ten years.

In Cairo on May 29 President Nasser gave a warning that Egypt must treat the United States and Britain as enemies for siding with Israel. Addressing the National Assembly soon after it had given him the power to rule by decree, he said, 'If the Western countries slight us and deny us our rights we shall teach them how to respect us. ... We are not facing Israel but those behind it. We are facing those who created Israel.' Speaking of the military situation, he declared that 'preparations by the UAR and her allies for the liberation of Palestine are complete'.

On Tuesday May 30 it was announced that Russia had informed Turkey of her intention to send ten warships through the Bosphorus into the Mediterranean during the following week. Under the Montreux Convention of 1936 warships from foreign countries can pass through the Straits if they inform the Turkish Government eight days in advance. Meanwhile, the authoritative Cairo newspaper *Al Ahram* reported that a United States tanker flying the Liberian flag had turned back from the Straits of Tiran after a warning shot had been fired across its bows. But in Washington and at the US Embassy in Cairo all knowledge of such a ship in the area was denied.

At a press conference in Jerusalem Mr Eban said that Israel would be prepared to accept any solution which guaranteed free passage for *all* ships through the Straits of Tiran but added that there must be a time limit of 'weeks or days' for diplomatic action. 'We will act alone if we must,' he said, 'to break the blockade but with others if we can. Let there be no mistake about the crucial character of the effort Israel is prepared to make.'

But the most dramatic event of May 30 was the unexpected arrival in Cairo of King Hussein of Jordan who, after a stay of only six hours, signed a defence agreement with President Nasser. This sudden turn of events surprised the Egyptian people as much as foreigners. The two men had for long been at loggerheads, President Nasser having often denounced Hussein in the past as a traitor to the Arab cause.

The following day President Aref of Iraq, who had previously rejected the King's invitation to send troops to Jordan, agreed to support his military confrontation with Israel. Iraqi troops and armoured units moved up into Jordan. The left-wing Syrian régime, finding itself odd-man-out after the Nasser-Hussein pact, showed its anger by denouncing Jordan as 'the home of treason'.

Meanwhile, in Amman, Ahmed Shukiary, the head of the Palestine Liberation Organization, was saying that it was 'possible and even most likely' that his Palestine Liberation Army would fire the first shot. If the Arabs took Israel, he said, the surviving Jews would be helped to return to their native countries. 'But my estimation is that none will survive.'

In Germany the Bonn Cabinet reversed their earlier decision not to supply gas masks to Israel, 20,000 of which would now be supplied as soon as possible. The Cabinet decided that the gas masks were of humanitarian value only and did not fall under the NATO ban on the export of military equipment to crisis areas.

The Defence Pact of May 30 was undoubtedly the turning-point between peace and war. Strategically, an alliance between Egypt and Jordan could scarcely be tolerated by Israel. For Israel would now be exposed to attack at its most vulnerable point, the 'soft under-belly' where Jordanian territory formed a salient into Israel and provided a hostile base for attack only twelve miles from the Mediterranean coast. Under the defence pact, the Egyptian Chief of Staff would command both Jordanian and UAR Forces in the event of war, so establishing a pincer which could be manipulated from Cairo.

Chapter Three
Israel Decides

While events in Washington and at the United Nations were moving slowly, if at all, in the Middle East the situation was developing with great rapidity. The talkers were being overtaken by events. While President Johnson and Prime Minister Harold Wilson were hawking a document around the world seeking to obtain the signatures and support of other maritime nations for concerting action to open the Straits of Tiran, if need be by force, the problem of the Straits had become a minor issue in the mounting crisis. While the eyes of the world were focused elsewhere four conditions had been fulfilled, any one of which had in the past been regarded as a cause for war by Israel – the closing of the Straits, a concentration of Egyptian forces in Sinai, a Nasserite Jordan and Iraqi troops on Jordanian territory. Few people imagined that Jordan could come under Nasser's control while Hussein remained in power; but, at least as far as the command of the armed forces was concerned, it had. A threat to Israel's shipping and access to the East was one thing: the direct and deadly threat of an Arab military build-up along her borders was another.

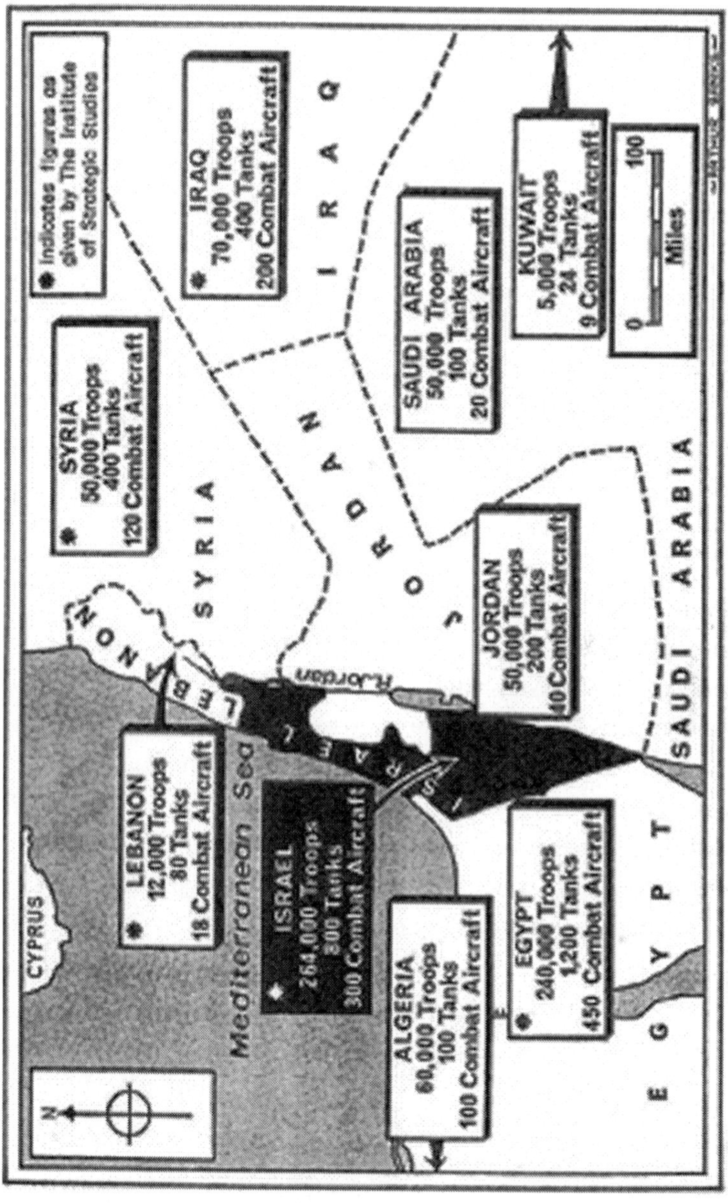

Armed strengths in the Middle East

Israel, with four out of every five men in her Army a civilian, could not afford to maintain her forces mobilized indefinitely. Already by the end of May many of the shops and businesses were closed, the factories were operating at a greatly reduced level and the corn was standing in the fields waiting to be harvested. But equally Israel could not afford to stand down from her high level of mobilization while the imminent danger of a surprise attack by her neighbours existed. It was an intolerable situation for her. Throughout the country and particularly in the Army, there was growing unrest and dissatisfaction. It was one of those rare occasions in a democracy when public opinion in a non-election year was able to bring massive and real pressure to bear on the Government. The country demanded a decision, and demanded that someone they knew and trusted should be at the helm. For many years Ben-Gurion, occupying the positions of Prime Minister and Minister of Defence, had relieved the Israeli people of any anxiety for their security. Now after ten years of peace Israel was faced with the gravest crisis since her war of independence of 1948, when one person in every hundred had died in defence of the State they had so recently, after so many years of wandering throughout the world, established in Palestine.

In the face of this crisis the Israeli people turned to one man – General Moshe Dayan, the victor of Sinai in 1956. Here was a man who had the knowledge and ability to assess the situation and make a decision. From Dayan they would accept a decision to fight or to wait with complete conviction that, whichever it should be, the decision had been taken for sound reasons.

Dayan is an Israeli hero, his career a matter of national pride. Born in Palestine in 1915, he joined the *Haganah* (the Jewish underground defence organization) at the age of 14, and was gaoled by the British for his underground activities in 1939. He was released after serving only a year of his ten-year sentence and joined the British Army. He took part in the Second World War in which he went on a commando raid attacking the Vichy French forces in Syria. As a result of this episode he lost his left eye and acquired a black eye-patch, which has become his trademark. In Israel's war of independence he fought as commander of a Jeep commando battalion: but it was as Chief of Staff during the victorious Sinai campaign of 1956 that Dayan won international fame and became a symbol of Israel's patriotism.

In 1960 Dayan became a member of the Knesset and was appointed Minister of Agriculture in David Ben-Gurion's Government. When Ben-Gurion seceded from Eshkol's ruling Mapai party in June 1965, and formed the small but influential Rafi group, Dayan followed. Shimon Peres, one of the leading lights of the Rafi Party, has described the problems which confronted Israel in the days leading up to the war: 'There were two questions to be resolved – the decision to go or not to go and secondly who should bear the responsibility for that decision. There was growing resentment in the country and in the Army, not because the Government hadn't decided on war – but because it had taken *no* decision.' Rafi was, broadly, the party of the 'hawks', while the 'doves' put their trust in Eshkol and Eban.

The divisions inside Israel at this time were not only political ones on party lines. There is a marked difference of outlook between the *Sabras,* the Israeli-born Jews, and what they contemptuously refer to as the 'Jews of the Ghettoes', the refugees from Europe and the survivors of the Nazi concentration camps. The native-born Israelis have the idea that, after nearly two thousand years wandering among alien people, European Jews had become cowed by their dependence on others to protect them rather than looking to their own defence. A notable exception to this was of course the valiant struggle put up by the Polish Jews in the Warsaw Ghetto when they tried to resist the overwhelming strength of their Nazi oppressors. The Sabras claim that it is the natural reaction of the European Jew, whenever Israel is threatened, to look to others – the Western powers – for their protection rather than relying on Israel's own resources. This was the reason, they claim, for Israel relying on the British and the French in 1956 as it was for the Government of Eshkol to look to the United States and the maritime nations to open the Straits of Tiran rather than take decisive action at the outset.

By May 24 Shimon Peres was the organizing centre of a political alliance which could muster 50 of the Knesset's 120 votes, and which aimed to overthrow Eshkol. Eshkol, 'very much an Attlee figure' as *The Observer* described him, and leader of Mapai, was considered to be weak and too inclined to appeasement. Peres was allied with Begin of Gahal, the second most numerous party, and with representatives of the religious parties, including Moshe-Haim Shapiro of the National Religious Party which, although aligned with the Government, was keen to have Ben-Gurion or Dayan as Prime Minister.

Begin went to see Eshkol and proposed that Ben-Gurion take his place. Eshkol was not happy with the idea. Shapiro then pressed for Ben-Gurion as Minister of Defence, though without Ben-Gurion's knowledge.

Meanwhile, it became clear that although many members of the Mapai party wished to broaden the Government, they would not tolerate the full expulsion of Eshkol. Ben-Gurion therefore let it be known that Eshkol would be welcome to stay on in any capacity except as Prime Minister or Minister of Defence.

Eshkol still demurred. Then, on May 30, Peres let it be known that the Rafi would dissolve itself as a party and re-join Mapai if a joint arrangement could be agreed. This considerably improved Rafi's bargaining position as many Mapai supporters favoured bringing Rafi back into the fold. It also strengthened Rafi's hand in the meeting of May 31 with Mrs Golda Meir, who was strongly opposed to giving any of the Rafi group a position of responsibility and power in the Government.

At the same time it became clear that Eshkol would not step down from the premiership *and* the Ministry of Defence in favour of his predecessor, Ben-Gurion. So Rafi proposed that Dayan should be put forward as the Rafi-Gahal candidate for power. Ben-Gurion was angry at the substitution.

The need for Dayan's inclusion in the Government became more pressing when King Hussein flew to Cairo for the signing of the military pact with Nasser on May 30. Some members of the Israeli Government tried to suggest that there was no particular significance in this meeting as similar moves had been made in 1956 and in 1964. But Gen. Yariv, the head of the Israeli Intelligence, stressed in very clear terms to the Government the implications of the pact. His fears were supported two days later when the Egyptian General Riadh assumed command of the Jordanian Army and the UAR established an advance command post in Amman.

Discussions with the Government went on throughout Wednesday May 31 in a vain attempt to get Dayan accepted in a position of authority, either as Prime Minister or Minister of Defence; Dayan was. pessimistic and depressed. Eshkol was prepared to have him in but only in an advisory capacity, offering him the deputy premiership or membership of the Government's inner committee for defence, which consisted of 13 people. Both positions would have involved responsibility without power. This was something that neither Dayan nor the Rafi leadership was prepared to accept.

Later that night (May 31) Dayan had a meeting with Eshkol in which he indicated that if the latter could not offer him a responsible position in the Government, such as Minister of Defence, he would accept any military post under General Rabin, the Chief of Staff, preferably the command of the Southern Front.

Eshkol agreed on the Wednesday night to Dayan's becoming Commander of the Southern Front. By the Thursday morning members of Mapai, believing that agreement had been reached with Rafi, called up Shimon Peres and others of the Rafi leadership to congratulate them on their statesmanship in reaching a settlement with the Government on the basis agreed between Eshkol and Dayan the night before.

Meanwhile, the leadership of the M'Arakh Alignment * were pressing for Yigal Allon to be appointed Minister of Defence. But this was not acceptable to many of the Mapai, who favoured Dayan. On Thursday June 1 at noon there was a meeting at Begin's house with the religious group where it was decided that they should demand that Dayan be given the Defence Ministry.

* See Appendix 2.

At 2 pm there was a meeting between Eshkol and the Gahal leadership at which Eshkol proposed Yigal Yadin (former Chief of Staff and now Professor of Archaeology at Jerusalem University) as Minister of Defence. Both Yadin and Rafi refused this proposal: Yadin, as he felt that public opinion and the morale of the army demanded that Dayan should fill this post.

At 3 pm on Thursday there was a meeting of the Secretariat of Mapai at which 24 people spoke. Of these, 19 supported Dayan and only 5 backed Allon. At 7 pm Eshkol and delegates of Rafi met, and it was agreed that Dayan should have the Defence Ministry. This meeting lasted no more than ten minutes. An hour later the Rafi leadership met in Ben-Gurion's house. After two hours of discussion Ben-Gurion changed his mind and approved Dayan's appointment as Defence Minister. By 11 pm the same night the Cabinet met and made provision for the inclusion of three extra members. Dayan (Defence) and Menachem Begin (Minister without Portfolio) were appointed immediately; the third, Joseph Saphir (also Minister without Portfolio), was appointed three days later.

It is now a controversial issue in Israeli politics as to who should have the credit for the decision to strike, and for the successful conduct of the war. Dayan's admirers claim that when he entered the Cabinet the decision to fight had yet to be taken, and add that no detailed plan of attack had been worked out. Eshkol loyalists tend to present contradictory evidence.

Brigadier-General Ezer Weizmann has said that when Dayan became Minister of Defence 'he knew that there was a possibility that the decision to go might not be taken'. Others claim that the Eshkol Government was too fearful to make the decision without him. They wanted Dayan included so that if the whole thing ended in disaster they would not have to carry the can alone.

The Foreign Secretary, Abba Eban, and the Minister of Labour, Allon, recall events differently. Eban says that the decision to fight had been reached by June 1 : it was dictated by the pact between Nasser and Hussein. Allon agrees. He says that prior to the Defence Pact there was a division in the Cabinet, a majority still hoping for a diplomatic solution. But after May 30 war was inevitable. It was just a question of timing.

The truth of the matter is perhaps more simple than political rivalries would indicate. Even Peres, a staunch Dayan man, was in no doubt as to the largest factor: 'Nasser and Hussein at Cairo airport. This was an historic and crucial kiss ... we were now surrounded by a sort of banana filled with Russian weapons.'

Dayan was included in the Cabinet because the Eshkol Government was being forced to two unavoidable conclusions: Israel had no alternative but to fight and the Israeli Government needed Dayan because the nation demanded it and because they needed his knowledge, courage and optimism. Just as it had taken Hitler to make Churchill Prime Minister in 1940, so, as Dayan put it shortly before the start of the war, 'It took 80,000 Egyptian soldiers to get me into the Israeli Cabinet.'

The appointment of Dayan received little attention in the English press the following day. Pride of place was given to the Anglo-American diplomatic moves to secure recognition of free navigation in the Gulf. But by the time Harold Wilson and Lyndon Johnson met in Washington on June 2, it was too late for a diplomatic formula to succeed. War was certain. Only the date was open.

✤ ✤ ✤

The Armed Forces that Dayan found under his command when he was appointed Defence Minister less than eighty hours before Israel was to be at war were a remarkable and unique military machine. They were composed of farmers, greengrocers, taxi-drivers and business men – four men out of five were civilians. Nevertheless, in defence of their own land, they were one of the finest armies the world has ever seen.

In May 1967 the Israelis had an army of 50–60,000 men, all but 10-12,000 of whom were National Servicemen. On complete mobilization the Israeli Army can put 264,000 men in the field. National Servicemen in Israel serve 30 months (it was increased from 26 months in November 1966) and then go on the reserve. They remain on the reserve until they are forty-five when they join the Civil Defence. Brigadier-General Sharon, who commanded the central axis in Sinai and was also in command of the paratroop brigade which captured Mitla in 1956, was in charge of training the Defence Forces. The basic training for officers on the reserve is 42/58 days annually, 36 for NCOs and 30 for privates. These figures are variable and depend on the specialized work of the reservist. Israel is the only democratic country in the world where women are automatically called up for military service. They serve for 18 months and when in reserve corporals and below serve 30 days a year and sergeants and above 42–47 days a year. Although women fought in the 1948 campaign, in 1967 they were not used as fighting troops. Nevertheless, many of them were in the front line and were to go through some of the toughest fighting, acting as radio operators, intelligence staff and as nurses. General Yoffe, commander of one of the Israeli divisions in the Sinai, paid tribute to the women of Israel's Armed Forces: 'When the men see the women enduring the same heat, flies, discomfort and exhaustion that they are, it spurs them to battle on and endure the sufferings and deprivations of war with even greater determination.'

General Yoffe also said:'I would like to make a point here that all my division, from the Commander down, are civilians and were civilians up to three weeks ago. I myself have been a civilian for two years after leaving the Army, and from Nature Conservation in Israel, I had to go and start protecting not nature, but the country. This is the common thing in Israel where today you are a soldier and the next day something else.'

A very substantial part of the Israeli Army can be mobilized within 24 hours and the process is complete down to the last man within 72 hours. Officers and company sergeants telephone or visit the house of each of the men in their unit to tell them to report for duty. Those who happen to be away from their homes at the time make it their business to find their own way to their units and in many cases even people abroad do all they can to return to their country. Or in the case of an emergency, a system of code messages broadcast over Kol Yisrael (Radio Israel) is used to call up reservists.

Each unit goes to a collection centre and from there the men are transported to their base camp where they are issued with all equipment, except boots which they bring with them. In the case of the reservist armoured units which, in the event of an emergency, it is essential should be in the field first of all, each man has his uniform and equipment hanging from a hook which bears his name and the tanks and armoured half-tracks are waiting, fully serviced and ready to go. In some cases in the recent war it was not possible to issue all the troops with weapons. Some of the units found that their mobilization was more than 100 per cent as many of the men who were still fit but disqualified by age or had received severe wounds in previous wars were reporting for duty and asking to be allowed to go with the Army – at least one unit had over 100 extra men. A man over sixty years of age who had been General Yoffe's driver with the British Army in the North African desert in World War II formed up and pleaded not to be left behind. Yoffe told him that if he found a jeep to drive he would have the job. Inside 24 hours the man reported for duty, jeep and all – no questions asked.

Israeli military planners have always envisaged Egypt as the major threat and believed that any confrontation would take place in the southern part of Israel and the Sinai peninsula. In times of crisis, therefore, the bulk of the Israeli Army would be deployed in the southern Negev along the Egyptian/Israeli border. Because of the small size of Israel and the concentration of her population, the Israelis know that they can never afford to let their own country be the battlefield – they must go out and meet the enemy in Sinai.

The threat posed by Jordan and Syria had always been regarded as a minor one compared with Egypt; and even up to the week immediately preceding the war few people believed that Jordan would involve herself from the outset and attack Israel. The plan was to maintain a defensive posture on the Syrian and Jordanian fronts, thus enabling the greater part of Israel's Army to be free for the battle royal in the Sinai arena. So that the whole Army, including all the reservists, should be free to fight outside Israel's borders, the territorial defence of the country was made the responsibility of the civil defence. In the case of the settlements along the borders, the inhabitants of the kibbutzim had the duty of looking after themselves and their families. Each kibbutz has its own armoury of small arms but in times of emergency mortars and machine-guns are brought in by the Army which also seconds an officer to advise and command the local force. The settlements along the Syrian border were particularly vulnerable as they lay on a low plain dominated by the Syrian ridge which rises steeply to the east making it easy for the Syrians to fire down on the settlements, but almost impossible for them to fire back. For a long time the situation on the border had been tense.

A woman would never know when she said goodbye to her husband in the morning, as he left on his tractor to cultivate the fields close to the border or in the demilitarized zones, whether she would ever see him again. This perpetual state of fear was heightened by the increasing number of sabotage raids made into Israel by terrorists based in Syria. In the event of an open war between Israel and Syria these settlements would be at the mercy of the Syrian artillery dug in in bunkers and fortifications to a depth of 10 miles from the border. These fortifications had been built up by the Syrians over the past 19 years and housed an incredible quantity of the most modern and powerful artillery, anti-tank and anti-aircraft equipment the Soviet Union could supply. The 250 or more guns could put out a sustained fire in the order of ten tons of shells per minute, stretching all along the border and some of them able to reach up to fifteen miles into Israel. In the course of the war, the buildings of those kibbutzim were to be almost flattened and their fields which were waiting to be harvested set on fire by the shelling. In spite of the heavy artillery bombardment to which they were subjected, few of the women and children in the settlements were killed as from previous experience they had built concrete walls to protect the children's sleeping quarters and had established deep and heavily sandbagged shelters from which they hardly moved during the week of the war. There was never any question of the women and children being evacuated from these front-line areas and it is one of the greatest strengths of Israel's territorial defence system that every man in the kibbutz knows he is fighting to defend not only his home and his land, but his wife and his children too.

The withdrawal of the United Nations Force had produced an atmosphere of tension on the Israeli/Egyptian border, especially along the Gaza Strip. A visit to the kibbutz at Kefar 'Azza after the United Nations had been withdrawn revealed that the workers in the field and soldiers of the Israeli Army on border patrol were fired on and shelled practically every day; and a few days before the outbreak of war incendiary shells destroyed 500 acres of wheat in a neighbouring kibbutz at Nahal Oz.

One of the greatest strengths of the Israeli Army is its flexibility and its use of tactics not to be found in military books. These tactics, unshackled by any elaborate preconceived and inflexible plan, were evolved in the fighting of 1948 and demonstrated in the Sinai Campaign of 1956. Moshe Dayan, who had master-minded Israel's victory in 1956, and Arie Sharon, who had led the paratroop drop on the Mitla Pass at the outset of that campaign, had between them very largely evolved and perfected the up-to-date techniques of the Israeli Army.

In the years since 1956 the Israelis have improved still further the strength, equipment and training of their armed forces. The basic principle of Israeli tactics which was in a large part responsible for their rapid victories in 1956 and 1967 was described by General Rabin, the Chief of Staff, in conversation after the war as being that of a 'mailed fist' – striking with massive concentrations of armour deep into enemy territory and throwing them off balance without establishing firm lines of communication or advancing along a front, which has been the textbook method for centuries. Under Rabin the training and efficiency of the Armoured Corps reached a very high level and he was the man largely responsible for preparing the innumerable separate and individual plans on which the campaign of 1967 was based. There was no overall plan of campaign nor did it have a code name – after the campaign was over the Israeli Army staff began scratching its head to think one up. As General Ezer Weizmann, Director of Operations, said: 'We have got a plan for everything – even for capturing the North Pole. The plans are like bricks. They can be used one by one to build up a structure as the situation develops. We don't go in for preconceived and, therefore, inflexible master plans.'

One of Israel's greatest achievements has been her ability to create a powerful military machine with very limited resources by establishing a very strict order of priorities. In the case of the Army it was to have a number of crack armoured brigades and to motorise all their infantry. 'No one walks in the Israeli Army today – that all went by the board years ago', remarked General Aric Sharon. In the air the establishment of correct priorities has been if anything of even greater importance. Although the credit for the state of readiness and the achievement of Israel's air victory go to General Mordechai Hod, the Commander of the Air Force, it is Brigadier-General Ezer Weizmann who over the past ten years has been architect of that Air Force. It was his decision to devote such resources as they had to creating a strong force of fighter bombers rather than squander them by having a bomber force as well. As far as he was concerned bombers were expensive animals and had little application to Israel's defence problems as their major role is to bomb centres of civilian population, which Israel had no interest in doing. He wanted to have an Air Force that could destroy any enemy force that might be sent against Israel and which could give support to Israeli ground troops. He therefore concentrated on building up a sizeable force of fighter bombers, adding to Israel's armoury the French Mystère and more recently the 1400 mph Mirage. 'We always went on the assumption that we would be fighting the finest air force in the world – then we set out to show that this was not the case,' Weizmann remarked.

In the early part of 1967 the Israeli Air Force put on a demonstration for the benefit of the air attachés of the foreign embassies in Tel Aviv. A squadron of Vautours, Israel's longest range fighter-bombers, landed and taxied in pairs up to a ramp. A stop watch was started the second they touched down. Within 7½ minutes the aircraft had been filled up with fuel and oxygen, their cannons had been reloaded with ammunition, ten bombs had been hung from their wings and they were airborne once again. After the war one of the attachés asked General Hod how long the turn-around time of the Israeli aircraft had been. Hod replied that he had seen for himself earlier in the year. 'But surely that was only a demonstration,' insisted the air attaché. There can be no doubt that it was not. This incredibly fast turn-around time – equalled by few Air Forces in the world – was to be a major factor in Israel's victory.

Whether among the pilots or among the soldiers sweating it out in the 100°F heat of the Southern Negev the mood was one of cool self-confidence. They knew that they were outnumbered in troops: they knew they were outnumbered in quantity and quality of equipment. Nevertheless, they never had any doubt of the outcome. In contrast to the Arab countries, it was hard to find anyone in Israel in the weeks before the war who openly wanted war. But there was a strong feeling among people of every walk of life that if the Arabs wanted a war they could have it.

One by one, without fuss or bother, the men – and women – had left their jobs in the cities and in the countryside to go and fight for their country. Their greatest strength was that they knew what they were fighting for. Every man realized that while defeat for the Arabs would mean the loss of an army, for Israel it would mean the end of her existence as a state and the annihilation of her people. As an Israeli officer who had served with the British Army in the Second World War and who had fought at Alamein put it: 'This would have been a second Masada. When the Egyptians got here they would have found no one alive. I would have killed my wife and daughter rather than let them fall into their hands. And I don't know anyone who wouldn't have done the same.'

⚜ ⚜ ⚜

It was quite fortuitous that Harold Wilson found himself in Washington just at the time of the Middle East crisis. He had had a long-standing engagement to visit Expo '67 in Montreal and to have a talk with the Canadian Prime Minister, Mr Lester Pearson. It has become the traditional custom for British Prime Ministers to visit the United States in the common course of business twice a year and he was, therefore, going to have a perfectly routine meeting to which no one need attach too much attention. Two weeks before, de Gaulle at his press conference in Paris on May 15 had again imposed an effective veto on Britain's immediate entry into the Common Market. For some days before the crisis in the Middle East it appears there had been a feeling among anglophile members of the Johnson administration that it might have been better if Wilson had not gone to Washington at all. It was felt that he would either make offensive remarks about the war in Vietnam to prove to de Gaulle that he was turning into a good European after all, or, alternatively, that he would say nothing about Vietnam and so add weight to de Gaulle's persistent mistrust of the Anglo-American relationship.

It must be remembered that at the time, especially in the aftermath of General Westmoreland's trip to Washington and his speech before the special joint session of Congress on Vietnam, the White House was steeling itself for a further increase in the Vietnam war effort. British MPs, including right-wing Labourites and some Conservatives (such as David Howell), had been in the United States during the Whitsun recess and been dismayed at the hardening White House mood. As Howell remarked, after seeing Johnson: 'He seems to be substituting prayer for policy.'

Word had reached Washington from London that Wilson was now having trouble not only with his left-wingers but some reputed right-wingers about his continued 'association' with United States Vietnam policy. Last August, on Wilson's previous White House trip, the President had pointedly reminded him that in an unfortunate Commons statement on the first Hanoi bombing he had 'disassociated' himself from something he had never been associated with.

It was clear that the President had got bored with Wilson. As he saw it, Wilson tried to make political capital at home by posing as being politically close to him 'when in fact the President had not even bothered to let him know he was indulging in direct correspondence with Ho Chi Minh. Johnson has little regard for British efforts to play the mediator. If its efforts were to be successful, the President would be happy but he and his administration remain distinctly sceptical.

Anglo-American discussions had produced no positive plan of action for the Middle East. Since Nasser's announcement that he would blockade the Gulf, London and Washington had been trying to prepare a declaration recognizing rights of passage, which the maritime nations would be invited to endorse. Reporting this to the House of Commons on May 31, George Brown was greeted by cheers from the Government front bench. Winding up the debate, the Prime Minister warned the House that time was running out, and added: 'One condition of a lasting peace must be the recognition that Israel has a right to live.'

He said that Britain reserved the possibility of action, in co-operation with other powers, should the Security Council fail to produce a solution. It was clear from his speech that, while there was little time, no physical action was imminent. Supposing that Nasser remained adamant, there was some idea of naval action to force a relaxation of the blockade. But at the time of the Wilson-Johnson meeting, such a possibility was still in the planning stage.

When Wilson reached Washington on Friday June 1 from Ottawa he was given a spectacular welcome. A full guard of honour turned out on the south lawn of the White House, and Wilson was saluted by trumpeters and the firing of guns. The NBC commentator, Joe Harsch, inquired: 'Is there any change in the special relationship with Britain, what with the flags and twenty-one guns . . .? It's just as if we were greeting the King of Patagonia.' He meant that it is more a mark of distinction at the White House to be received without fuss.

Wilson spent two hours alone with Johnson before lunch, and two hours afterwards with him and the Cabinet.

At 4.30 he appeared at a press conference at the British Embassy. In the ensuing half hour he gave away as little as possible, and later that evening, replying to Johnson's toast to the Queen, he remarked that he had twice that week spoken about the Middle East crisis: once in the House of Commons, and once at the press conference. 'And it was important that I should say nothing on either occasion,' he commented, 'so I said nothing! '

⚜ ⚜ ⚜

While diplomacy was taking its course in Washington, New York and London, the Israeli vision of a US-backed international flotilla to open the Straits of Tiran was rapidly evaporating. Even if in the initial phases the British and American Governments had given assurances of support in opening the Straits it had become quite clear to the Israeli Government by the beginning of June that both the Americans and the British were becoming more and more reluctant to take any effective action. Although this might have been a disappointment to those in the Israeli Cabinet who still favoured reliance on diplomacy and international action, other developments had taken place which favoured those who demanded action.

The efforts of the Israeli Foreign Minister Abba Eban, although the subject of derision and deprecation by many of his countrymen and even some of his colleagues in the Cabinet, had managed to secure for Israel in his two weeks of peregrinations backwards and forwards to Washington, London and Paris a climate of opinion in which it was possible for Israel to take decisive action. Public opinion in most western countries had come round to the side of the Israelis when it saw the recklessness and provocation of Nasser's action coupled with Israel's reluctance to take decisive action without first seeing what diplomacy could achieve. When it was becoming daily more evident that diplomacy would achieve nothing and that the Governments of the United States and Britain were unlikely to carry out their half-promises, there was a general feeling, particularly in the United States and Britain, but also in some of the smaller countries of Europe such as Holland, that it was not for them or their Governments to be angry if the Israelis should decide to look after their own affairs.

By the first weekend in June two things were clear to the Israelis. First that they would not incur the wrath of the President of the United States as they had done in 1956. Secondly, the Soviet Union would not intervene. Whether this was merely a shrewd assessment of the situation by Israeli Intelligence or whether in fact some wink had been received through unofficial channels from Johnson is impossible to say. Certainly the State Department, through their Ambassador in Tel Aviv, Walworth Barbour, were giving the Israelis the 'red light' against war. Nevertheless the Israelis felt that it was safe for them to act should the situation demand it. The situation as outlined by General Yariv, head of Israeli Intelligence, was a very black one. In addition to the fateful kiss between Nasser and King Hussein at Cairo airport the Israelis now knew that Egypt's General Riadh had arrived in Amman to establish an advance command post and that Jordanian forces had been placed under his command. Besides this, on the evening of Sunday June 4 the vanguard of an Iraqi Infantry Division reinforced by more than 150 tanks would begin crossing the Jordan river into the West Bank area. This Iraqi build-up would be complete by the middle of the week and posed a grave threat to the security of Israel. While she could cope with 800 or more Egyptian tanks in Sinai, Israel felt that the presence of 3–400 enemy tanks so close to her major air bases and centres of population was an intolerable danger. In addition to this, the Egyptian Air Force was getting very cocky. For ten years since 1956 there had been no intrusion or violation of Israeli air space by Egyptian aircraft. Now in the past two weeks at least three overflights had been made by Egyptian MiG-21s, making a sweep over Israel from the Dead Sea towards El Arish – a route that took them over some of Israel's major air bases and the area in which the bulk of her armour was deployed. These run-ins had been made at 50–60,000 feet at mach 1.7. They were only over Israeli territory for 4 minutes and hence could not be intercepted. Although the Israelis knew that with the camera equipment they carried they would get a picture equivalent to only 1–150,000 on a map, it was the growing presumption of the Egyptian Air Force that worried them. They believed that a further, more detailed reconnaissance of their air bases and military installations might be undertaken.

Another factor enabling the Israelis to act was the fact that Israel had regained – something realized by few people in Israel or elsewhere – the element of surprise. Observers of the Middle East scene, whether journalists, diplomats or military strategists, almost without exception believed that Israel's strategic position had altered gravely to her detriment in the three weeks since the Egyptians began their build-up of 90–100,000 men and upwards of 800 tanks in the Sinai. In the week preceding the outbreak of war the Israelis with one accord were complaining: 'We've missed the boat.' There is no doubt that Cairo after several days of tension and anxiety in Government circles was beginning to relax and feel that victory had been won without a war.

In these circumstances the Israelis took the decision to strike. Meeting in secret session on the night of Saturday lune 3 and the morning of Sunday June 4 the final doubts and hesitations were swept away or overcome. By the Sunday evening the soldiers and airmen knew that the following morning they would be at war.

It had been an agonizing and anguished decision for the Cabinet, composed to a very large extent of civilians with little pretensions to military knowledge. When General Hod, the head of the Air Force, told them that their Air Force could destroy the Air Force of Egypt and any other Arab power that intervened without Tel Aviv being subjected to enemy bombardment they found it hard to believe. So much had been heard of the new Russian-trained Egyptian Air Force equipped with more than 400 modern jet fighters and bombers – how was it possible to knock out such a force with one blow and be sure that Tel Aviv would not be bombed? Many of them had visions of tens of thousands of civilian casualties – this was something that made the decision to strike so difficult. But Dayan was an optimist and his inclusion in the Government meant that at last there was somebody with a deep understanding of the military as well as the political situation of Israel. Dayan, together with Weizmann and Hod, was one of the few who knew that the Air Force could do what it promised. This was, perhaps, Dayan's most decisive contribution to the victory. As a senior Army officer put it, 'Rabin was Dayan's Chief of Staff – Dayan was Commander-in-Chief.'

When, on the night of Thursday lune 1, Dayan assumed the office of Defence Minister he was already very clearly in the picture. For the previous two weeks, with the permission of both the Prime Minister and the Chief of Staff, General Rabin, he had been visiting the troops in the field and, in particular, going over all the plans with the individual commanders. Between the Thursday and the Sunday night he made several alterations to the plans within the framework of the original conception of the battle. These envisaged holding the line on the Jordanian and Syrian fronts while destroying the Egyptian Army in Sinai.

Even before he was appointed to office, Dayan was offering his advice freely to the individual commanders and although he was still technically a civilian his intrusion was resented by few of the people to whom he spoke. For instance, on Wednesday May 31, the day before his appointment, he visited General Narkiss, the central commander, whose task it was to guard Tel Aviv, the densely populated coastal strip and the Israeli part of Jerusalem from attack, principally by Jordan. They met in Jerusalem and went over the plans, then went up to Castel, a vantage point outside the city of Jerusalem from which they surveyed the whole area. Dayan suggested that Israeli troop movements be kept to the bare minimum so as to offer no provocation to the Jordanians. There was no intention whatever on the part of Israel to attack Jordan unless she attacked first. For this reason General Narkiss had been assigned only limited forces to defend Tel Aviv and Jerusalem and the coastal plain from close to Beersheba in the south to Natanya in the north.

In case of a Jordanian attack, which it was felt would probably be a local one and in the nature of a demonstration of solidarity with his fellow Arabs by King Hussein, Dayan warned Narkiss: 'Don't bother the General Staff with requests for reinforcements. Grit your teeth and ask for nothing.' Dayan was known to be a man of action and on hearing of his inclusion in the Israeli Government many people felt that this meant that a decision to fight would come in the course of the next few days. One of the first tasks he set himself was to disabuse the world of any such idea and regain the element of surprise which was vital for Israel, so as to achieve a speedy victory and avoid large-scale civilian casualties. It was at once pointed out that the army, which after two weeks of mobilization and waiting in the desert was demanding that a decision be taken, would more readily accept a decision not to fight from a Government which included Dayan. He was a 'civilian' they knew they could trust. If such a decision were to come from him they knew that it would be for sound military reasons.

Dayan's first public appearance as Minister of Defence designate was at a Press Conference in Tel Aviv the evening of Saturday June 3. According to the *Jerusalem Post* the following morning: 'Defence Minister Dayan, speaking at a press conference here yesterday, said that it was too late for a spontaneous military reaction to Egypt's blockade of the Tiran Straits – and still too early to draw any conclusions of the possible outcome of diplomatic action.' 'The Government – before I became a member of it – embarked on diplomacy: we must give it a chance,' Dayan declared.

The next day – the day before war broke out – newspaper offices not only in Israel, but throughout the world, received pictures of Israeli troops on leave relaxing on the beaches. As part of the general plan of deception, several thousand Israeli soldiers had been sent on leave that weekend. An Egyptian spy in Tel Aviv might well have sent back reports of a nation in a holiday mood.

Other aspects of the deception plan later became apparent. The Israeli Government itself did its part towards lowering the temperature. Following Cabinet sessions at which the decision to strike had been taken, the following communiqué designed for use by Monday's papers (June 5) was issued:

> The Cabinet at its weekly session yesterday heard reports on the security situation by the Prime Minister and the Minister of Defence-designate, and a survey of political developments by the Foreign Minister :
>
> Decided to co-opt Mr Joseph Saphir MK to the Cabinet:
>
> Approved the following draft laws :
>
> (a) State of Israel Bond Issue (Second Development Loan – 1967)
>
> (b) Defence tax – 1967
>
> (c) Defence Loan- 1967
>
> Approved an amendment to the Employment Services Regulations, extending the period during which immigrants and discharged servicemen enjoy priority in obtaining employment :
>
> Ratified the following treaties :
>
> (a) An accord on technical and scientific co-operation between the Israel Atomic Energy Commission and the Peruvian Committee for Control over Atomic Energy.
>
> (b) A cultural accord between Israel and Belgium.
>
> (c) A convention between Israel and Britain on legal procedures in civil and commercial matters.

There can be no doubt that overall the Israeli deception achieved its purpose. Egyptian generals were seen on the tennis courts of Cairo; there was little to indicate that anyone there had any inkling just how soon the blow would fall.

The grounds on which those who believed that Israel had 'missed the boat' were that she had lost the initiative and that with an army of more than 80,000 with some 800 tanks poised just south of her border the strategic balance had turned sharply against Israel; but this was to forget the situation in the air where the fortunes of war would be decided. Whichever side achieved a position of supremacy in the air would have the armies and the civilian population of the other at its mercy. But in the air there had been little change in the strategic balance. On the debit side as far as Israel was concerned was the higher probability of Jordanian and Iraqi involvement. On the credit side, there was the greater number of Egyptian aircraft deployed in the forward Sinai bases, close to Israel's borders where they were far more vulnerable to a surprise attack.

On the evening of Friday June 2 the correspondent who was representing the *News of the World* visited General Dayan at his home in Zahala on the outskirts of Tel Aviv and suggested that it was not true that Israel had 'missed the boat' and could not act – the outcome would be decided in the air where the strategic balance had altered little. The newly appointed Defence Minister replied: 'Things are rarely so black and white – they are much more often grey. It is most unlikely that any one side could achieve total air supremacy.' On the strength of that interview, the correspondent took plane for London on the Sunday morning – the day before the outbreak of war. He was followed at 8 am the following morning by a *Sunday Times* news team.

Israel, like a cowboy of the old Wild West, did not wait for her enemy to draw – she had seen the glint in Nasser's eye.

⚜ ⚜ ⚜

THE MILITARY BUILD-UP

May 15. Israeli Independence Day Parade. Egyptian troop movements through Cairo towards Sinai. Israel alerted forces.

May 16. Egypt declared state of emergency. All military forces said to be 'in a complete state of preparedness for war'. All the country's armed forces had been alerted, and were moving into defensive positions on the Israeli frontier.

May 17. Statements from Cairo and Damascus said that both UAR and Syria were in 'combat readiness'. Strong movement of Egyptian forces east across Sinai. In Amman, an announcement was made that Jordanian forces were being mobilized.

May 18. Cairo Radio continued to say that Syrian and Egyptian troops were on maximum alert. Iraq and Kuwait announced mobilization the same day, and in Tel Aviv it was stated that 'appropriate measures' had been taken.

May 19. The UNEF officially withdrawn; at Gaza the UN flag was hauled down and the force declared to exist no more.

May 20. Israel completed partial mobilization.

May 21. Ahmed Shukairy announced that 8,000 men of the PLA had been placed under the command of the UAR, Syria and Iraq. Egyptian reserves called up.

May 22. Mr Eshkol said that in the past few days Egypt had increased her forces in Sinai from 35,000 to 80,000 men. In Cairo it was announced that Nasser had accepted an offer of Iraq Army and Air Force units to assist in the event of war.

May 23. King Feisal of Saudi Arabia, who was in London, announced that he had ordered Saudi Arabian forces to be ready to participate in the battle against Israeli aggression.

May 24. The US Sixth Fleet (about 50 warships) was reported to have taken up positions in the eastern Mediterranean. In Amman, it was officially announced that general mobilization had been completed, and that the Government had given permission for Iraqi and Saudi Arabian troops to enter Jordan; 20,000 Saudi Arabian troops were said to be standing by on the Saudi/Jordanian border on the Gulf of Aqaba.

May 26. President Nasser said in Cairo that if war came Israel would be totally destroyed: the Arabs were ready and could win.

May 28. General mobilization was proclaimed in the Sudan.

May 29. It was announced in Algiers that Algerian military units were being sent to the Middle East to help Egypt.

May 30. Nasser/Hussein defence pact.

May 31. Iraqi troops and armoured units were reported to be moving into Jordan.

June 1. Iraqi aircraft left Habbaniyah air base near Baghdad for H3, Iraq's westernmost air base not far from the Israeli border.

June3. The Egyptian Commander-in-Chief, General Mortagi, issued an order of the day to his soldiers in Sinai: 'The results of this unique moment are of historic importance for our Arab nation and for the Holy War through which you will restore the rights of the Arabs which have been stolen in Palestine and reconquer the plundered soil of Palestine ...' The same day a fair proportion of the Israeli forces were sent on leave and were seen (by the foreign press and on television) sporting themselves on the beaches.

Chapter Four
The Air-Strike

At 0745 on the morning of Monday June 5 the first wave of the Israeli air-strike went in. It was directed against ten airfields of which nine were hit at precisely the same moment. The tenth, Fayid, was attacked a few minutes later, as it was still half covered by the morning mist over the Canal. The aircraft had been timed to take off at carefully measured intervals so that they should all arrive on target at the same moment and thereby achieve the maximum surprise. Each attack was made by four aircraft flying in pairs. Every aircraft reached its target, carried out its mission exactly as instructed and every single bomb exploded. The ten airfields attacked in this strike were: El Arish, Gebel Libni, Bir Gifgafa, Bir Thamada, Abu Sueir, Kabrit, Inchas, Cairo West, Beni Sueif and Fayid.

By far the greater part of the Egyptian Air Force was caught on the ground. The only Egyptian aircraft airborne at the time the Israeli strike went in was a training flight of four unarmed aircraft flown by an instructor and three trainees.

There were four reasons why the Israelis chose 0745 (Israeli time) as the hour for attack:

1. The Egyptian state of alert was past its peak. It was safe to assume that the Egyptians, ever since the'y began their aggressive troop concentrations in Sinai three weeks before, had several flights of MiG-21s waiting at the end of the runway on five-minute alert at dawn every morning. They were also probably flying one or two MiG-21 airborne patrols at this time of day, a most likely time for an enemy to attack. However, it was calculated to be most unlikely that they would have stayed at this state of readiness indefinitely. When no attack had materialized within two or three hours after dawn the Egyptians would more than likely have lessened their alert and switched off some of their radar scanners. The Israelis felt it safe to assume that by 0730 (0830 Cairo time) the Egyptians had lowered their guard.
2. Very often attacks are made at dawn. But since pilots have to be on deck at least three hours before getting airborne that would have meant their getting up at about midnight or in fact getting no sleep at all that night. By the evening of the first day of war they would have had had no sleep for 36 hours with the whole night and possibly the next day of action ahead of them. By making the initial strike at 0745 the pilots were able to sleep until 0400 or so.
3. At this time of year there is a morning mist over much of the Nile, the Delta and the Suez Canal. By 0730 this has just about dispersed. Around 0800 the weather is usually at its optimum. The visibility is at its best because of the angle of the sun, and the air is at its stillest, which is important when it comes to placing bombs accurately on runways.
4. 0745 (Israeli time) is 0845 Egyptian time. Why 0745 rather than 0800 or 0815? – Egyptians get to their offices at 9 am. Striking 15 minutes before that time would catch Generals and Air Force Commanders on their way to their offices, and pilots and Air Force personnel on their way to training courses and other activities.

General Hod was in the command centre when the last of the Egyptian early morning patrols got airborne and appeared on the Israeli radars. He pressed his stop-watch. He knew very well how long the MiG-21 can stay airborne – by 0745 the patrol would be almost out of fuel and on the point of landing.

The primary objectives of the first strike were to make the runways unusable and destroy as many MiG-21 s as possible. The MiG-21 s were the only Egyptian aircraft that could effectively prevent the Israeli Air Force achieving its objective – the destruction of Egypt's long-range bomber force which posed such a threat to the civilian population of Israel. Eight formations of MiG-21 s were destroyed as they were taxi-ing to the end of the runways. Earlier the Israelis had managed to persuade the Egyptians to move 20 of their front-line aircraft – twelve MiG-2Is, eight MiG-19s – from the area around Cairo and the Canal where Egypt's major air bases are concentrated, to Hurghada in the south where they were effectively *hors de combat.* The Israelis had achieved this a few days before by sending several strong probes of aircraft south over the Gulf of Aqaba which persuaded the Egyptians that the Israelis might well be planning to attack with a left-hook around the southern end of the Sinai Peninsula instead of, as in fact was the case, by a right-hook out over the Mediterranean. At Hurghada they were effectively removed from the chief area of Israeli activity. These twenty MiGs, once the Israeli sledge-hammer had fallen, instead of heading south to Luxor and other bases in Upper Egypt, to which they might have been able to afford at least some protection, headed north to the bases near the Canal where they found they had no runways to land on and fell prey to the Israeli Air Force.

Apart from these, only two flights of four MiG-21s were able to get airborne, and these succeeded in shooting down two Israeli aircraft which were attacking Egyptian air bases before they themselves were shot down.

The Israeli aircraft in flights of four made their way by various routes – some by a short circular right-hook over the sea to the bases around Cairo – the Canal and in Sinai. Others went straight across to attack the bases in Upper Egypt. 'We went in right on the deck,' Brigadier-General Ezer Weizmann, the Israeli Chief of Operations, said later. The Israeli strike aircraft flew at extremely low altitudes, probably no more than 30 feet above ground or sea level, so as to remain beneath the Egyptian radar. And not only Egyptian radar. The Israelis were probably more worried about the Russian and American radar than they were about the Egyptian.

Radar activity in the Middle East at this time was intense. Besides the Egyptians, who had sixteen scanners in the Sinai Peninsula alone, there were others poking their noses in to see if they could catch wind of what was going on.

Russian naval vessels in the area were keeping a close watch on the situation, as was the United States Sixth Fleet which, besides using its seaborne radar and the Elint (Electronic Intelligence) vessel USS *Liberty*, was flying airborne radar patrols with carrier-based aircraft. Even the British were surveying the scene from their lofty perch on top of Mount Trudos, Cyprus.

Electronic Countermeasures (ECM) have come a long way since they were first used by the British in the Second World War to disrupt, confuse or, by deliberately feeding into it false information, mislead the enemy's radar. Nor are the Israelis themselves new to this art of misleading the enemy. During World War II the British used high-powered radio transmitters with German-speaking controllers to feed false instructions to the German fighter and bomber pilots on the frequencies they were known to be listening out on. From where were these German-speaking controllers recruited but from the lews who had fled from Germany before the war. It can safely be assumed that the Israelis are well to the fore in the use of ECM and similar activities.

Although 23 Egyptian radar stations (including the 16 in Sinai) were put out of action by the Israeli Air Force this was not done until the Monday afternoon. ECM were probably not used before 0745 on Monday morning as this might well have given the enemy warning that something was up. But there can be little doubt that thereafter the Israelis 'played' with the Egyptian radar, and not only with the Egyptian radar – probably there were also 'games' specifically reserved for the others whose big ears were flapping in this part of the world.

As the first wave of Israeli aircraft struck their targets, the second wave was already on its way and the third wave had just got airborne. They were spaced at 10-minute intervals. Each flight of four aircraft were given seven minutes over their targets – enough for three or four passes, one bombing run and two or three strafing passes. An extra three minutes was allowed for navigational error or for an extra run over the target. The Israelis were operating an incredibly fast turn around time. For aircraft striking the main Egyptian bases in the vicinity of the Canal the rotation would have been as follows:

Time to target : approx 22½ minutes.
Time spent over target : approx 7½ minutes.
Return to base : approx 20 minutes.
Ground turn around time : approx 7½ minutes.
Total: approx 57½ minutes.

This means that the Israeli aircraft were over their targets for the second time within an hour of their first attack.

Behind them, to guard Israel and their home bases, the Israeli Air Force had left only twelve aircraft – eight flying top cover, four on stand-by at the end of the runway. Israel was playing for high stakes. It was a question of win or lose all – but she had calculated the risks with great care and played her hand with confidence and decision.

Discussing the actual bombing of the Egyptian airfields General Weizmann said that there was an American phrase : 'with only one pass, you hold on to your arse, but our boys do not go for this'. The Israeli pilots had made several passes over their targets in the interests of greater accuracy and therefore greater damage to the enemy's Air Force. They used dive-bombing to a considerable extent and with great effect. 'This is why we don't go in for strategic bombers – we have no interest in bombing the civilian population: for the destruction of runways and aircraft, fighters are more efficient,' remarked Weizmann.

The almost total destruction of the Egyptian Air Force on the ground was due not merely to surprise but in part at least to an ingenious bomb which the Israelis have devised and perfected for the specific purpose of destroying runways. As soon as the bomb leaves the aircraft a retro-rocket is fired to stop its forward impetus. Then a booster rocket drives it into the runway. Once it has penetrated the concrete a time fuse explodes it. The fuse may be instantaneous or may be set on a variable time-delay. Normally runways are considered easy to repair, but it is rather more difficult when the runway keeps exploding.

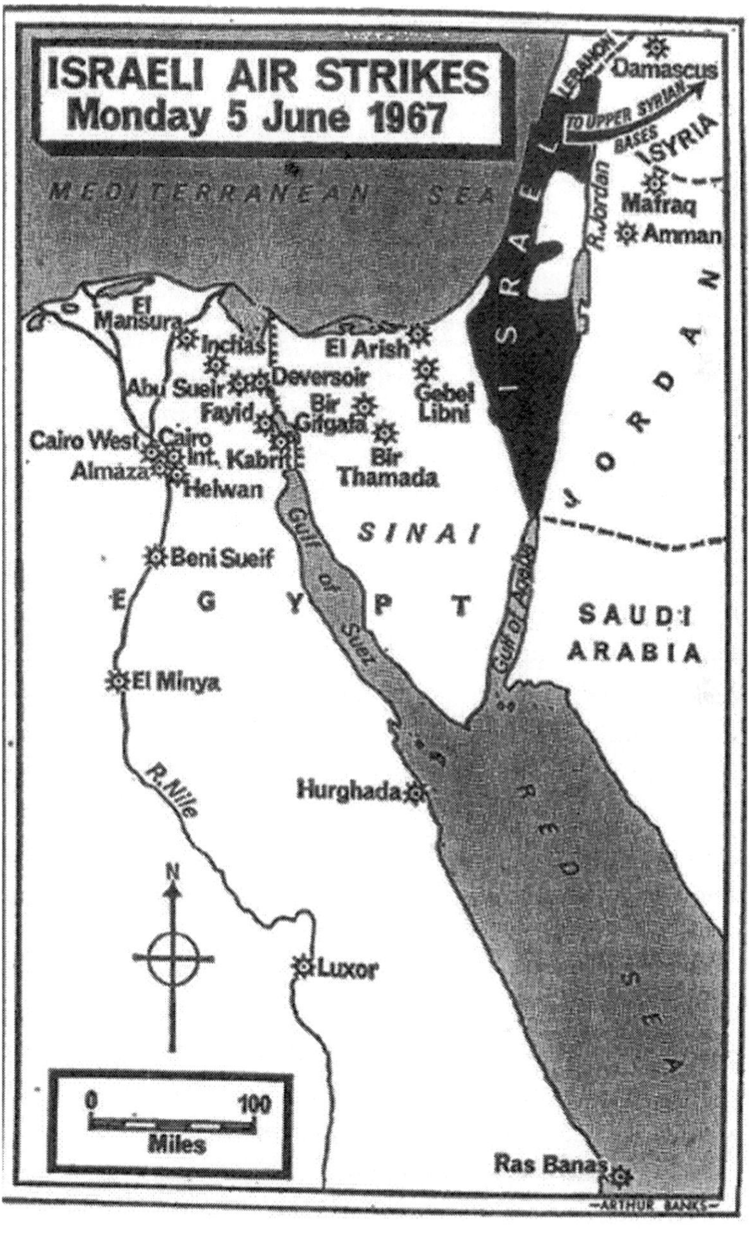
ISRAELI AIR STRIKES
Monday 5 June 1967
MEDITERRANEAN SEA
LEBANON
Damascus
TO UPPER SYRIAN BASES
SYRIA
ISRAEL
R.Jordan
Mafraq
Amman
JORDAN
El Mansura
Inchas
El Arish
Abu Sueir
Deversoir
Gebel Libni
Fayid
Bir Gifgafa
Cairo West
Cairo Int.
Kabrit
Bir Thamada
Almaza
Helwan
SINAI
Gulf of Suez
Gulf of Aqaba
Beni Sueif
EGYPT
SAUDI ARABIA
El Minya
R.Nile
Hurghada
RED SEA
N
Luxor
0
100
Miles
Ras Banas
ARTHUR BANKS

The point of this unique bomb is to enable an aircraft to bomb runways while flying at low level and high speed. A conventional bomb released in this way would bounce and do only superficial damage. The Israeli bomb obviates the necessity of flying down the barrels of the enemy anti-aircraft guns in a dive-bombing attack. Nevertheless, by no means all the Israeli aircraft were armed with this weapon and many of the runways were destroyed by dive-bombing from 5,000-6,000 ft with conventional 500 lb and 1,000 lb bombs. Enemy aircraft both on the ground and in the air were destroyed almost exclusively with cannon-fire.

Anti-aircraft fire over the Egyptian bases was lighter than the Israelis had expected and not particularly accurate. Although the Egyptians loosed off several of their Soviet-made SA-2 surface-to-air missiles not one Israeli aircraft was shot down by them. At the levels at which the Israelis were operating, the missiles proved totally ineffective. They gain speed very slowly and for this reason are useless below 4,000 ft above ground level. On one occasion an Israeli pilot out of the corner of his eye saw what appeared to be another aircraft moving in in a leisurely way as if to join in formation with him. He looked again and realized it was a missile. It was flying in the same direction as his aircraft and closing in on him from the side. He moved his aircraft smartly towards it and let it pass under him. It flew on out of sight. This missile is still the mainstay of Russia's anti-aircraft defence. Its uselessness, coupled with the fact that several of the missiles have fallen into Western hands, must be a considerable anxiety to the Soviet defence planners.

There had been considerable apprehension among the civilian population of Israel about Nasser's much vaunted surface-to-surface missiles which he had claimed could hit

Tel Aviv. For a number of years it has been known that a team of German and East European scientists have been at work at a Research Complex established by Nasser on the outskirts of Cairo and the 'missiles' had been given pride of place in Cairo Revolution Day parades. In the event nothing came of them and it would appear that for the time being, at least, they are a myth. The Israeli Air Force did not take the opportunity that it undoubtedly had of destroying this Research Centre, which has probably been responsible for the manufacture of the poison gas Egyptian forces have been using in the Yemen. A senior Israeli Air Force officer lamented: 'This is a decision we might live to regret.'

For 80 minutes without let-up the Israeli Air Force pounded the Egyptian airfields. Then, after a 10-minute break, there followed a further 80 minutes of Israeli air-strikes. In these 2 hours 50 minutes the Israelis destroyed the offensive potential of the Egyptian Air Force and effectively broke its back as a fighting force.

Altogether nineteen Egyptian airfields were hit on the first day of the war. As well as the ten mentioned above, Mansura, Helwan, El Minya, Almaza, Luxor, Deversoir, Hurghada, Ras Banas, and Cairo International were also attacked that morning. The Israeli Air Force estimates that in these 170 minutes it destroyed over 300 out of about 340 serviceable Egyptian combat aircraft, including all 30 of the long-range TU-16 bombers.

The major Sinai airfield of El Arish was the only one of the bases attacked whose runways were not put out of action, since Israeli plans called for its use as a forward supply and casualty evacuation base. Already by the Tuesday evening it was in use as such.

At more than one of the Egyptian bases the Israeli Air Force had destroyed all the aircraft but left the dummy mock-ups under camouflage covers untouched. When asked if this was because they were such bad dummies or because Israeli Intelligence was so good, an Israeli officer said that it was a combination of both but he added that at Abu Sueir, which is near Ismailia, they had in fact blown up some dummies as well as hitting all the actual aircraft. He said that as far as the Sinai airfields were concerned, where their intelligence was even better than for the main Egyptian fields, they had made no mistakes.

Just as the Israelis had reckoned against the Soviet warships in the Mediterranean having a direct link with the Egyptian Command and being able to pass information from their radar to the Egyptians inside ten minutes, so too General Hod counted on having a couple of hours head-start in which to deal with the Egyptian Air Force before having to cope with those of Jordan and Syria. In the event he had four hours. They did not join in the fray until about midday. By that time the Israelis had completed the destruction of the greater part of the Egyptian Air Force and were in a position to turn their full power against these new enemies that had come belatedly into the battle. 'We were able to deal with Syria and Jordan in twenty-five minutes,' Hod remarked dryly.

Shortly before noon on the Monday morning the Syrian Air Force dropped bombs near the oil refinery in Haifa Bay and attacked the airfield of Megiddo, where they succeeded in destroying a few dummy aircraft. The Israelis retaliated by attacking the Syrian Air Force base near Damascus.

Following a Jordanian attack at noon on the Israeli sattelite air base at Kefer Sirkin, where they destroyed a Noratlas transport aircraft on the ground, the Israeli Air Force bombed Mafraq and Amman airfields in Jordan, putting them out of action together with the Jordanian radar at Ajlun.

Before dusk on the Monday the Israelis paid further visits to most of the twenty-three airfields they had struck earlier in the day. Besides using regular bombs they used delayed-action bombs so that they would go off periodically throughout the night and hamper any attempt to repair the runways. As if this was not enough the Israelis continued with their air-strikes against these bases throughout much of the night.

When the Iraqi Air Force next morning attacked the Israeli town of Natanya the Israelis at once attacked their westernmost air base, H3, near the Iraqi/Jordanian border.

Up to nightfall on the second day of the war, the Israelis had destroyed 416 aircraft, 393 on the ground. The breakdown of those figures is shown in the table on page 87.

After making a demonstration just north of the Sea of Galilee with a pair of Hawker Hunters, one of which was shot down, the Lebanese, honour satisfied, made a graceful withdrawal from the war.

In the first two days of the war the Israeli Air Force flew more than 1,000 sorties, many of the pilots flying up to 8 sorties a day. By night-fall on the Tuesday Israeli losses amounted to 26 aircraft, including six Fouga Magister trainers (equipped with 68/80 mm rockets for tank-busting). They lost 21 pilots of whom about one half were taken prisoners of war in Syria or Egypt. Two pilots were subsequently returned by Iraq and a further two by Jordan. One pilot was reported to have been lynched in Egypt, although another was returned safe to Israel and negotiations took place for the release of two others held by the Egyptians. At least two of the pilots whose aircraft had been hit over Syria preferred not to observe the instructions of the Israeli ground control that was telling them to bail out – they chose to crash with their aircraft rather than fall into the hands of the Syrians.

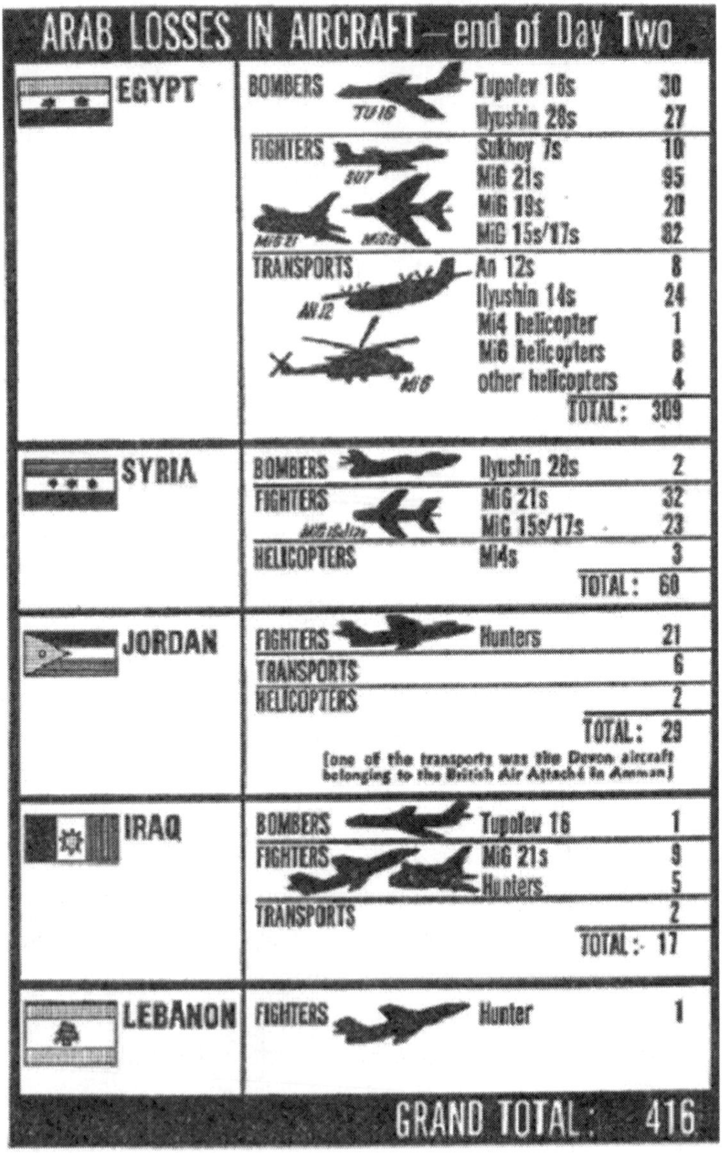
ARAB LOSSES IN AIRCRAFT—end of Day Two
EGYPT
BOMBERS
TU16
Tupolev 16s 30
Ilyushin 28s 27
FIGHTERS
SU7
Sukhoy 7s 10
MiG 21s 95
MiG 19s 20
MiG 15s/17s 82
TRANSPORTS
AN12
An 12s 8
Ilyushin 14s 24
Mi4 helicopter 1
Mi6 helicopters 8
MI6
other helicopters 4
TOTAL: 309
SYRIA
BOMBERS
Ilyushin 28s 2
FIGHTERS
MiG 21s 32
MiG 15s/17s 23
HELICOPTERS
Mi4s 3
TOTAL: 60
JORDAN
FIGHTERS
Hunters 21
TRANSPORTS 6
HELICOPTERS 2
TOTAL: 29
[one of the transports was the Devon aircraft belonging to the British Air Attaché in Amman]
IRAQ
BOMBERS
Tupolev 16 1
FIGHTERS
MiG 21s 9
Hunters 5
TRANSPORTS 2
TOTAL: 17
LEBANON
FIGHTERS
Hunter 1
GRAND TOTAL: 416

The damage sustained by the Egyptian Air Force in these two days has been estimated to be in the region of $500 million. Nor was the loss only in aircraft: ground equipment including 23 Egyptian radar stations together with several surface-to-air missile sites were destroyed, 16 of them in Sinai. Nevertheless runways can be patched up fairly quickly and, if the Russians decided to, the Egyptian Air Force could be back to where it was within six months.

Equipment is not everything of course and it will probably take many years to rebuild the spirit and morale of the Egyptian Air Force. It is estimated that about 100 of Egypt's 350 Air Force pilots were killed in the strike. In view of the large number of MiG-21s destroyed while taxiing on the ground, this figure probably includes a high proportion of their most experienced men.

Nasser knew very well that by Egyptian standards, at least, the Israelis did not have a large air force. They had a total of about 300 aircraft, some 50–60 of which were Fouga Magister trainers that had been equipped with rockets for the specific purpose of tank-busting. Yet reports had come into him of wave upon wave of Israeli aircraft attacking some 19 of his airbases at 10-minute intervals for 2 hours and 50 minutes with scarcely a break.

In his resignation speech of June 9, President Nasser declared: 'If we say now that it was a stronger blow than we expected we must say at the same time and with assurance that it was much stronger than his resources allowed. . . . The enemy attacked at one go all the military and civil airfields in the United Arab Republic. This meant he was relying on something more than his normal strength to protect his skies from any retaliation from us. . . . It can be said without fear of exaggeration that the enemy was operating an air force three times its normal strength.'

The reference by President Nasser to the Israeli Air Force being 'three times its normal strength' is perhaps significant. He was no doubt basing himself on the turnaround time of his own Air Force. The Israelis have learnt from top secret Egyptian Air Force plans they captured at El Arish that the Egyptians based their plans on their aircraft being overhead their targets every three hours instead of every hour or less, as was the case with the Israeli Air Force. And this in spite of the fact that many of the Egyptian aircraft had a far shorter distance to go to reach the main Israeli air bases from their Sinai airfields, than the Israelis had to reach the complex of bases around Cairo and the Canal. Compared with the ground turnaround time of 7–10 minutes of the Israeli Air Force, that of the Egyptians was more than two hours.

While the Egyptians reckoned on two sorties a day per aircraft – many of the Israeli pilots flew eight, a few even more on the Monday of the war.

The disparity in these figures speaks for itself and in it undoubtedly lies a major cause of Israel's victory.

No wonder Nasser found it inconceivable. Perhaps it was not only a good excuse for the lamentable failure of the Egyptian Air Force when he made the accusation of British and American aircraft involving themselves in conflict on the side of Israel, maybe he really believed it.

On Thursday June 8 an Israeli spokesman revealed a telephone conversation which they had monitored between Nasser and Hussein at 4.50 am on the Tuesday, the second day of the war. The conversation went as follows:

Nasser: How are you? The brother wants to know if the fighting is going on all along the front.

Nasser: Will His Majesty make an announcement on the participation of Americans and British?

Hussein: (Answer not clear.)
Nasser: Hello, will we say the US and England or just the US?
Hussein: The US and England.
Nasser: Does Britain have aircraft carriers?
Hussein: (Answer not clear.)
Nasser: Good. King Hussein will make an announcement and I will make an announcement.
Nasser: We are fighting with all our strength and we have battles going on on every front all night and if we had any trouble in the fighting it does not matter, we will overcome despite this. God is with us. Will His Majesty make an announcement on the participation of the Americans and the British?
Hussein: (Answer not clear.)
Nasser: By God, I say that I will make an announcement and you will make an announcement and we will see to it that the Syrians will make an announcement that American and British airplanes are taking part against us from aircraft carriers. We will issue an announcement. We will stress the matter and we will drive the point home.
Hussein: Good. All right.
Nasser: A thousand thanks. Do not give up. We are with you with all our heart and we are flying our planes over Israel today, our planes are striking at Israel's airfields since morning.

However incredible Nasser may have found the destruction of his air force, this conversation makes it very plain that he was trying to cook up an entirely fabricated allegation against Britain and the United States and to involve the unfortunate Hussein in this absurd enterprise. He was also lying to his ally about the activity of his planes. He had none. Since the end of the war King Hussein has stated in London that he no longer believes this story. And two days later, on

July 4, the Egyptian Foreign Minister, Mahmoud Riad, when asked by *The Times* correspondent in Cairo:

> 'Do you really think British bombers or pilots had been attacking Arab people during the fighting?' Riad said he had no proof of such attacks, adding that the Arabs did not think this point important, although I had explained that it was very important to the ordinary people in Britain.

The fabrication about British and American air intervention was not believed by the Russians. Indeed, it is known that it made them very angry. Thus, when it had failed in its objective of dragging in the Russians on the Arab side, it was abandoned by Egypt and by Jordan. However, the peoples of the Arab countries still believe it.

It has been suggested that Nasser had visions of a grandiose Battle of Britain-type confrontation over the Sinai Peninsula of the Egyptian and Israeli Air Forces which would engage in good old-fashioned dogfights. But even supposing the Israelis had not got in their first decisive blow, catching virtually all the Egyptian Air Force on the ground, there is little reason to suppose that the outcome would have been any different. According to the Israelis, in the sixty-four dogfights that took place, fifty Egyptian MiGs were shot down for the loss of no Israeli Mirages. Even the subsonic Vautours and Mystères were able to shoot down MiG-21s.

The Israeli aircraft destroyed, were either shot down by ground fire or 'jumped' from above while carrying out ground attacks. General Hod was insistent: 'In actual dogfights between aircraft the score was 50-nil. We shot down 50 MiGs in aerial combat without losing one single one of our aircraft.'

How did the Israelis manage to achieve such absolute success in so short a time? General Hod gave the following reasons.

1. Sixteen years planning had gone into those initial 80 minutes. 'We lived with the plan, we slept on the plan, we ate the plan. Constantly we perfected it.'

2. Intelligence – of enemy air movements and activities: the location and details of the enemy air bases: the deployment of his aircraft: the location of his radar and missile sites – was good.

3. Operational control – the ability to absorb and integrate with the existing plan new information as it comes in, and to pass new information and new targets to the pilots in the air – played a vital part in the success of the operation.

4. The execution of the plan by the pilots [average age 23] was the fourth vital link in the chain of success. It reflected years of training – in flying, navigation and bombing precision. 'Normally we expect results in war to be some 25% less than in peacetime exercises, because of the excitement of the situation and because of the distraction of antiaircraft fire. As it turned out the results were even better than in the peacetime practices. This was perhaps because the pilots were so keyed up and concentrated all their efforts on achieving the maximum precision and effect. Also perhaps because they did not need to observe the peacetime air safety regulations. We would have been happy with each aircraft destroying one enemy aircraft every mission. In fact the figures were usually many times this.' On one occasion two Israeli aircraft destroyed sixteen Egyptian bombers on the ground in the space of four minutes.

The Israelis have been practising this sort of attack for years. There are four or five ranges in the Southern Negev which have each been hit with several thousand bombs in practice raids. At least once a year they do all-out raids on these targets, and, as a result, when it came to the real thing not one aircraft failed to reach its target at precisely the correct moment, even though they only were using dead reckoning for their navigation.

But quality of manpower and high level of training played its part not only in the air – it was equally vital on the ground. To turn around modern combat aircraft in 7–10 minutes and to keep an Air Force that is flying more than 500 sorties a day in the air, requires tremendous skill and co-ordination. General Hod has remarked since the war: 'At 0745 Monday morning the serviceability of our combat aircraft was better than 99% and we maintained that level of serviceability throughout the week of the war. Although it might have taken up to an hour to patch up holes in one or two of our aircraft, at no stage was any of our aircraft unserviceable, if you exclude our losses. Never did we have the situation of pilots waiting for aircraft.'

General Weizmann recalled : 'Three or four months before the war a large contingent of Americans from their Air Force Staff College came to Israel. They had been to Cairo and had been very impressed there, they had visited Jordan and had been equally impressed by what Hussein had told them. When I had to talk to them – I had the feeling they thought we were in a tight spot – I told them how during the Second World War we used to say:

'"The Germans have surrounded us again – poor bastards." And I added that it was still true today: "The Arabs have surrounded us again – poor bastards." I had the impression that they thought we were rather cocky. We were and with good reason.'

⚜ ⚜ ⚜

By 1035 (Israeli time) on the Monday morning the Egyptian Air Force had been destroyed. It no longer constituted an effective fighting force and was unable to give either cover or close support to the Egyptian Army in Sinai. Time was now vital to the Israelis. The greater part of the Israeli Cabinet was terrified at the prospect of a premature cease-fire. They had vivid and uncomfortable memories of '56 when United States pressure had forced ignominy and defeat on the British, French and Israelis when victory was but a few short hours away. The whole of the Israeli plan had been conceived on the basis that time would be short and that the Israeli victory would have to be as swift and decisive as possible. Their plan was a bold one – some might have said reckless. But unlike the British and the French in the inglorious fiasco of '56, the Israelis had a very just appreciation of their enemy and his capabilities. This was to be the secret of their success.

Forty-eight hours was all the Israelis needed to break the back of Nasser's 100,000-man army in Sinai. (It was also to prove enough for their forces to reach the Suez Canal, seize Sharm el-Sheikh and take Jerusalem and most of Jordan's West Bank.) But did they have 48 hours? Dayan was certainly anxious. If Nasser had been informed by his Air Force commanders of the true situation of his Air Force, and if he had had the best interests of his people at heart, he might well have demanded an emergency session of the Security Council and requested an immediate and unconditional cease-fire. Had Nasser done this, he would have placed Israel in a most awkward position. For this reason Dayan exhorted the Israeli commanders to press forward with the utmost speed – but few needed the exhortation.

Chapter Five
A Naval Impertinence

On the night of Monday June 5 the Israeli Navy attacked Port Said and Alexandria harbours – the two main bases of the Egyptian Navy in the Mediterranean. As Israeli forces, consisting of a destroyer and some MTBs, approached Port Said, two Egyptian OSSA missile-carriers came outside the breakwater of the harbour to meet them. The Israelis opened fire on them with 20 mm cannon and the OSSAs turned tail and ran back into harbour without firing a shot. Both were damaged. Israeli frogmen then entered Port Said harbour where they believed there were three Egyptian MTBs and three anti-submarine craft besides the two OSSA missile-carriers but they were unable to discover them. All that they could find were two oil tankers which they left untouched because of the damage that would have been caused to the civilian population of Port Said had they been blown up. The Israeli force patrolled the entrance of the harbour throughout the night in case reinforcements were to be sent from Alexandria, but these in fact did not materialize as the Israeli Navy was at work there too.

Although the Israeli Navy's attack on Port Said was not a success in terms of enemy vessels destroyed, it achieved one major objective – to guard Tel Aviv from the eighteen

Egyptian missile-carrying craft whose missiles had a range of thirty-five miles and carried a 1,000-lb explosive warhead. The following morning (Tuesday June 6) the Egyptian Navy evacuated Port Said harbour and retreated to Alexandria, from which the OSSA and KOMAR vessels no longer had the range to reach Tel Aviv.

At the same time as Israeli Naval forces were attacking Port Said, Israel's only operational submarine made its way stealthily to the entrance of Alexandria harbour. A force of frogmen, loaded with explosive charges for blowing up Egyptian Naval vessels, made their way out of the submarine's escape hatch and penetrated into the harbour. It was a dark and moonless night – ideal for such operations. The Israelis believe that the frogmen succeeded in damaging, possibly destroying, two Egyptian submarines and two of the OSSA missile-carriers. However, although the submarine waited until it was nearly dawn before making for the open sea the frogmen did not return. The submarine went back again the following night when a further rendezvous had been set in case the frogmen had needed more time or had run into trouble – but in vain. The Government-controlled Cairo newspaper, *Al Ahram,* reported that at about midday on Tuesday June 6 four Israeli frogmen had been seen in the water in the vicinity of the yachting harbour just east of Alexandria and had been taken prisoner. A further two were captured about four hours later. It is thought they might have been trying to seize a power-boat and make a getaway when they were caught.

The only offensive action undertaken by the Egyptian Navy that came to the notice of the Israelis, was on the night of June 6 when a force of three submarines approached the shores of Israel – one just north of Haifa, one to the south of it and one near Ashdod. Whether they came with the intention of attacking shipping or of landing saboteurs, as the Israelis had done in Port Said and Alexandria, is not clear. However the Israelis, although they had only four sonar devices in the whole of their Navy, succeeded in detecting all three of the Egyptian submarines and attacked them with depth charges. At least one was damaged, as was evidenced by a large slick of oil that came to the surface, but they all managed to escape. General Erell, Commander of the Israeli Navy, commented afterwards: 'They used their periscopes too much. With the equipment they had, the Egyptians could have had picnics here outside Haifa.'

An Israeli seaborne assault in conjunction with a para-troop drop had been planned for the Monday night against El Arish, the main Egyptian military and logistic base in Sinai. However, the operation was cancelled on the Monday afternoon when it was seen what good progress the armoured forces under General Tal were making through Khan Yunis and Rafa towards El Arish. The paratroopers were promptly diverted to the Jerusalem area and the Jordanian front where, somewhat to the surprise of the Israelis, the Jordanian forces had attacked within a matter of hours of the outbreak of war between Egypt and Israel.

Israel, a nation of only 2½ million people, has devoted virtually all its military budget to its Air Force and Army – hardly anything was accorded the Navy. It has long been a joke in the Israeli Navy that if they want new equipment they have to find it for themselves – as they did in 1956 when they took the destroyer *Ibrahim-Al-Awal* from the Egyptians.

The Egyptian troop movements into Sinai found the Israeli Navy with only one of their three destroyers in service. And of their three submarines, all pre-World War II vintage, one was in mothballs and another, the *Rahaf*, so old that it could not submerge. The Israeli Navy had twice the number of sailors as it had ships to accommodate them. Starting on May 19 the Israeli Navy launched a crash programme to bring their forces to as high a state of readiness as the limited number and age of their naval vessels permitted. A new naval base was established at Ashdod, from which MTBs and other light naval craft could operate. New radar sets were installed on several vessels and in many cases new guns were fitted. Trawlers were armed for patrol duties and the submarine *Rahaf* was fitted out with sonar and depth-charge launchers for anti-submarine work. The former Egyptian destroyer *Ibra-him-Al-Awal*, seen towards the end of May by the British Consul in Haifa coated in red oxide paint undergoing a refit in Haifa harbour, miraculously turned grey within forty-eight hours and put out to sea. A landing craft that was due to be ready in August was completed within five days by the civilian yard in which it was being built. 'It only had two of its three engines and a make-shift rudder – but it was good enough for us,' said General Erell.

On the day war broke out the comparative strengths of the Israeli and Egyptian Navies were as follows:

Type	*Israel*	*Egypt*
Destroyers	3	7
Submarines	3*	12
Missile-carriers	—	18
Anti-submarine craft	1	12
MTBs	8	32

* One, the *Rahaf*, was unable to submerge.

Because of its ludicrously small size and the antiquity of its equipment compared to that of the Egyptian Navy, deception of the enemy was of even greater importance to the Israeli Navy than it was to the Israeli Army and Air Force, both of which made use of the art. The major interest of the Israeli Navy was that Egyptian naval forces in the Mediterranean should be as weak as possible – only there could they pose a major threat to Tel Aviv and Israel's populated coastal regions. The Israelis therefore set about persuading the Egyptians to move some of their vessels from the Mediterranean down to the Red Sea. They did this by sending four landing craft overland across the Negev Desert to Eilat, the Israeli port at the northern end of the Gulf of Aqaba. The landing craft were seen arriving in Eilat by day. But the same night, under cover of darkness, they were taken back into the desert ten or fifteen miles north of Eilat and brought down for a second time by daylight the following day. By the time the Israelis had repeated this manœuvre a few times and had sent the only three MTBs they had in Eilat on patrols towards the Red Sea, the Egyptians evidently believed that the Israelis might be preparing an assault on Sharm el-Sheikh as they had in '56. (The Israeli vessels only had the range to get to Sharm el-Sheikh and back if the wind was from the north on the way down and southerly on the way back.)

The outbreak of war found 30% of the Egyptian Navy bottled up in the Red Sea where they were little threat to Israel. Two Egyptian destroyers seen in the Mediterranean on June 3 had already passed through the Canal to the Red Sea by the time the war started two days later. All that this force, by itself more powerful than the whole of the Israeli Navy, was able to do in the course of the war, was to send a flotilla, consisting of two destroyers and six MTBs, up the Gulf of Aqaba towards Eilat on the night of June 6. When the flotilla got half-way up the Gulf it thought better of it, turned round and headed for home. This was no doubt a prudent decision – the three Israeli MTBs were lying in ambush for it just twenty miles south of Eilat.

Even after the war was over the Egyptian naval forces in the Red Sea were unable to return to their Mediterranean bases – the Canal had been blocked on the orders of President Nasser with barges and a couple of unusable Egyptian ships that had long been tied up in Port Said harbour The Egyptian ships had to make their way to the Yemeni port of Hodeida at the southern end of the Red Sea.

⚜ ⚜ ⚜

On the afternoon of Thursday 8 June, the US Navy Elint (Electronic Intelligence) vessel USS *Liberty*, was steaming west-north-west at 5 knots some 14 nautical miles north of the Sinai Peninsula not far from El Arish. According to a statement issued by the United States Defence Department in Washington later the same day: 'The *Liberty* departed Rota, Spain June 2 and arrived at her position this morning to assure communications between United States Government posts in the Middle East and to assist in relaying information concerning the evacuation of American citizens from the countries of the Middle East.' No explanation was forthcoming as to why the sophisticated and efficient communications systems, installed in US Embassies throughout the world, should suddenly have become so inadequate to their task.

Out of a clear blue sky Israeli fighter aircraft flying in pairs from the south-east, made a dive-bombing attack from 5,000–6,000 feet and strafed the *Liberty* with their cannon. Minutes later, three Israeli MTBs approaching from the north-east also joined in the attack, raking the *Liberty* with machine-gun fire and firing two torpedoes, one of which struck home, ripping a forty-foot gash below the water-line in her starboard side amidships.

By the time the Israelis realized their mistake and called off the attack, 34 officers and men of the *Liberty* were dead and a further 75 had been wounded. The vessel had been riddled with 821 hits and fires were blazing both for'ard and amidships.

One of the Israeli MTBs signalled the *Liberty* asking if she needed assistance. The reply is reported to have been a curt one. It is a considerable tribute to the bravery and efficiency of the men in the USS *Liberty* that within half an hour of the attack all the fires had been put out and she was steaming north at 10 knots despite a 30° list.

Explanations of the attack have been many and far-fetched. One is that the Israelis believed they had a monopoly of listening in on other people's conversations in this part of the world and resented the intrusion; another, that the Israelis had done it at the request of the CIA to disprove Egyptian-inspired claims of collusion between Israel and the United States. However, there seems no reason to doubt the explanation given by the Israelis and accepted by the Americans that it was just one big mistake. The Israeli Air Force has blamed the Navy which it says was responsible for identifying the vessel prior to the attack. The Navy reported it first as an Egyptian ship, then as a Soviet ship, then once again as an Egyptian ship, and finally as 'anyway a warship and it's too damn close'. Three days earlier the Israeli Government had asked the Americans what vessels they might have in the area in the course of the week – no reply had been received. According to an Israeli naval officer, the *Liberty* was flying no flag at the time the attack went in. 'Not a soul could be seen on her decks, she was like a ghost ship – deserted.' A United States navy court of enquiry, however, after a seven-day investigation, reported that 'the USS *Liberty* was in international waters properly marked as to her identity', adding that a 5 ft by 8 ft Stars and Stripes was flying from her gaff.

Perhaps one of the explanations of the Israelis' jumpiness and hasty action was the fact that earlier in the day the airborne radar of one of the Israeli reconnaissance aircraft on patrol over the Mediterranean had shown a large number of blips approaching Israel from the west that might have indicated an all-out Egyptian naval attack. With the Egyptian Navy in the Mediterranean still virtually intact, in spite of the Israeli forays into Port Said and Alexandria harbours on the night of June 5, the Israelis were, not surprisingly, apprehensive. Later it was established that the blips on the radar had been echoes from unusual cloud formations in the area.

The Israeli Navy, feeling that its exploits were in no way comparable with those of the Israeli Army or Air Force, and ashamed of the *Liberty* incident, prefers to remain the 'silent service'. Nevertheless, starved of resources and with no modern equipment, it had successfully protected the coasts and the population of Israel from a seaborne attack, it had assured the safe passage of merchant ships to and from Israel's Mediterranean ports throughout the war and it had succeeded in penetrating the enemy's main naval bases at Alexandria and Port Said, in the face of a navy many times its strength and equipped with some of the most modern naval vessels – Z-class destroyers, W-class submarines, KOMAR and OSSA missile-carriers – that the Soviet Union could supply. As General Erell himself put it: 'It was a gross impertinence on our part.'

Chapter Six

Sinai: The Mailed Fist

Many conquerors have trodden the wastes of Sinai, from Alexander the Great on his way to Egypt in 332 BC, to Napoleon who at the end of the eighteenth century led his army to Acre following the Battle of the Pyramids, where he had exhorted his troops before their victory over the Mamelukes: '... from the summit of these pyramids, forty centuries look down upon you.' Here too the children of Israel wandered forty years before entering the Promised Land and here Moses received the tablets on which the ethical codes of both the Jewish and Christian religions and of Western civilization are based.

Sinai, whose sand seas and barren mountain ranges divide Africa from Asia and the Mediterranean from the Indian Ocean, is a place of the utmost desolation. With the exception of a narrow coastal strip in the north, the Peninsula rarely receives rain and its sole inhabitants are the nomadic bedouin who have roamed its parched and hostile wilderness for centuries in search of the meagre scrub-grass for their goats. Here the silence of the desert is disturbed only by the moan of the wind that passes over its burning sands.

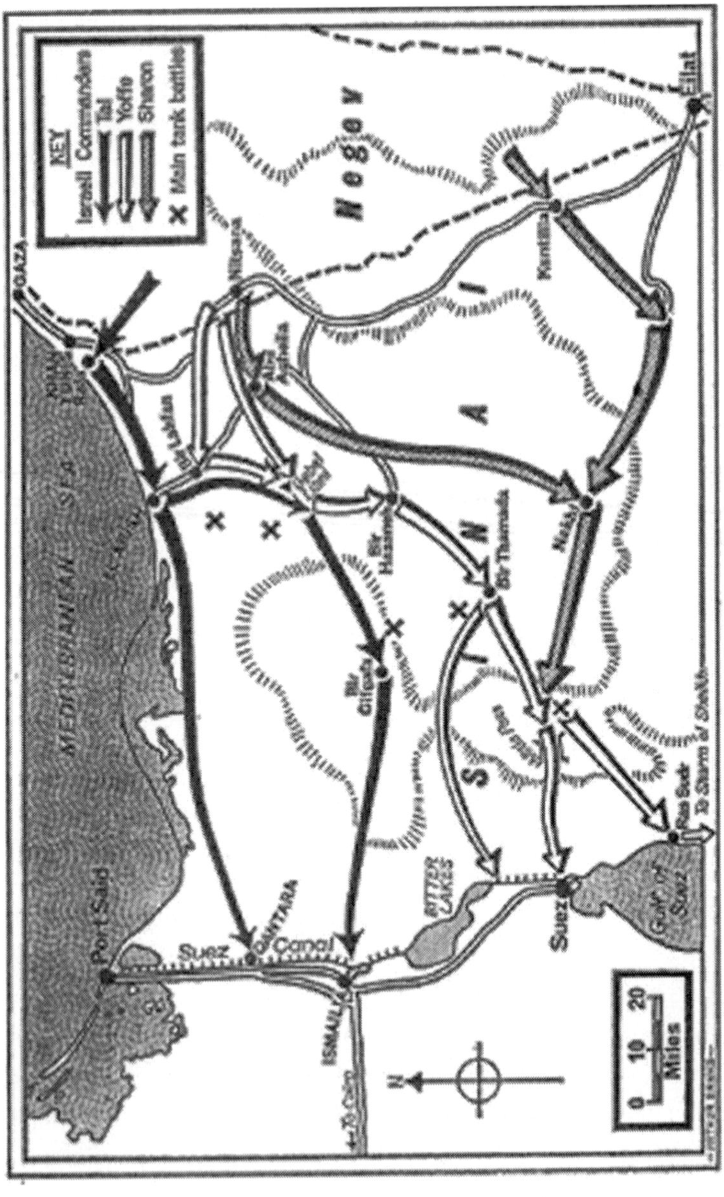
KEY
Israeli Commanders
Tal
Yoffe
Sharon
Main tank battles
GAZA
Negev
MEDITERRANEAN SEA
Port Said
Suez Canal
QANTARA
ISMAILIA
BITTER LAKES
Suez
Gulf of Suez
Eilat
Bir Gifgafa
Bir Thamada
S I N A I
N
0 10 20
Miles

As a battle-ground for modern warfare Sinai has few rivals. It is an arena where the protagonists can clash without involving civilian populations, where in a single battle a thousand tanks can manœuvre and bludgeon each other in the swirling dust of the desert. In 1956 this was the scene of the first battle between Egyptians and the founders of a new Israel. And in 1967 it was to be the battle-ground Israeli Commanders Tal Yoffe Sharon of an even more momentous clash between the forces of Zionism and of Arab nationalism.

Before May 15 there had been two Egyptian divisions stationed in the Sinai peninsula: the 20th PLA (Palestine Liberation Army) Division in Gaza and the 2nd Division which was spread out the length of the Israeli/Egyptian border. Between May 15 and the end of the month these two were reinforced by five more Egyptian divisions: the 7th Division (Rafa-El Arish); the 3rd Division (Gebel Libni-Bir Hassneh); the 4th Armoured Division (Bir Gifgafa-Bir Thamada); the 6th Infantry Division (Nakhl-Kuntilla); and a Special Armoured Force of division strength (West of Kuntilla). Once these new forces were deployed the 2nd Division was concentrated in the Abu Agheila–Kusseima area. The total force comprised some 100,000 men with between 900 and 1,000 tanks.

According to General Tal, Commander of the Israeli Armoured Corps, the Egyptians were well deployed, both for offensive action and for defence. On the one hand, they were in a position to thrust eastwards across the southern Negev with their Special Armoured Force and 6th Infantry Division, poised to the west of Kuntilla, and link up with Jordan, thereby cutting off Eilat from the rest of Israel. With Israel deprived of its port on the Gulf of Aqaba the proposed British- and American-backed flotilla would have been rendered useless. On the other hand, as a defensive deployment the Egyptians were, according to General Tal, 'blocking all the main lines of advance through the desert with massive troop concentrations and strongly fortified positions, some of which had been prepared over the last 20 years. The only line of advance westwards from Israel's southern border that was not blocked, was the one taken by General Yoffe and his armoured brigade across the dunes – the Egyptians evidently believed them to be impassable.'

Just as the Israeli Air Force and Navy succeeded in persuading the Egyptians to move some of their aircraft and naval vessels from the north, which was to be the theatre of war, to the vicinity of the Red Sea, the Israeli Army also played its part in the deception. A photograph taken by an Egyptian reconnaissance aircraft in the days immediately preceding the outbreak of war would have appeared to indicate an Israeli force of up to two, possibly three, armoured brigades positioned close to the Israeli/Egyptian border opposite Kuntilla. In fact there was only one – heavily reinforced by dummy tanks under inadequate camouflage netting to make it appear much stronger than it really was. Clearly there was an overall plan of deception devised by the Israelis to persuade the Egyptian High Command that they were planning another dash down the coast to Sharm el-Sheikh as they had done in 1956. And clearly it was successful.

But the Israelis could not repeat in 1967 the same strategy they had used in 1956. Sharm el-Sheikh, by reason of its situation and lines of communication, is untenable in the face of a large concentration of hostile forces in the northern part of the Sinai Peninsula. The Israelis were only able to make their dash down the coast to Sharm el-Sheikh in '56 because Egyptian forces to the north were weak, the greater part of the Egyptian Army being deployed around Cairo and the Suez Canal to resist the Anglo-French invasion. In 1967 the situation was very different. Even the Egyptians must have realized the indefensibility of Sharm el-Sheikh, for on the morning of Wednesday June 7, evidently beginning to appreciate the extent of the Israeli victory in the northern part of the Peninsula, they withdrew their troops a full two hours before the Israeli assault forces arrived.

The Israelis knew that this time they had no alternative but to engage the main force of the Egyptian Army concentrated along their southern borders and break it in the Sinai desert. If this could be achieved the opening of the Straits would follow automatically. Israel could never afford to let her country become the battlefield – she had to move out to meet her enemy. Unlike the Egyptians, who dispersed half of their tanks throughout their army on the basis of one tank battalion for every infantry brigade and one armoured group for each infantry division, the Israelis believed in keeping their armour together. In conversation since the war, General Rabin, the Israeli Chief of Staff, has said: 'We use our armour like a mailed fist, thrusting with speed and massive momentum deep into the enemy territory – not to take his positions, but to throw him off balance and make his positions untenable.'

The plan devised by General Rabin and his staff had three phases: first, to break through the Egyptian defences at two of their strongest points; secondly, for an armoured division to leap forward to the range of mountains just east of the Suez Canal, blocking the escape routes of the Egyptian forces; thirdly, the final destruction of the Egyptian Army.

Facing the seven Egyptian divisions in the Sinai were three Israeli 'divisions' under Generals Tal, Yoffe and Sharon. (The basic unit of the Israeli Army is the brigade group, a completely self-contained fighting unit of about 3,000 men with its own detachments of armour, artillery, support troops, HQ and medical units. An Israeli 'division' consists of two, three, or even four brigade groups.) The task of breaking through at the two selected points was given to the forces under General Tal and General Sharon. General Yoffe's division, composed entirely of reservists from the commander downwards, had the duty of making a dash across the desert to the Mitla and the other passes in the range of mountains to the east of the Canal, blocking the enemy's escape routes to Egypt. Once the overall plan had been conceived, it was left very largely to the individual commanders to plan its execution; the commanders' plans were then referred back to the General Staff for comment and criticism. General Sharon, to give but one example, formulated his plans for the assault of Abu Agheila, the second point of the Israeli attack, only a few days before the battle.

The *élite* of the Israeli Armoured Corps (perhaps 250-300 tanks), under the command of Brigadier-General Tal, was charged with the task of achieving the initial breakthrough. The point selected was Rafa, close to the Mediterranean shore at the southern end of the Gaza Strip. The objective was El Arish, on the coast, 30 miles to the west of Rafa. It lies on the railway line from Qantara on the Canal to Gaza and was the Egyptians' main logistic base through which they supplied their army in Sinai.

The Rafa–El Arish area was held by the Egyptian 7th Infantry Division in strongly fortified positions. Rafa itself, defended by a force of brigade strength, was surrounded by a deep minefield in the shape of a horse-shoe that reached almost to the coast. The Egyptians had established themselves in strong defensive lines running south from Rafa to a sea of impassable dunes. In front of these positions, where two infantry brigades were heavily dug in behind barbed-wire and anti-tank guns, was an extensive line of minefields. To the rear of the positions was a brigade of artillery equipped with 122 mm guns together with a battalion of long-range 100 mm guns, which between them could launch some 5 tons of shells per minute.

Tal planned his attack with two considerations in mind: to avoid the Egyptian artillery and to avoid their minefields. This led him to the decision to penetrate the defences of Rafa by way of the neighbouring town of Khan Yunis, although it would mean tackling part of the 20th Palestinian Division as well as the Egyptian 7th Infantry Division. But Tal knew that his forces would be almost out of range of the Egyptian artillery and that once in Khan Yunis they could smash their way into Rafa, avoiding the minefields by advancing swiftly in column using the Egyptians' internal roads. Knowing that there were more than 100 Egyptian tanks deployed inside the Rafa–El Arish defensive area and that they must maintain their freedom of manœuvre, Tal felt it safe to assume that his forces would not be hampered by minefields once they had broken through the Egyptian defences. While one brigade attacked Khan Yunis on the northern flank, Tal planned to send a second brigade to outflank the Egyptian minefields and entrenchments that ran south from Rafa. These forces were to assault and silence the Egyptian artillery and then take the entrenched positions from the rear.

This was to be the first land battle of the war. 'My men knew,' Tal said later, 'that on this battle depended the outcome of the war – possibly the fate of Israel. More than ten years had passed since we had last clashed with the Egyptians. We could not tell what effect the Russian training, the modern Russian equipment and the new morale of the Egyptian Army would have on their fighting capacity. We knew that we would be fighting forces whose equipment was superior both in quality and quantity to our own. For its size the Egyptian Army is probably the richest in the world, after the US Army.'

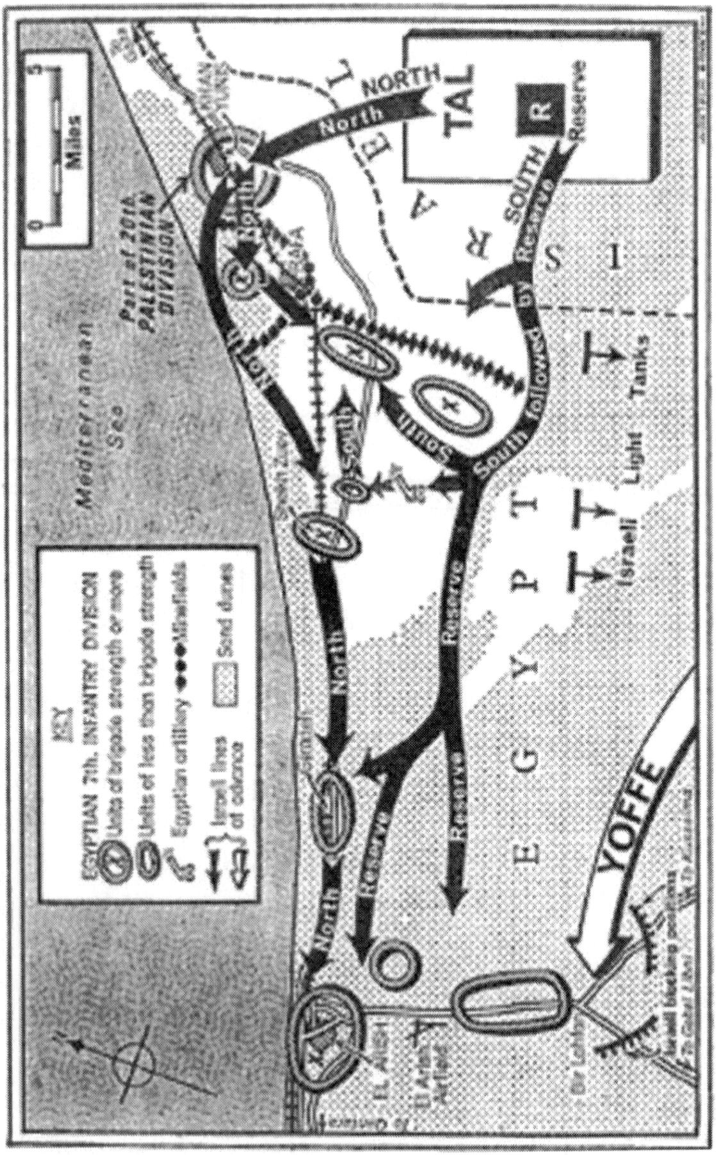
Mediterranean Sea
KEY
EGYPTIAN 7th. INFANTRY DIVISION
Units of brigade strength or more
Units of less than brigade strength
Egyptian artillery
Minefields
Israeli lines of advance
Sand dunes
Miles
PALESTINIAN DIVISION
NORTH
TAL
R
Reserve
SOUTH
North
South
South followed by Reserve
ISRAEL
EGYPT
Israeli Light Tanks
YOFFE

Before the battle Tal told his men: 'If we are to win the war, we must win the first battle. The battle must be fought with no retreats, every objective must be taken – no matter the cost in casualties. We must succeed or die.'

At 0815 on the morning of Monday June 5, on receipt of the long-awaited order from HQ Southern Command, Israeli ground forces attacked. Half an hour earlier, the first wave of the Israeli air-strike had gone in. Already, a major part of the Egyptian Air Force had been destroyed. At more than a dozen airfields, whole squadrons of MiG-21s – among the fastest and most modern aircraft in the world – had been reduced to a charred, smouldering litter of twisted metal. But neither the Israeli tank crew racing across the sand towards the Egyptian entrenchments, nor the Egyptian soldier lining up his anti-tank gun at the rapidly approaching targets, knew anything of this.

Under intense fire from artillery, machine-guns and anti-tank guns, Tal's northern brigade reached the Palestinian positions outside Khan Yunis and began its assault. The Israeli tanks charged the fortifications. Almost immediately six of them were destroyed by the defenders and a bitter battle ensued. However the speed and momentum of the Israeli thrust carried all before it and their tanks burst through the Palestinians' positions and into Khan Yunis. But this speedy break-through was achieved only with heavy casualties which included 35 tank commanders, one of them a battalion commander. It is a matter of pride in the Israeli Army that their tank commanders fight with their turrets open even under the heaviest fire so as to have a clear view of the battlefield. Although this involves heavy casualties in tank commanders, there can be no doubt that it is a major factor of the Israeli success.

From Khan Yunis two battalions of the northern brigade by-passed Rafa, making their way between the Egyptian positions and the sea, and advanced rapidly in a southwesterly direction towards Sheikh Zuev, a strongly fortified position held by an Egyptian brigade blocking the Israelis' line of advance. The rest of the tank brigade forced its way into the Egyptian defences at Rafa, advancing in line-ahead down the road from Khan Yunis thereby avoiding the minefield.

Meanwhile Tal's second brigade of tanks had been rolling forward on a more southerly line of advance to outflank and get behind the Egyptian entrenchments and minefields running south from Rafa. The Israelis moved up one battalion of tanks opposite the Egyptian lines and began shelling them so as to persuade the Egyptians to open fire and give away their positions. This they were successful in doing and the Israeli forces came under intense anti-tank fire. Almost immediately one of their leading tanks, carrying a company commander, was destroyed. The tank burned furiously and a dense column of black smoke rose several hundred feet above it. The commander of the southern brigade was able to use this smoke column as a marker to enable him to skirt along the northern edge of the dunes and outflank the Egyptian positions without making any wrong turns which might have led his forces to a dead-end with their line of advance blocked by impassable waves of soft sand.

The Israeli forces succeeded in breaking through the dunes at the southern end of the Egyptian lines and getting behind them. However, they missed the southernmost Egyptian brigade which they were unable to see because of the lie of the ground, and began to attack from the rear the next one to the north of it without realizing that they had left a whole Egyptian brigade intact just to the south.

One of the Israeli tank battalions was detached from the southern brigade and made a dash for the Egyptian artillery which had, moments before, been hit by an Israeli air-strike. The battalion destroyed 20 Stalin tanks which were protecting the artillery and then rushed the Egyptian guns which they succeeded in silencing. This Israeli tank battalion, after achieving its initial objective, was due to turn east to link up with the other Israeli forces attacking the Egyptians from the rear. Instead, they got too far north before beginning their swing eastwards and ran into a further force of 20 Egyptian tanks which they also engaged and destroyed. But this had not been in accordance with Tal's plan and, meanwhile, the southern brigade commander, who was attacking the Egyptian positions of brigade strength with only one battalion, found himself encircled. The fighting was bitter. The Israeli battalion was fighting for its life against superior Egyptian forces. 'When I spoke to the brigade commander on the radio,' Tal said later,'I could hear that he was firing his machinegun with one hand while holding the microphone in the other.'

Tal, who had kept one of his brigades in reserve, now sent in one battalion of armoured infantry with instructions to follow the trails north of the dunes made by the southern brigade a couple of hours before. At the same time he ordered the northern brigade commander, who was by now advancing fast in a westerly direction along the coast, to turn round and come back eastwards with one of his tank battalions to assist the encircled Israelis. In addition he instructed the armoured infantry of the northern brigade, that had broken into Rafa itself and was engaged in overcoming the Egyptian positions in the town, to head south through the minefields encircling Rafa and also try to link up with their beleaguered comrades.

In fact it was the battalion commander whose force had destroyed the Egyptian artillery, and who should not have let his forces get separated for so long from the other battalion under the southern brigade commander, who first broke through to them. He arrived only just in time. The Israeli tanks were down to almost their last round of ammunition. However the arrival of these reinforcements immediately turned the balance and the Israelis overcame the whole of the Egyptian brigade leaving more than 1,000 Egyptians dead. Shortly afterwards General Tal arrived on the scene and joined the southern brigade commander whose men were completely exhausted – only one tank company was in a position to continue fighting without reorganization.

On hearing that the brigade had 50 casualties awaiting evacuation a few miles to the south, Tal sent a helicopter to bring them out. However the helicopter, as it attempted to land beside the Israeli casualties, was met by intense Egyptian groundfire. Only then was it realized that the southernmost Egyptian brigade, hidden by the uneven lie of the ground, had been missed earlier in the day and remained intact in its fortified positions. Immediately the southern brigade commander, together with a battalion commander, led the only remaining tank company to assault the Egyptian entrenchments. By then it was already night and for two hours in the darkness the battle raged. The Egyptians fought fiercely but in vain. By the time firing ceased their positions had been overwhelmed and 1,500 Egyptians lay dead on the battlefield. When the remains of the Israeli tank company joined up with the rest of their brigade both the brigade commander and the battalion commander collapsed. The Israeli southern brigade had suffered 70 dead and several times that number wounded.

Earlier in the afternoon, seeing the progress that Tal's forces were making in the direction of El Arish, an airborne and sea assault that was due to attack El Arish that night had been cancelled and the paratroopers who had been scheduled to make the drop were diverted to Jerusalem and the Jordanian front where heavy fighting had broken out shortly before noon. At 1600 hours Tal had ordered the remainder of his reserve brigade to advance in the direction of the El Arish airfield in order to cut it off from the fortified area around the town itself.

Meanwhile, on Tal's northern line of advance, the leading Israeli tank battalions had overcome the Egyptian defences at Sheikh Zuev and had made contact with the heavily defended Egyptian positions at Giradeh, five miles east of El Arish.

While Tal's forces had been achieving their breakthrough at Khan Yunis, General Yoffe, twenty miles further south, was advancing across a sea of sand dunes towards Bir Lahfan with one of his two armoured brigades. This was the only line of advance that the Egyptians had left unblocked by fortified positions; evidently they believed that it was impassable. However, the Israelis had reconnoitred the route with jeeps in 1956 and although the jeeps had frequently become stuck because of the softness of the sand, the reconnaissance party had reported that the route might be suitable for tracked vehicles. In more than one place Yoffe's advance was held up by minefields which had to be cleared by engineers on foot, using prods to discover where the mines lay. However, he lost none of his tanks. 'We could tell the places where it was natural for mines to grow,' Yoffe explained with a broad grin and an expansive bear-like gesture. In the space of 9 hours his brigade advanced some 60 miles, reaching the Bir Lahfan area at about 1800 hours on the Monday evening. There Yoffe established his brigade in a blocking position across the roads from Gebel Libni and Abu Agheila to El Arish, so as to prevent Egyptian reinforcements reaching El Arish which was already under heavy attack from Israeli forces under General Tal. As expected, the Egyptians did try to reinforce their troops in El Arish by sending an armoured brigade and part of a mechanized infantry brigade up the road from Gebel Libni. At Bir Lahfan they ran into Yoffe's tanks. Battle was engaged and 14 Egyptian tanks were destroyed. Fighting continued intermittently throughout the night but by 1000 hours the next morning [Tuesday], following an air-strike by the Israeli Air Force, the Egyptians beat a retreat closely pursued by a detachment of Yoffe's tanks.

By midnight on Monday Tal's advance tank battalions had smashed through the Egyptian position at Giradeh and the northern brigade commander was able to report that he had one battalion of tanks in El Arish. When, going through the plans before the war, Tal had told Rabin, the Chief of Staff, that he would have El Arish in his hands within 20 hours, Rabin had hold him: 'Don't show off.' Although there was still heavy mortar and machine-gun fire from isolated Egyptian units scattered throughout the area, the Israeli armoured forces had succeeded in the space of little more than 12 hours in breaking the back of the Egyptian 7th Division and fighting their way into El Arish.

But the battle was by no means over. The Egyptian position at Giradeh was heavily fortified with concrete trenches and bunkers that made it the strongest position in the vicinity of El Arish. And although the leading Israeli tanks had succeeded in breaking through and reaching El Arish the rest of the northern brigade found its advance blocked by the Egyptians. Tal diverted all but one battalion of his reserve brigade that was just passing south of Giradeh on its way to the El Arish airfield and instructed it to head north to the assistance of the northern brigade. Halfway to Giradeh this force got stuck in the dunes and was unable to advance any further. Tal therefore sent an armoured infantry battalion from Rafa, where it was attempting to secure a line of communication for vehicles carrying fuel and ammunition, to advance westwards and attack Giradeh. After a heavy fight, the northern brigade commander succeeded in breaking through the Egyptian defences with the loss of 10 tanks and many casualties including one battalion commander and two company commanders. The two battalions of the reserve brigade that had got stuck in the dunes south of Giradeh thereupon continued their advance to the El Arish airfield, where they destroyed 10 Egyptian tanks and forced a further 10 to retreat towards Bir Lahfan.

Dawn found Tal with two armoured brigades in El Arish. Tal described it as 'a brutal battle' and said that his forces had been greatly hampered in their advance by the strength and accuracy of the Egyptian anti-tank fire. General Tal said after the war: 'The Egyptian tanks gave away their positions with their first or second shell. But the anti-tank guns, concealed among the dunes in concrete bunkers, always fired in salvo; it was like a line of lightning along the battlefield. It was impossible to see where they were and few were destroyed by tank fire. We just advanced on the flashes with our tanks and crushed them.'

Only the total air supremacy achieved in the first three hours of the war by the Israeli Air Force, had made possible the speedy Israeli advance through Rafa to El Arish. Even on the Monday morning, when the Israeli Air Force was coping with the Air Forces of Egypt, Syria, and Jordan, the Israeli ground commanders had been able to call in air-strikes on particularly strong enemy positions.

The Rafa-El Arish battle had been fought by the Israelis 'regardless of cost', but now the battle had been won, Tal's chief interest was to save Israeli casualties. He therefore ordered the southern brigade commander to launch what he called a 'sophisticated attack' against Egyptian positions outside Bir Lahfan, to the south-east of El Arish. The brigade commander was told to send one battalion of tanks forward to make contact at long range. No further units were to be committed and no assaults begun until Tal himself gave further orders. By shelling the Egyptian positions at long range the Israeli Centurion tanks were able to destroy the anti-tank guns in their concrete bunkers as well as the T-54 tanks that were lined up behind them, because of the superior range of their British 105 mm guns and the accuracy of their gunners. Seeing that the action was going well, Tal allowed a second battalion to advance through the dunes on the east side. Many of the Israeli tanks got stuck in the soft sand and were, for a while, in considerable danger. However, as the second Israeli battalion advanced, the Egyptians, anxious not to be out-flanked, retreated parallel with the Israeli advance. By this means the Israelis were able to break through into the Egyptian positions without so much as one casualty while destroying more than 30 Egyptian anti-tank guns, 15 tanks and 2 radar-controlled anti-aircraft guns. Tal did not want a repetition of what had happened at Giradeh where, after the initial Israeli break-through, the Egyptians had been able to re-form and block the advance of Israeli reinforcements. He therefore sent an infantry battalion from his reserve brigade to follow closely behind the advancing Israeli armour. At noon on Tuesday, these forces broke through the defences of Bir Lahfan, the last of the fortified Egyptian positions in the area.

Following the break-through achieved by Tal's forces at Khan Yunis and Rafa, an Israeli brigade entered the southern end of the Gaza Strip and advanced north-east towards the town of Gaza, clearing out the Palestinian positions as they went and taking the town itself at 1245 hours on Tuesday afternoon. Meanwhile, as one of his armoured infantry battalions was fighting its way through El Arish street by street, Tal sent a special task-force of engineers, tanks and self-propelled artillery to strike westwards along the coast towards Rumani and the Suez Canal.

From El Arish Tal himself headed south with the rest of his forces to meet General Yoffe at Gebel Libni, which was the 'limited objective' of both Tal's and Yoffe's forces. There they were to formulate their plans for the next stage of the campaign and to receive their further orders by radio from General Gavish, Commander of the Southern Front.

⚜ ⚜ ⚜

While General Tal's forces were effecting the initial Israeli break-through at Rafa and General Yoffe's armoured brigade was battling its way across the dunes, General Sharon was moving up his men and equipment from their defensive positions around Nitsana so that by nightfall [Monday] the encirclement of the Egyptians in Abu Agheila would be complete and all would be set for a night assault.

Abu Agheila was the second break-through point selected by the Israelis. It was a fortified defensive position lying among the dunes some fifteen miles west of the Egyptian/Israeli border. Its fortifications consisted of three parallel lines of trenches nearly three miles long, with three hundred yards between the first and second, and six hundred yards between the second and third. The trenches had all been concreted and the front line was set in the middle of a minefield with mines both in front and behind it. These entrenchments were strongly supported on either flank by infantry and armour. Within the fortifications were deployed a large number of Egyptian tanks and anti-tank guns together with artillery. Behind them were further dispositions of infantry and armour to guard the positions from the rear. Many of the entrenchments had been there since as long ago as 1948 but had been considerably increased and elaborated on since then. The position was held by a reinforced brigade of the Egyptian 2nd Infantry Division made up of four battalions of troops supported by 80-90 tanks (T-54s and T-34s), six regiments of artillery with 122 mm Russian guns, several anti-tank squadrons and detachments of heavy mortars.

Abu Agheila, commanding the junction of the roads from El Arish, Gebel Libni and Kusseima, effectively blocked the main line of advance of Israeli forces in the vicinity of Nitsana to the central part of the Sinai peninsula. The Israelis could not afford to advance further into Sinai while leaving such a strongly held Egyptian position behind them, blocking their supplies of fuel and ammunition which were essential if they were to maintain the momentum of their rapid advance. Furthermore, the advance of General Yoffe's second brigade could not take place until Abu Agheila had been taken.

The man assigned the task of taking Abu Agheila was Brigadier-General Ariel Sharon who, as a brigade commander, had led the paratroopers sent to capture the Mitla Pass in 1956. More recently he had been in charge of the training of the Israel Defence Forces. Sharon is a powerful, stocky man with a swashbuckling air. He has the face of a Roman general under a tousled mop of greying hair. Stuffed in his epaulette he keeps his crimson paratrooper's beret (his is a more brilliant colour than any of the others in the Israeli Army – a gift from French paratrooper friends).

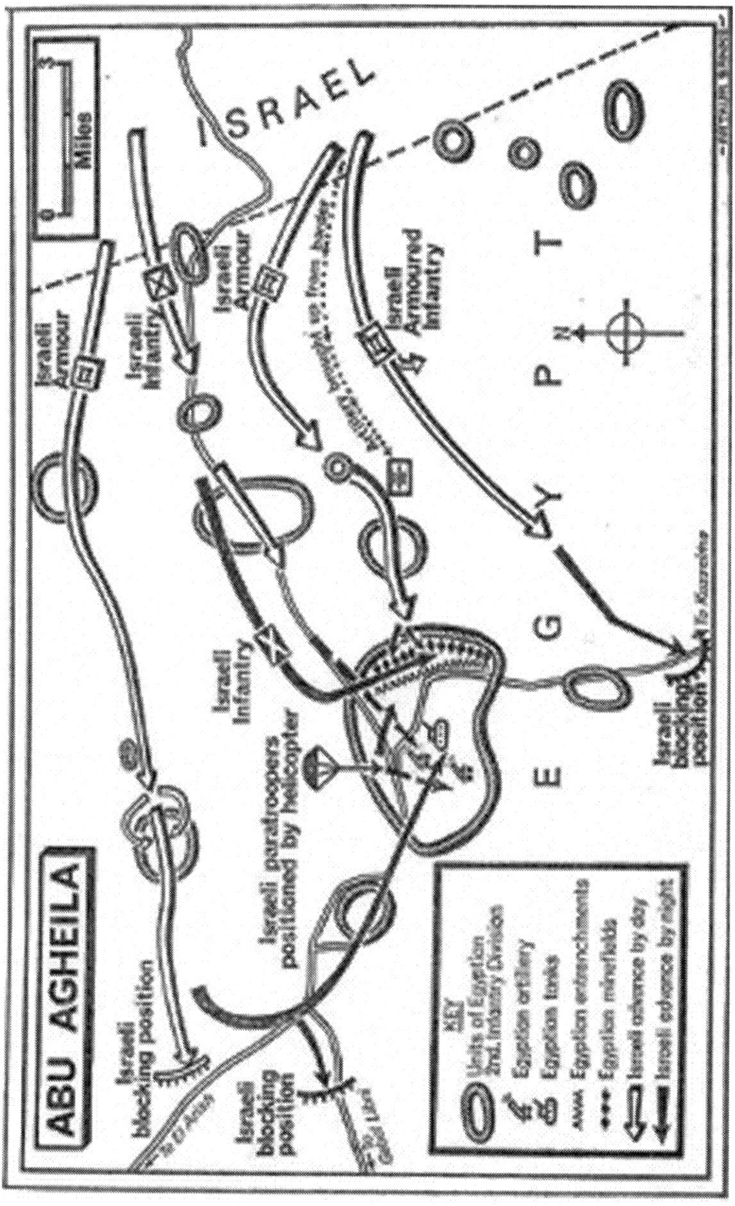
ABU AGHEILA
ISRAEL
EGYPT
Miles
Israeli blocking position
Israeli blocking position
Israeli Armour
Israeli Infantry
Israeli Armour
Israeli Armoured Infantry
Israeli Infantry
Israeli paratroopers positioned by helicopter
Israeli blocking position
KEY
Units of Egyptian 2nd Infantry Division
Egyptian artillery
Egyptian tanks
Egyptian entrenchments
Egyptian minefields
Israeli advance by day
Israeli advance by night

According to Sharon, the system of defence used by the Egyptians at Abu Agheila was very largely Russian, but he added: 'That is convenient for us since we try to avoid frontal attacks.' Sharon had evolved his plan of attack only two or three days before. He had precise information about the fortifications at Abu Agheila and of the disposition of Egyptian forces in the area. He said later: 'I had a sand-table made of the whole area and went over it with every one of my officers so that each one had a clear picture of it in his mind and knew exactly what had to be done – this was most important since we were to attack at night.' Sharon had decided on a night attack because, as he put it: 'The Egyptians do not like fighting at night nor do they enjoy hand-to-hand combat – we specialize in both.'

Sharon's plan of attack was as follows: to establish his artillery in a forward position from which it could direct an intense and accurate fire on the Egyptian entrenchments. Secondly, to block the Egyptians from behind to stop any reinforcements reaching them and to attack them from the rear with a regiment of tanks. Thirdly, to use heli-borne paratroops to attack Abu Agheila from the north, behind the main defensive lines and silence the Egyptian artillery. Fourthly, to assault the Egyptian left (northern) flank with infantry to clear out the front trenches so that engineers could be brought in to clear a path through the minefields. Fifthly, to break through with tanks into the fortified area itself.

Sharon's armoured brigade had crossed the border at 0900 on the Monday morning. They advanced towards Abu Agheila, engaging and over-running the forward positions of the 2nd Egyptian Division by noon and destroying several tanks. Behind the armour came six regiments of Israeli artillery with all their ammunition in one tremendous convoy.

They advanced under a heavy barrage of Egyptian artillery fire and by 1500 they had established themselves in a position not more than five miles from Abu Agheila. From there they could pour a fierce and concentrated fire on to the Egyptian entrenchments. They fired ranging shots until all their guns were spot on their targets and then ceased fire. Also following behind the armoured brigade's advance was one of Sharon's infantry brigades, which began its advance from the border in civilian buses. 'We smeared all our buses and civilian transport with mud,' General Sharon explained, 'not so much to camouflage them but to make them appear a little more military.' (Evidently they were not particularly successful for an Israeli Air Force Colonel who was in charge of the ground control of the Israeli air-strikes in Sinai said afterwards: 'We did not make many mistakes in identifying our own vehicles from the air. Whenever we saw an ice-cream wagon, a hot-dog van or milk trucks, we knew they could only be ours.')

After covering less than ten miles, the infantry had to abandon their buses which had become stuck in the soft sand and could go no further. They then advanced ten miles on foot across the desert before nightfall and, under cover of darkness, moved up to positions from which they would be ready to assault the Egyptians' left (northern) flank.

Meanwhile a reconnaissance group, supported by a regiment of tanks, some engineers and heavy mortars, advanced along a more northerly route to outflank the Egyptian positions and block them from behind. At about 1500 these forces ran into an Egyptian position of battalion strength which stood in their path NNW of Abu Agheila. Heavy fighting ensued in which the Israeli attack was repulsed and seven Israeli tanks were destroyed. The Israeli commanders radioed for close air support but, in spite of several attempts, the Israeli aircraft were unable to find the place because of a sandstorm blowing in the area which reduced visibility to a few hundred yards at ground level. However, soon after 1530, the Israelis attacked again and succeeded in taking the position at the second attempt. They then advanced to the El Arish-Abu Agheila road where they fought a battle with more than twenty T-54 tanks and established themselves in a blocking position across the road.

After dark they advanced south-eastwards to the junction of the road from Gebel Libni, which they also blocked. Here further supplies of fuel and ammunition caught up with them and they awaited orders to advance down the road to Abu Agheila and attack the Egyptians from the rear. Sharon at the same time had sent a second force of reconnaissance troops – tanks, jeeps and mortars – by a southern route to the Kusseima-Abu Agheila road on which it took up position after nightfall. By these two movements the Israelis had cut off all the Egyptian lines of reinforcement – from Kusseima, El Arish and Gebel Libni. By the same token they had cut off all the Egyptian lines of retreat from Abu Agheila. The encirclement was complete.

At dusk two pathfinder helicopters flew in low over the dunes and landed little more than a mile to the north of the Egyptian defences. Their task was to guide the main helicopter force by the use of flares to the point from which they were about to attack. As soon as it was dark, a whole battalion of paratroopers were lifted in by helicopter. 'Helicopters are a much more accurate and speedy way of positioning troops than to drop them out of aircraft when they land all over the place,' commented Sharon.

By 2145 the Israeli troops were ready. The blocking positions behind the Egyptians had all been established and the Israeli tank regiment north-west of Abu Agheila was poised to attack the Egyptians from the rear. The Israeli infantry had moved up to within a few hundred yards of the Egyptian trenches and the bulk of the armour, which had been kept to the rear so as not to expose it to direct Egyptian artillery fire in daylight, had also been brought up into forward positions opposite the Egyptian lines.

Sharon himself was standing on the dunes no more than a thousand yards from the Egyptian trenches. 'It was as light as day, with high explosive and incendiary shells exploding all over the place, lighting up the whole area', Sharon commented afterwards. At 2200 a suggestion came from HQ Southern Command to consider delaying the assault until the following day when air support could be provided – so far, on the Monday, there had been only one Israeli air-strike on the entrenchments at Abu Agheila. One of the pilots had been shot down by anti-aircraft fire, but was later rescued. Sharon said afterwards: 'I had a very real anxiety about the lives of our soldiers. I felt that even with air support it would be too big a job to take such a heavily fortified position by day. I had seen the lines of our soldiers marching forward across the dunes earlier in the day. I had seen the confidence in their faces and knew they were ready to go. I could not keep them waiting. I was sure we could take it.'

At 2245 Sharon gave the order to attack. Instantly the six regiments of artillery, which he had moved up earlier in the day and which were out of sight behind the dunes to the east of Abu Agheila, opened fire. Sharon himself takes up the story: 'For half an hour the fire was tremendous – I have never seen such fire in all my life. I then ordered the paratroopers to break through the Egyptian defences and assault the artillery. At the same time I instructed the tank regiment positioned to the north-west of the El Arish road to advance and attack the enemy from the rear. Moments later I gave the word for the whole armoured brigade to move up close to the Egyptian positions and open fire, but the smoke and dust was so thick they could not shoot.

'At 2315 our artillery ceased fire, our tanks opened up. and the infantry assault went in. Each battalion had a trench to clear. Earlier on I had sent someone to acquire 150 torches – I had a friend at the Ordnance Depot. I told him I wanted 50 with red lights, 50 with green and 50 with blue; he slapped some paint over the bulbs and I had them in two or three hours. Each battalion had a different colour. In this way our tanks knew exactly where our men had got to and were able to keep their fire ahead of them. We used searchlights to light up the whole area and enable our tanks to shoot accurately.

'By 0030 hours [Tuesday] the Egyptian artillery was beginning to slacken. The paratroops had been doing their job but they had several casualties. Of one group of 150 men, 5 were killed and 15 wounded. I ordered them not to leave the wounded – we never do – but I wanted them to keep their wounded with them in case the Egyptians counter-attacked. Since it takes two men to carry each wounded man nearly half our troops in this unit were out of action.

'The infantry which only had orders to clear one mile of trenches in fact ran through all three miles of them fighting hand-to-hand all the way. I immediately ordered the engineers to start clearing the minefields. This they did on foot with prods and with flails mounted on tanks. It was essential to get our tanks inside the fortifications before dawn otherwise they would be very vulnerable to the Egyptian artillery. At one point the Egyptians blew up the road in such a way that the crater was too deep for the tanks to climb out of it.

They therefore had to turn off the track – immediately one was blown up on a mine. This delayed their advance. But very soon Za'ev, our engineer, managed to open up another path advancing with flails under heavy fire and the tank brigade was able to break into the fortifications.

'Meanwhile the tanks from the north broke in on the Egyptians from behind.

'By 0300 hours I was able to radio the Southern Command that Abu Agheila was in my hands, although the main tank battle inside the fortified area which measured 8 miles by 4 miles did not take place until dawn and continued from 0400 to 0600.

'At 0600 hours the battle was over and I was able to order my troops blocking the Kusseima-Abu Agheila road to the south to advance towards Kusseima. The attack on Abu Agheila was the most complicated our army has ever carried out. Our men had succeeded because they believed – they knew – they could take it.

'The second of General Yoffe's brigades had to pass through ours. So that they could do this we had to clear hundreds of vehicles off the road – all the buses and milk wagons that we had advanced in the day before. It was impossible to turn them round and drive them back, we just pushed them off the track into the sand. Once we had cleared the road, Yoffe's men were able to advance towards Gebel Libni.

'In Abu Agheila I said goodbye to the infantry and paratroop commanders and advanced with only my armoured brigade southwards towards Nakhl to meet up with other forces that were being attached to my command.'

The Israelis, with their break-throughs at Rafa and Abu Agheila achieved, were now behind the bulk of the Egyptian Army and two gateways into the heart of Sinai were open to them. General Yoffe's second brigade reached Gebel Libni at 0600 hours on the Wednesday morning with fresh troops. All was now set for the final encirclement and destruction of the Egyptian Army in Sinai.

Chapter Seven
Jerusalem and the West Bank

While the battle was raging in Sinai, even more momentous events were taking place in Jerusalem. Brigadier-General Uzzi Narkiss, the Israeli Central Commander, had been envious of the commanders on the southern front, feeling that they would have the major part of the fighting, while he might see no action at all. However, he was to be in luck. Already by midnight on the first day of the war, Monday June 5, he was to be told, in the midst of the fighting, by the Chief Army Rabbi, General Schiomo Goren: 'Your men are making history – what is going on in Sinai is nothing compared to this.'

On the Monday morning Israeli forces in the central sector, opposite Jordan, and the northern sector, opposite Syria, were in a purely defensive deployment. The Israeli plan was to hold the line on both these fronts since the bulk of their forces would be engaged in the destruction of the Egyptian Army in Sinai. It was the Israeli hope and indeed, until the fateful kiss between Nasser and Hussein in Cairo on Tuesday May 30, the Israeli belief that Jordan would not involve herself in any conflict between Israel and Egypt. Jordan had held aloof in '56 and it was strongly felt that she would do so again.

As soon as the Nasser-Hussein pact became known on the Tuesday evening before the outbreak of war, General Narkiss, whose area of responsibility included Jerusalem, Tel Aviv and the whole of the heavily populated coastal plain of Israel, received specific instructions from the Israeli General Staff not to be in any way provocative but to maintain a strictly defensive posture. One of his major preoccupations, in the event of war, would be the situation of Mount Scopus which was an Israeli-held enclave cut off from the Israeli part of Jerusalem and surrounded completely by Jordanian territory. Mount Scopus is the seat of the old Hebrew University and acquired its anomalous position when the Armistice Commission lines were drawn in 1948. Under the terms of the 1948 Armistice Agreement the technically de-militarized zone was held by 120 Israeli soldiers who were stationed there on a fortnightly-basis. One Israeli convoy was allowed to pass each way every two weeks – the UN checking the numbers of soldiers. There was also a strict limitation on the amount of arms and ammunition that the Israelis could take into Mount Scopus. Nevertheless, they evidently found ways of getting military supplies through, for by the time the war started they had a sizeable arsenal in Mount Scopus although they still had no more than 120 troops to defend the area. A few days before the outbreak of hostilities the Israelis deferred to a request by the Jordanians to cancel the regular fortnightly convoy which was due to go to Mount Scopus. It seems that this request from the Jordanians came because they felt they were unable to control the mobs in Jerusalem in view of the tension since the closing of the Gulf of Aqaba. This surprising readiness on the part of the Israelis, who can, when they wish, be particular about such matters, underlines the care that Israel was taking to avoid any provocation of Jordan.

Narkiss' other concern was the status of the old Government House in the UN area just south of Jerusalem which was being used by the United Nations as their headquar ters; it was his responsibility to make sure that this wasn't taken over by the Jordanians.

These, although important, were in the nature of local threats. There were, however, two graver threats that Narkiss had to guard against. The first was that the Jordanians might encircle and cut off the Israeli part of Jerusalem; the second, and even more serious, that they attempt to cut Israel in two by thrusting westwards to the coast in the vicinity of Natanya. Here at its waist Israel is no more than ten miles wide. To have their already small country divided in this way would be strategically, economically and politically disastrous for the Israelis and would have gravely weakened their defensive position since their lines of communication going north and south would have been totally disrupted. With the bulk of the Israeli armour in the south of the country it would have made the north particularly vulnerable to Syrian and Jordanian attack.

The Jordanian deployment in the southern part of the West Bank area in the weeks preceding the war consisted of the 27th Infantry Brigade, with a battalion of the 3rd Armoured Brigade, between Jericho and Jerusalem and, slightly further to the north, the Jordanian 60th Armoured Brigade with more than 80 Patton tanks. These forces could pose a considerable threat to Mount Scopus and Government House.

But the arrival in Jordan on May 24 of a whole Iraqi infantry division backed up by some 150 tanks made a much more serious situation for Israel. A force of this size, combined with the Jordanian forces, could easily pose a major threat to Israel at its most vulnerable point, the narrow coastal strip between the Jordanian border and the Mediterranean.

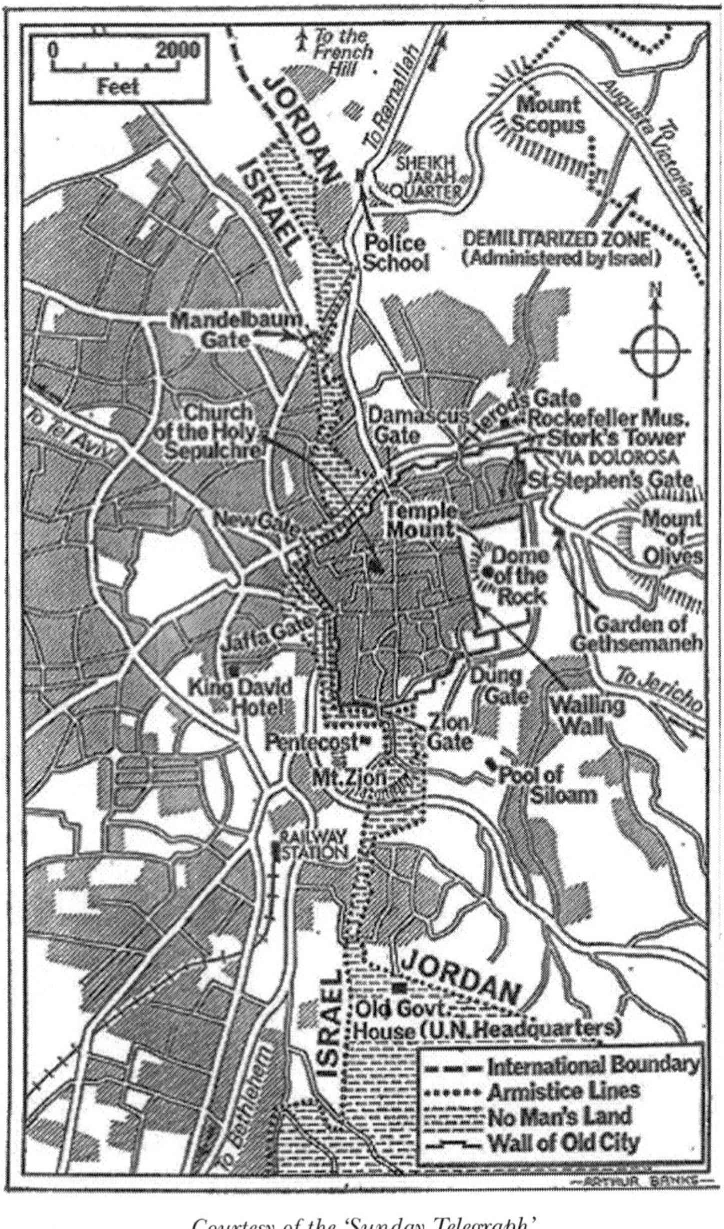

Courtesy of the 'Sunday Telegraph'

On Wednesday May 31 Moshe Dayan, not yet a member of the Government, visited Narkiss on the authorization of Eshkol, and told him: 'Don't bother the General Staff with requests for reinforcements. Grit your teeth and ask for nothing.' In the event of an attack Narkiss' plan, which he had evolved two or three days before Dayan's visit, was to break through with his infantry to Mount Scopus from Jerusalem and to move his armour up to the high ground between Jerusalem and Ramallah where he would be in a position to dominate the whole of Jerusalem and defend Mount Scopus and Government House.

This was at the same time the indirect approach to the Old City of Jerusalem. In conjunction with this Narkiss planned to use his infantry to take and hold Sur Bahir so as to cut the enemy's route between Jerusalem and Bethlehem, but he asked to be allocated a paratroop brigade to take the Police School, a Jordanian stronghold between the Israeli sector of Jerusalem and the Mount Scopus enclave.

From the vantage point of Castel (Narkiss' advance command post just off the Jerusalem–Tel Aviv road, 5 miles west of Jerusalem) Narkiss and Dayan surveyed the area and went over all the plans. Dayan suggested cancelling some small troop movements that had been planned, so as to offer no provocation to the Jordanians.

Later in the week immediately preceding the war, it was learnt that the Iraqi division was advancing through the eastern part of Jordan and was due to cross the Jordan River on the Sunday night and would come under the command of the Egyptian General Riadh, in Amman. It was also learnt on the evening of Saturday June 3 that one battalion of Egyptian Commandos had arrived in Amman.

Narkiss, having been told that he could not expect reinforcements, got everyone busy in his sector digging miles and miles of trenches. All the villagers, townspeople and members of the kibbutzim in the area got hard to work digging. Women and school children filled sand-bags. Mines were laid everywhere but there were not enough of them. 'We did all we could to be ready to absorb an attack,' said Narkiss.

On the morning of Monday June 5, shortly after the first wave of the Israeli air-strike had gone in against Egypt, the Israeli Prime Minister, Mr Eshkol, sent the following message to King Hussein via General Odd Bull, the UN commander: 'We shall not initiate any action whatsoever against Jordan. However, should Jordan open hostilities, we shall react with all our might and he (King Hussein) will have to bear the full responsibility for all the consequences.' General Bull confirmed that this message had been received by King Hussein.

Nevertheless, shortly after 0830 sporadic firing broke out along the Jerusalem perimeter from the Jordanian side of the border and soon afterwards shells began falling on the Israeli part of the city. Either Hussein could not believe that the Egyptian Air Force was already virtually destroyed or he was no longer in control of his armed forces who were now taking their orders from the Egyptian General Riadh. By 1130 there was firing all along the Jordanian border and shells from the Jordanians' Long Tom guns in Kalkilya were falling on Tel Aviv while others, from positions further to the north, were exploding in the vicinity of the major air-base of Ramat David.

The Israelis were surprised but not dismayed. For them this was the chance of a lifetime. By 0910 General Nar-kiss who, just over an hour before, had ordered a full alert in all the Central Command area and had given instructions for the air-raid alarms to be sounded, was telling Teddy Kollek, the Mayor of Jerusalem, on the telephone: 'It's a war but everything is well under control. You may well be Mayor of a united Jerusalem.'

The following account of the fighting in the Jerusalem area is based on a diary of the campaign kept by General Narkiss' assistant together with extracts from accounts of the battle given by Colonel Morechai Gur, the paratroop commander who led the ground forces in the fighting in Jerusalem, and Colonel Uri Ben-Ari, commander of the armoured forces in the area. The latter are referred to as Motta and Uri, respectively.

Monday June 5 1967.

0911 Jordanian troops were in position. Amman radio declared that Jordan was being attacked.

0927 Hussein declared on the radio: 'The hour of revenge has come . . .'

0930 'I spoke to the Commander of the Jerusalem area and asked him if he had enough tanks. These were being held well to the rear as there were restrictions under the Armistice on what we could have in Jerusalem itself. I reminded [him] that he should be prepared to take Abdul Aziz Hill (1 mile from Castel) and perhaps Government House as well.'

0933 'I talked to Rabin and told him: "My forces are ready to take Latrun, Government House and Abdul Aziz." '

0955 'I ordered the trains [from Tel Aviv to Jerusalem, which for nearly ten miles of their journey pass within 200 yards of the Jordanian border] to continue running – but empty.'

1030 Cairo radio announced that Government House had been taken.

1130 'There was fire all along the line. I spoke with Rabin (Chief of Staff) and asked his permission to occupy the places mentioned. He said: "No." 'Moments later Mount Scopus came under bombardment by 25-pounders and artillery, as did Ramat Rachel.

1150 Narkiss again called Rabin and suggested action. Again he was told: 'No.'

1200 The United Nations asked for a cease-fire. Narkiss agreed.

1210 Narkiss spoke to Barlev (Deputy Chief of Staff) and told him: 'I think we must act. I consider the Jordanians would like only to be able to say that they have fought, then they will shut up. But I would very much like to get in and take the positions mentioned.'

Barlev: 'Niet!'

1220 'The Jordanians were bombing and shelling our positions and Hunters strafed a village near Natanya. The shelling continued.'

1230 'I spoke with the Commander of the Jerusalem area to tell him: "If Mount Scopus is attacked Uri (commander of the mechanized brigade) will penetrate to the north." I cancelled the movement of the trains.'

1240 Jordanian Hunters bombed near Tel Aviv. (Little damage sustained and no loss of life.)

1245 Radio Amman declared: 'Mount Scopus has been occupied.'

1250 'Immediately afterwards I received authorization to order the mechanized brigade near Ramla to move towards positions near Castel.'

1300 'I ordered Uri to be ready to move. He was to use three roads from Ramla to reach his positions close to Jerusalem.' [All the tank transporters were in the Southern Negev where by far the greater part of the Israeli armour was deployed. The transporters would be needed if it proved necessary to rush tanks from the southern front to the Jordanian or Syrian fronts.]

Uri asked that he be allowed to go in to the attack as soon as he reached his access point. He did not want to have to stop and wait at the border and reform his tanks but wanted to go straight in with momentum. Narkiss spoke with Dayan who said that if Mount Scopus was in danger he could go. Dayan proposed that the mechanized brigade should go by a more direct route passing just north of Jerusalem. Narkiss told him he preferred to stick to his original plan as he believed that he would reach the Ramallah-Jerusalem road sooner this way even though it was further.

Uri's mechanized brigade began its climb up the road towards Jerusalem.

Narkiss told the Infantry Commander to be ready to shell the Police School.

1400 The General Staff informed Narkiss he would receive one battalion of paratroopers to fight in the Jerusalem area.

1405 Uri arrived at Narkiss' HQ. Narkiss: 'This was to be a revenge for '48. We had both fought here – that time we had been defeated.' [Rabin had also fought for Jerusalem in '48. All three had been born there.] Narkiss told Uri to get to Mount Scopus as quickly as possible.

1410 The Brigade Commander of the Jerusalem area informed Narkiss that Government House (the UN HQ) had been occupied by Jordanian forces.

'We had begun at 0800 in a defensive posture. By 1200 hours this was all changed.'

Narkiss asked authorization to counter-attack.

1415 A second battalion of paratroopers under their commander, Motta, was committed to Narkiss' command. Narkiss decided to use them for the attack on the Police School and Sur Bahir.

Motta:

On Monday we were ready in the vicinity of one of our airfields to embark for airborne action [against El Arish]. At about 1400 hours we received the order to take one battalion to Jerusalem, but before long it turned out that a whole brigade was wanted. We were entrusted with a mission which we realized was one of extreme difficulty – to break through into a built-up area.

In every army this is considered to be the most formidable type of combat area. We were to connect up with Mount Scopus and create a situation in which we could conveniently break through into the Old City. A few days before this I had gone to look over the terrain, to observe the positions, the fortifications, and to take stock of the enemy's position.

1425 Narkiss was ordered to counter-attack. Meanwhile General Odd Bull (UN Commander) asked again for a cease-fire.

1430 Narkiss asked Intelligence for the location of the 60th Jordanian Armoured Brigade. Dayan telephoned and said he was on his way to Jerusalem. Narkiss told him to go by a southerly route.

As Uri left Narkiss' HQ Motta (the Paratroop Commander) arrived to be briefed.

1550 Government House, together with the fortified zone behind it, was taken by Israeli forces at the cost of eight Israeli dead.
Narkiss asked permission to take Latrun – permission not granted.

1600 Narkiss went with three vehicles to his advance command post at the Castel.
By now the whole paratroop brigade (three battalions) had been committed.

1645 Narkiss gave orders that the Israeli flag be flown from Government House. At the same time he instructed his Operations Officer to equip Motta with flags for the capture of the Police School so that it would not be shelled by Israeli forces once it had been taken.

1700 A village near Castel was shelled.

1715 The Air Force was ordered to attack the 60th Jordanian Armoured Brigade.

1730 'Uri was ready to go – he entered Jordan. None of the tanks were equipped with flails for dealing with mines. [They were all in the south.] Uri had men walking in front of his tanks to detect and uncover the mines. Because of the rapid speed of his advance forty of his men were injured by exploding mines.'

1920 Abdul Aziz hill was taken.
'Uri reported that the radar position was in our hands. But he reported that without mine detectors or flails the going was slow.' Beit Iksa was also taken.

Uri:

At 1300 hours we received the order to seize the mountain ridge between Ramallah and Jerusalem. The positions in this area had been known for a long time. The radar site I remember from 20 years ago when I attacked it several times. We took it once, then somebody else lost it. It was a concreted position as was Abdul Aziz, while Beit Iksa was a fortified village. If anyone had taught at the Command and Headquarters School that it was possible for an armoured brigade from the plain to attack the Jerusalem positions within four hours he'd have been thrown out; but my men did it. The problem in these positions was the bunkers. One tank was detailed to each bunker and between 1700 and 1900 they were all silenced. Then the armoured infantry went in and with great persistence removed the mines with probes, one by one in the darkness.

Narkiss decided that it was likely that the Jordanian 60th Armoured Brigade would try to set an ambush for Uri at the junction on the Ramallah-Jerusalem Road but he reckoned that Uri would get there first.

2000 Narkiss arrived in Jerusalem.

'Sur Bahir was in our hands; but there were signs of a counter-attack.'

Narkiss went to the Knesset to see Dayan who should have gone there to be sworn in as Minister of Defence. Dayan was not there and the ceremony was postponed. He was not in fact sworn in until after hostilities had finished.

Narkiss met Motta who told him that he planned to attack after midnight.

Narkiss told his HQ to press the General Staff for permission to take Latrun.

Narkiss requested that the Air Force continue its strikes on the Jordanian 60th Brigade. He had a dispute with Barlev on the timing of Motta's attack.

Motta's troops had left for Jerusalem at 1900 hours and would be ready to attack at 0200 hours (Tuesday).

The General Staff wanted to make the attack at 0800 the following morning coupled with artillery bombardment and air-strikes. Narkiss told them that it was too close to Jerusalem for air-strikes and persuaded them to agree to the 0200-hour timing.

2400 The Chief Army Rabbi, General Schiomo Goren, visited Narkiss at midnight and told him: 'Your men are making history – what is going on in Sinai is nothing compared to this.'

Narkiss told him to prepare his trumpet.

Tuesday June 6 1967.

0140 Narkiss accompanied Motta to his command post not far from the Police School. All of the Israeli part of Jerusalem was under artillery and mortar fire. As the two commanders took stock of the situation from the roof of a building, a shell from a 25-pounder hit the roof on which they were standing. Fortunately for them it hit the parapet and neither was hurt.

Motta:

At 0220 we began to give artillery support and the tanks rolled forward down the slope of the street and took up position. As soon as the noise of the tank tracks was heard, the enemy opened fire along the entire length of the line. The shelling increased in intensity. But as the tanks moved forward they began to silence the enemy positions. A great many of the men in the tanks were Jerusalemites. They began to smash the emplacements and at the same time our forces opened a strong artillery fire.

We were moving forward with two battalions, one operating in the Police School sector on 'Ammunition Hill', the other in Sheik Jarah. This was fighting of a sort I had never experienced. The men had to break through at least five fences before they reached the emplacements. They passed the first line of positions and entered the trenches. The fighting was going on in the trenches, in the houses, on the roofs, in the cellars, anywhere and everywhere. We passed from one position to another and saw the marks left by our artillery which had been outstandingly effective. Some of the concrete bunkers had received direct hits and been destroyed.

The battle in the trenches lasted from 0220 hours until about 0700 hours. We had reached a bunker with two heavy machine-guns we did not know about as it was hard to place from an aerial photograph. The commander was on top of it, and did not realize that there was a bunker there. It had a wall that projected into the trench. Just then a soldier jumped up, above the bunker, and dropped a grenade from above, despite the fact that he was completely exposed. The grenade exploded, but the firing from the bunker kept up. Then one of our men threw three charges of explosives. The first soldier jumped back to the other side of the trench and detonated the three charges. The bunker exploded but only three soldiers were killed and the two survivors continued to shoot. An [Israeli] soldier then came over from the other side and flung another grenade in – and that was the end of that.

A young fellow by the name of Naphtali who stood at an observation post and noticed the beginnings of a left flank movement ran all over the position, shooting and reconnoitring until he was hit. Thus the fighting went on with officers and men running back and forth carrying ammunition and encouraging the fighting forces. All this time, we in the brigade command room had no idea how bitter the fighting was. We knew there had been casualties, but did not know exactly what had happened.

The second sector, also in the centre, was the Sheikh Jarah quarter, which is dominated both by the Police School and by the Mandelbaum Gate sectors. Fence after fence was opened, casualties were evacuated behind the lines, and the advance continued. Every time we ventured to cut in on communications and ask what was happening the answer was – 'It's O.K. Everything is going according to plan.' The only thing on their mind was that t–e casualties should be evacuated in time and according to their needs.

0345 The Police School was taken: 'This was the heaviest fighting of all [40 men were killed out of 500 in the paratroop battalion]. The Police School was held by more than 200 of the Arab Legion. You should be at least three times as strong as the enemy for an attack against a heavily fortified position.'

'The Arab Legion fought like hell. It took us several hours of street-to-street fighting before we took the Police School.' When the Police School was finally taken, 106 Arab Legionnaires lay dead in and around the building.

The Israeli forces were given supporting fire by 120-mm mortars and by artillery from the vicinity of Castel and two searchlights on top of the Histadrut (Federation of Labour) building were used to illuminate the area and enable air-strikes to continue during the night, the Police School being their principal objective.

Motta's paratroopers continued their advance and entered the American Colony:

Our two regiments continued to advance and at about 0600 hours the Ambassador Hotel was in our hands; the whole of the American Colony fell to us a little later. Some of the legionnaires retreating from the front line took cover inside the buildings, and so there was house-to-house fighting. Sometimes it was necessary to deal with the same house twice, since our boys were running forward all the time. Here we suffered casualties in the streets, for the legionnaires continued to fire from those houses which had not yet been dealt with, and some of our boys were shot from behind. As dawn broke a little after 0400 hours, we engaged our tank battalion, distributing the tanks between the regiments, and fighting proceeded to the inner courts while we went on mopping up along our main lines of advance up to the Rockefeller Museum. We now threw in our third regiment, the one that had been fighting in the Mandelbaum Gate area, and its orders were to reach Herod's Gate – a very important point, since it was through this gate that we planned to pour our infantry into the Old City.

0600 Uri with his armoured brigade reached the cross-roads on the Ramallah-Jerusalem road shortly before the Jordanians and prepared an ambush for them in which he destroyed at least fifteen of their tanks. The Jordanian armour was too close to the Israelis for them to use air-strikes against the Jordanians.

Soon after midnight Narkiss had told the General Staff that he wanted Motta and his paratroopers to enter the Old City in the morning but the General Staff said he must wait.

0700 A mechanized force of paratroopers attached to Uri's command entered and took Latrun, an enclave of Jordanian territory jutting into Israel from the south-western corner of the West Bank area. The Israelis had terrible memories of it from the war of '48 when hundreds of their comrades had died trying to seize this strongly defended Arab position. [In the war of '48 6,000 Jews out of 600,000, or one in every hundred of the population, had been killed. In 1967 the figures were to be incomparably lower: just under 700 out of a population of 2,600,000, or 1 in 3,700.] This time Latrun fell easily and the Israeli paratroopers were able to advance quickly along the road towards Ramallah. Before they reached Ramallah, the towers and minarets of Jerusalem suddenly came into view. As one of them put it: 'We had never seen Jerusalem from this side before. It was a fantastic feeling, knowing that the rest of our brigade was fighting there, to think that after all this time Jerusalem would once again be ours. We wished we could be there.'

0922 Narkiss asked his own staff to tell the General Staff that if they didn't authorize him to take the Wailing Wall it would be their mistake. Meanwhile he ordered Motta to try and penetrate the Old City.

Motta:

The mopping up outside the walls was all over at about 1000 hours, with our forces in control of all the areas designated. We were now ready to break through into the Old City. All through the day we engaged in minor actions and the impetus of our attack, through no fault of our own, declined somewhat. We had gone into action quickly, but it is difficult to keep up speed in open areas with only infantry troops and no tank cover. The Arabs held the wall, and it was impossible for us to move. Hardly did our men start moving when they were hit and it was clear that so long as we had not taken the wall it would be impossible to move along the streets.

1200 Uri joined up with the paratroopers on the French Hill after a fierce fight in the gully below where the Israeli attack had initially been repulsed by the Jordanians. A few moments later Dayan arrived.

1225 Narkiss and he went to Mount Scopus by half-track. Dayan said : 'On this day 6 June '67 what a fantastic view.' He told Narkiss that he must seal off the Old City of Jerusalem by taking the heights behind it to the East.

Dayan feared that the United Nations Security Council might impose a cease-fire before the Israelis had achieved their objectives, and had obtained a satisfactory and lasting result. He wanted the Israeli forces to be in as commanding a position as possible.

1300 Narkiss gave the order to take the heights behind Jerusalem but warned Dayan it would be difficult. Motta had only one tank company assigned to him; Narkiss gave him another. After one hour Motta reported that he was having difficulty and he was sustaining losses. Dayan returned by helicopter to Tel Aviv.

Motta:

The same situation held for the Augusta Victoria area, which is dominated from two heights – and so the tank battalion attached to our units had to regroup. This battalion had come into action fast, had suffered many losses and it therefore took some time to regroup. In the end we decided to resume the attack towards evening.

Narkiss decided to postpone the taking of the hills until dark.

1715 Uri headed north towards Ramallah leaving behind a company of tanks for Motta. Meanwhile the paratroopers slept and organized themselves for the assault. H-hour was set for 2300 hours.

Motta:

At nightfall we went out again, to take Augusta Victoria heights. Our programme called for two reduced tank battalions, one for cover and one to advance straight up the road to Augusta Victoria.

We sent our tanks forward, and then one of our infantry regiments began its advance, but the units near the wall came under heavy anti-tank fire. One of our tanks went up in flames at once, as did a number of our reconnaissance jeeps. We had casualties from the very first moment and decided to make slight changes in our schedule.

2220 Troops on top of Mount Scopus heard the clanking of tanks coming up the road towards Jerusalem from Jericho. It seemed likely that the Jordanians were about to counter-attack. Narkiss cancelled the night attack planned for 2300 hours and told his men to prepare instead for a Jordanian counter-attack.

Wednesday June 7 1967.

0500 Barlev telephoned authorization to take the Old City and said: 'We are already being pressed for a cease-fire. We are at the Canal. The Egyptians have been carved up – don't let the Old City remain an enclave.'

0830 The paratroopers began their attack to the accompaniment of a half-hour aerial bombardment and artillery barrage.

Augusta Victoria was found to be empty and Motta reached Isoric with his tanks.

Motta:

This was an action in which we adopted all sorts of moves which, under ordinary circumstances, we might not have done. One regiment was to drive straight uphill from Mount Scopus to Augusta Victoria. Another regiment would conduct a daylight frontal attack with the Old City wall behind it. Since it would also have to advance through built-up areas, I decided to take whatever risk there might be and gave the order to go into action. The third regiment was to push on along the wall from Herod's Gate and, regardless of fire from the wall, was to break through the wall and reach the Temple Mount.

Not knowing for sure what the enemy position was, we decided to disregard our lack of information and proceed according to plan. We therefore brought in the Air Force at 0830 hours. Although the Mount Scopus regiment asked for another 15 minutes, I could not let them have it, and gave orders to attack at once. I instructed our tanks to start moving up and see where contact was being effected with the enemy, and to determine the battle plan accordingly. We laid down a heavy artillery cover. Our tanks advanced firing in every direction, and, after them, I sent a mechanized unit with recoilless guns. Now everything broke loose. We jumped into the command half-track and pushed forward, giving the Mount Scopus regiment its orders to advance at top speed and the second regiment to start its frontal attack. We knew there were tanks further on, so we turned our column along the ridge and swept it with heavy fire. This same thrust brought us to the square facing the Old City. The Temple Mount was before us, with its gold and silver cupolas, and all the New City beyond.

At this point, I ordered my brigade to attack the Old City. The plan called for a tank advance along the road to the gate, three infantry regiments were also ordered to move as far forward as possible – and whoever came first, well, that would be his luck.

We now started shelling the Moslem quarter of the Old City which borders upon the wall and might have prevented our forces from breaking through Herod's Gate. The shelling lasted 10 minutes and was highly effective. All our tanks opened fire, as did our recoilless guns; we swept the whole wall and not a shot was directed at, or hit, the Holy Places. The breakthrough area underwent concentrated fire : all the wall shook and some stones were loosened – but all the firing was to the right of St Stephen's Gate.

Seeing the tanks advancing towards the wall, we got into our half-track and went on to catch up with them, while ordering them to go faster. The infantry was ordered to keep up with the tanks. For a moment, I stopped the artillery fire but after our tanks had spotted the enemy positions, we renewed our firing and continued our advance up to the bridge beneath St Stephen's Gate. There the tanks found it more difficult to manœuvre, but it was by this time impossible to check our impetus.

I told my driver, Ben Tsur, a bearded fellow weighing some 15 stone, to speed on ahead. We passed the tanks and saw the Gate before us with a car burning outside it. There wasn't a lot of room, but I told him to drive on and so we passed the burning car and saw the Gate half-open in front. Regardless of the danger that somebody might drop grenades into our half-track from above, he pushed on and flung the door aside, crunched over the fallen stones, passed by a dazed Arab soldier, turned left and came to another gate. Here, a motorcycle blocked the way but, despite the danger of a booby-trap, my driver drove right over it and we reached the Temple Mount. Here there was no more firing, for it is a Holy Place. Our tanks could not get there but the infantry regiments did. The operation was completed; there only remained the mopping up to be done. At this point the Governor of the City came up to me together with the Kadi (Moslem Religious Dignitary) and informed me of the solemn decision not to defend the City. He assured me that the [Jordanian] troops had all left and there would be no further resistance. I promised him that we would start mopping up without shooting and would only do so as a last resort if we met resistance. While he told me that he could not be responsible for bandits opening fire, there was really no more resistance inside the City although we lost 4 of our men, and 2 of our officers were hit during the fighting for the Wall, when charging up to a house and climbing up to the roof.

0950 Motta entered the city by way of St Stephen's Gate.

1000 Narkiss, following close behind Motta, arrived at the corner of the 'Stork's Tower' where a battle with snipers was in progress.

1015 Narkiss was near the Wailing Wall with the Chief Rabbi, Barlev and Motta. 'Operation Old City' was almost over.

1400 Dayan entered the Old City accompanied by Rabin and Narkiss. They made their way to the Wailing Wall where Dayan, following an old Jewish tradition, scribbled a prayer on a scrap of paper and slipped it between the stones of the wall. It read: 'Let peace reign in Israel'.

The Wailing Wall is supposedly the last remains of the Temple, destroyed by the Roman Emperor Titus in the year 70 A D. As he stood beside it Dayan affirmed: 'We have returned to our holiest of holy places, never to be parted from it again.' Ben-Gurion, too, when he visited the wall declared, in a voice charged with emotion: 'This is the greatest day of my life.' Then, noticing a sign in English and Arabic that was defacing the wall, he asked that it be taken down. A soldier climbed up and prised it off with a bayonet, to the admonitions of Ben-Gurion not to damage the stones. A few days later, to guard the wall from the hordes of pressmen and throngs of sightseers, a crudely lettered sign appeared at the foot of the Wailing Wall which proclaimed in Hebrew characters: 'Beyt Knesseth.' – This is a Temple.

⚜ ⚜ ⚜

On the evening of Tuesday June 6, as soon as the outcome of the fighting in Jerusalem had been decided, Uri had pressed northwards to Ramallah with two battalions of his mechnized brigade. His forces entered the town at 1900 hours on the Tuesday evening. Uri gave the following account of its capture: 'For the first time in my life we had to capture a city almost in the dark – and that's a problem. We decided to go into Ramallah with a battalion of tanks, shooting on all sides. We crossed and recrossed the city several times and it slowly fell silent. There was some resistance from bazookas, etc., but within three-quarters of an hour the town was silent. We cleared out of it that night and took up positions to the north and to the south. By morning there was no resistance and the town was mopped up.

Meanwhile, as Uri was taking Ramallah and advancing on Nablus from the south, forces under Brigadier-General Elazar, the Israeli Northern Commander, were sweeping southwards from Jenin. The Israeli plan was for a coordinated pincer movement directed against Nablus, the main town on the high ground of Jordan's West Bank area, which, in conjunction with the operations around Jerusalem and Hebron in the south, would secure the whole of the West Bank for Israel.

At 1725 hours on the Monday afternoon one of Elazar's mechanized infantry brigades supported by a detachment of tanks crossed Jordan's northern border to take Jenin and silence the long-range Jordanian artillery which was threatening the major Israeli airbase of Ramat David. By 0200 Tuesday morning this force was heavily engaged with the Jordanian 25th Infantry Brigade in the hills to the north-west of Jenin. In the fierce fighting that ensued the Israelis believe that they severely mauled two of the Jordanian battalions and completely wiped out a third. 'We attacked them at night – and at night it is impossible to take prisoners,' commented General Elazar. Soon after dawn, another Israeli infantry force entered and took Jenin.

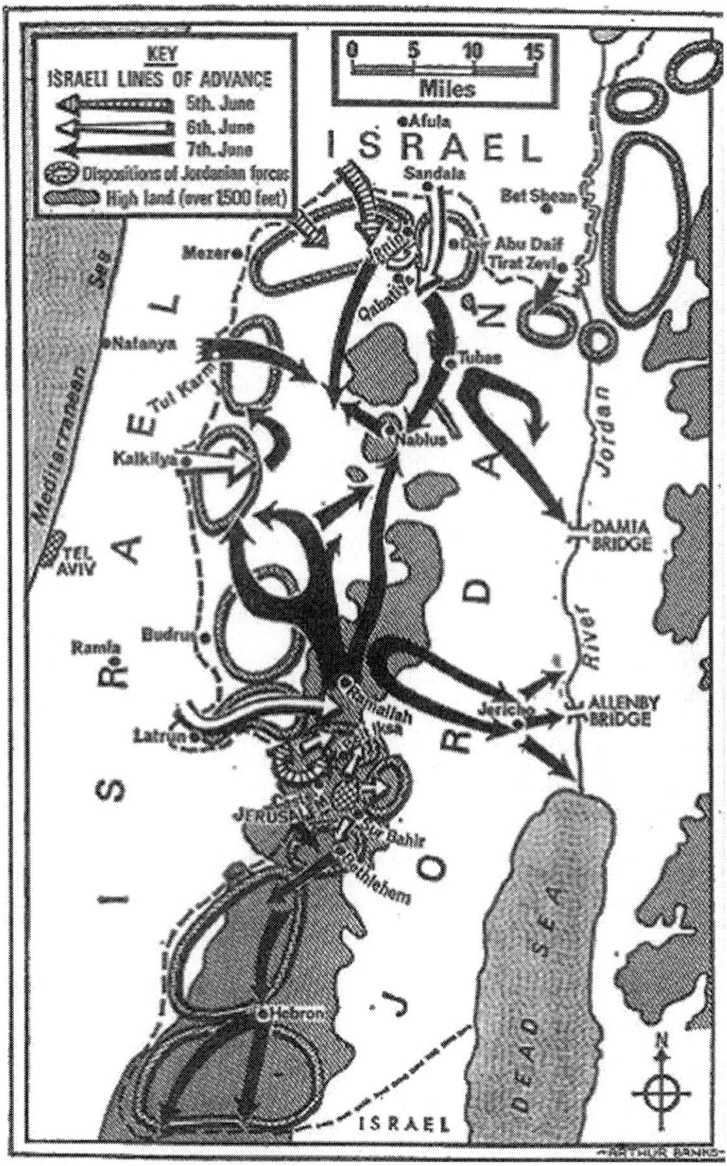
KEY
ISRAELI LINES OF ADVANCE
5th. June
6th. June
7th. June
Dispositions of Jordanian forces
High land (over 1500 feet)
0 5 10 15
Miles
Afula
ISRAEL
Sandala
Bet Shean
Abu Daif
Tirat Zevi
Mezer
Qabatiya
Natanya
Tubas
Tul Karm
Nablus
Kalkilya
Mediterranean Sea
TEL AVIV
DAMIA BRIDGE
Jordan
River
Budrus
Ramla
Ramallah
Jericho
ALLENBY BRIDGE
Latrun
Sur Bahir
Bethlehem
Hebron
ISRAEL
JORDAN
DEAD SEA
ISRAEL
N

The Jordanians, with 30 M-47 Patton tanks around Jenin and two battalions of the 40th Armoured Brigade with a further 88 Pattons near the Damia Bridge on the River Jordan, had a slight superiority in numbers of tanks over the Israelis who had just over 100. The Israelis therefore made a demonstration of military activity in the vicinity of the Israeli town of Beit She'an not far from Jordan's northern border and persuaded the Jordanians to split their forces and send one battalion of the 40th Armoured Brigade up towards the border at this point. Meanwhile the Israelis broke through with an armoured brigade north of Jenin and, in the course of the Monday night, made their way through the hills to the east of the town to take Nablus from behind. One battalion of the Jordanian 40th Armoured Brigade from the Damia Bridge had already passed through Nablus to reinforce units of the Arab Legion under heavy attack around Jenin. Their plan was to hold the Israeli advance at Kaptir, to the northwest of Nablus; however when they reached it the Israelis were already there and the Jordanians had to attack the Israeli forces which had taken up defensive positions. By the time the other battalion of the 40th Armoured Brigade, which had gone on the wild goose chase towards Beit She'an, got to Nablus it found that the town had already been taken by the Israeli armoured force from the north. 'The Jordanians failed to recognize our main effort,' General Elazar remarked afterwards.

The Israeli Mirage and Mystère jets together with the little – Fouga Magister trainers with their rockets hit the Jordanians mercilessly day and night. Although the aircraft were not particularly effective against the Jordanian armour and, as inevitably happens in a fast moving war, they hit their own troops and vehicles on more than one occasion, the Israeli air-strikes succeeded in blocking many of the narrow roads that wind their way through the Jordanian hills. This severely restricted the movement of Jordanian armour, supplies and reinforcements. Many of the Jordanian tanks ran out of fuel since their supplies were unable to reach them; others were abandoned or became easy prey to the Israeli tanks when their lines of advance or retreat were blocked by the wreckage of their own vehicles. In this way the Israelis destroyed 45 of the Jordanian tanks and captured a further 40–45 which were found abandoned but undamaged. According to General Elazar's estimate all the equipment and the greater part of the men of the Jordanian 25th Infantry and 40th Armoured Brigades had been destroyed. He put at 3,000 the number of Jordanians killed, wounded or taken prisoner in the northern part of Jordan's West Bank.

While Elazar's forces were taking the north and Motta's paratroopers were clearing the last snipers out of Jerusalem, Uri's mechanized brigade made its way from the high ground around Ramallah and Nablus down to the Jordan Valley and the arid banks of the Dead Sea several hundred feet below sea-level. Uri :

'We continued on to Jericho. We had a few trumpets with us – all that was needed. When you go down to Jericho, it's a long time before you see it. The road is difficult. There was no resistance *en route,* but our reconnaissance group, which kept 10 kilometres ahead of our brigade, saw the rest of the Pattons in the distance. Anyone who has travelled the road knows that suddenly there opens up before you the entire Jericho landscape and the Dead Sea.

'We advanced along two lines. One battalion attacked the police station, the strongest point in Jericho, another, using our Ramallah tactics, went through Jericho and back again, wiping out all resistance on the way. Sniping and enemy movements went on throughout the night but, when morning came, we mopped up the town once again and it fell silent. We then went down to the shores of the Dead Sea where we had once had a kibbutz – not one stone of it remained.'

Further to the west Israeli forces had meanwhile taken the towns of Tul Karm and Kalkilya, close to the Jordan/ Israel border. These were the towns from which Tel Aviv and the coastal plain had come under intensive shelling. In these towns the Israeli soldiers were none too scrupulous about private property. Later many of the houses were dynamited and the contents of the others smashed – Kalkilya was virtually flattened. Nevertheless, within little more than a week, Moshe Dayan, beaming beneficence, ceremoniously returned what was left of the town to its inhabitants and promised them help with the rebuilding.

In the southern part of Jordan's West Bank, Israeli forces under Colonel Amitai, the Jerusalem area commander, were completing the conquest of the area. On the Wednesday morning shortly after 1000, as Motta and his paratroopers had been about to break into the Old City, Colonel Amitai had concentrated his forces near Rachel's Hill and at 1400 they attacked the Jordanian positions to the south of Jerusalem. From there they sped forward to Bethlehem and Hebron which they took by evening having encountered only very light resistance. Already by noon the Jordanian forces had abandoned the Hebron area.

The total air supremacy achieved by the Israeli Air Force throughout the Middle East on the Monday undoubtedly played a vital part in the Israeli victory. Even from the first day of the war the Jordanian soldiers in the field, like their comrades in Sinai and Syria, had no air cover whatever, let alone close air support. To fight in open country for several days on end under constant aerial bombardment and strafing, both night and day, is impossible.

The Jordanians, with far smaller armed forces and incomparably less modern, sophisticated equipment than many of her Arab neighbours, had been the only ones to strike Israel and inflict damage on her. Neither the Egyptians nor the Syrians undertook any aggressive action of significance throughout the whole war, apart from shelling farm settlements from the far side of the border with notable lack of effect. The Jordanians who had, against their own interest, taken the path of duty as laid down by the dictates of Arab Nationalism, were the only ones, of all the dozen Arab states who declared war on Israel, to acquit themselves honourably on the field of battle. But Jordan was fighting against impossible odds with virtually no outside assistance against a neighbour many times her strength. It was an unequal struggle. Her losses have been enormous. Several thousand of her men have been killed and she has lost nearly half her country, including all of Jerusalem and the Holy Land, the basis of a potentially enormous tourist industry and her richest agricultural land.

Thus, by nightfall on Wednesday June 7, the Israelis had in their hands Jerusalem, the city of King David, Hebron, the city of Abraham, and all the Holy Land. Just a couple of weeks before, there were few Jews who would have believed they would see any of these places in their lifetime. For Jews the world over but particularly for those who had come to make their homes in Israel, this was the fulfilment of a hope of centuries. After the fighting was over Brigadier-General Ezer Weizmann remarked to one of the authors : 'You must understand why Israel was built here rather than in Uganda or Canada. We could never have fought the way we have for a Jewish state in any other part of the world. Jerusalem, the West Bank of the Jordan, indeed the whole of Palestine has a very deep significance for us. It is the basis of Zionism.'

Chapter Eight
World Reaction

On Monday June 5 Europe awoke to find Israel at war with her Arab neighbours. Across the Atlantic the news broke at a less convenient hour for those involved in the crisis. It was 2.50 am when Walt Rostow, President Johnson's Special Assistant For National Security Affairs, was roused by the White House duty officer. At 4.30 am Rostow, by then established in the Situations Room at the White House, woke the President.

Soon after dawn the Russian teletype machine in the Pentagon began to chatter, printing out Cyrillic characters, which were immediately translated and relayed to the White House Situations Room on another machine. It was a message from the Kremlin. Officials were taken by surprise – for this was the first use of the hot-line since its installation in August 1963 following the Cuban missile crisis. During the course of the week a dozen messages were to be exchanged. Kosygin wanted Johnson to know that Russia was against war in the Middle East and would not intervene if the US acted similarly; and Kosygin hinted that the two super-powers might work together to restore peace. Though Johnson was still in his bedroom when the message arrived he lost no time in drafting a reply. Dean Rusk was already at the White House.

At 5.55 am Press Secretary George Christian released the first White House statement on the war. It said:

> The United States will devote all its energies to bring about an end to the fighting and a new beginning of progress to assure the peace and development of the entire area. We call upon all parties to support the Security Council in bringing about an immediate cease-fire.

At 8.15 am, Rusk, McNamara, Rostow and Christian were present with Johnson at the first formal policy meeting. They discussed the possibility of co-operating with the Soviet Union to bring about a cease-fire. Later in the morning, Johnson recalled McGeorge Bundy from his post as director of the Ford Foundation, and made him one of his inner circle of policy-makers.

At a midday briefing the State Department Press Secretary, Robert McCloskey, declared that the US would be 'neutral in thought, word and deed'. The statement was inspired by Rusk and Rostow, and he checked with both of them before he made it. But it violently antagonized the Jewish community and many US politicians; and Johnson soon realized that a political blunder had been made.

Later in the afternoon of the first day, reporters were asking whether McCloskey's statement on neutrality meant an abandonment of Israel. Johnson called in Rusk, briefed him and sent him to make a fresh declaration describing the United States as 'non-belligerent'.

Rusk stated :

> I want to emphasize that any use of this word 'neutral', which is a great concept of international law, is not an expression of indifference and, indeed, indifference is not permitted to us because we have a very heavy obligation under the United Nations

Charter, and especially as one of the permanent members of the Security Council, to do everything we can to maintain international peace and security.

Of course, from start to finish, everyone including Russia, Egypt and Israel knew that the US would never sit idly by if it were to be a question of the destruction of Israel.

In the House of Commons, George Brown declared that Britain's first aim was an early and general cease-fire. He received general support for his contention that 'the British concern is not to take sides...'. He could not say which side had begun the fighting. Emmanuel Shinwell, who like other MPs still believed the outcome of the war in the Middle East to hang in the balance, warned that if the Security Council failed to bring about a cease-fire, Arab States might overwhelm Israel.

In Moscow the news of the war broke at 10.47 am Moscow time. All day, after the momentous announcement, the Soviet radio and news agencies were accusing Israel of aggression against the UAR. Later that night, Tass reported that the Soviet Government had condemned Israeli aggression and had demanded that Israel cease hostilities. It said that the Soviet Government 'reserves the right to take all the steps that may be necessitated by the situation'.

At the United Nations, Russia sought to condemn Israel as the aggressor while Britain and the United States preferred to make a straightforward and urgent call for a cease-fire. But although the three major Powers moved along predictable lines of policy, the fourth major Power, France, surprised all the political pundits, not for the first time in recent years.

It was expected that she would support Israel. In the past she had done so: in fact, Israel's Air Force was composed of French-built aircraft. When the news of the war reached Paris, French public opinion reacted with spontaneous expressions of sympathy for Israel. Even the traditionally anti-Semitic extreme right became passionate Zionists overnight. Veterans of the 'Keep Algeria French' campaign paraded boulevards chanting 'Israel will vanquish' to the same rhythmic beat as they once shouted: *'Algérie Française'*. In spite of these demonstrations for Israel, the French Government decided to preserve a studied silence.

De Gaulle announced that France's ties with Israel were less important than France's long-term and carefully nurtured interests in the Middle East. If these were not to be endangered France had to make a display of neutrality. In fact, de Gaulle was displeased because Eban, on his way through Paris, had disregarded de Gaulle's advice not to take the initiative.

The French position was ably summed up in the BBC-TV programme, *The World Today*, by Edouard Sablier, a leading French political commentator, on June 7.

> There is no doubt that there is nothing in common now between the position adopted by the present Government and the Mollet Government in 1956 . . . there is a growing difference between the cold-blooded position adopted by the de Gaulle Government and the very passionate position adopted by 90 per cent of the French people in favour of the freedom to live of Israel.

In effect de Gaulle's neutrality was modified by the proviso that he would oppose the country which had attacked first. As it was not then clear who had fired the first shot, this declaration was on a par with many others that have fallen from the enigmatic lips of the President.

His Prime Minister, M. Georges Pompidou, had formerly been manager of the Rothschild banking house in

Paris. Like the Rothschilds, he is a fervent Zionist. He did all he could to see that Israel received such military supplies as were possible, despite de Gaulle's ban on all further arms shipments. Some spare parts for aircraft may have been flown from Holland instead of from France to obviate the difficulty.

President Tito happened to be in Vienna on June 5. He was an old friend of Colonel Nasser and he made it plain that he regarded Israel as the aggressor. He was the first Communist statesman to comment on the outbreak of hostilities. He pledged full support for the Arab countries in their 'just confrontation with Israel'. His past friendship with Nasser stemmed from the mid-'fifties when an attempt was made to form an alliance of non-aligned powers, including India, Yugoslavia and Egypt.

Eleven other Arab countries rallied to Nasser's support that Monday: Jordan, Syria, Lebanon, Iraq, Saudi Arabia, Kuwait, Algeria, Morocco, Yemen, Sudan and Tunisia. Of these countries the only one which from the outset vigorously joined battle with Israel was Jordan. Drawn into conflict against his will by the pressures of the Arab world, King Hussein and his army played an honourable part. He fought promptly and with tenacity. Syria, the most malevolent towards Israel of all the Arab countries, did little in the first two or three days, apart from firing across the border; but a fierce vengeance was inflicted on her at the end.

Of the others, Lebanon had little war potential and prudently made small use of it. On the first day Lebanese pilots claimed to have shot down an Israeli jet over central Lebanon. Before the war started Iraq had sent one division and 150 tanks into Jordan. Though they never put in an appearance on the battlefield, they remained as unwelcome guests long after the cease-fire. Iraq declared a state of war with Israel and warned that any country helping her would be considered as committing an act of aggression against Iraq. It was claimed that Iraqi aircraft had destroyed seven Israeli aircraft in a raid on one base and bombed Tel Aviv. Neither report was true.

King Feisal of Saudi Arabia – who was in Paris having been orange-juiced and dined by the Queen and British Government in London, the latter wishing to conclude a deal to sell him £150M of arms – sent a message of support to Nasser. Mecca Radio said that Saudi Arabian troops had entered Jordan 'to fight on the side of our Arab brothers'. However, these gallant troops passed the war unnoticed by Israel. King Feisal wisely stayed away in Europe until July 21.

In Kuwait the Amir, Shaikh Sabah, proclaimed a 'defensive war between Kuwait and Zionist gangs in occupied Palestine'. The Amir said: 'The hour of sacrifice has come.' Before the outbreak of war he had already sent a detachment to Egypt which had been posted for the special defence of Sharm el-Sheikh.

Although the rich Arab states are traditionally loth to support the refugees from Palestine about whom they make so much fuss, Kuwait did offer prompt financial assistance to Egypt, Iraq, Jordan and Syria for the war. This amounted officially to about £50M but they were reported to have given a further £8M to Egypt and Jordan. Since Kuwait belonged to the sterling area this meant drawing on Kuwait's balances in London and its generosity coupled with the war scare naturally led to a weakening of the pound, as became more apparent in the days that followed. The other Arab countries confined their support for Nasser to demonstrations outside and damaging of American and British embassies and cultural institutes. In the Egyptian capital on the first day the scare had not yet begun.

On June 5, the first day of the war, Mr James Reston, reporting from Cairo, had a front-page piece in the *New York Times* cabled the day before saying:

> An alarming fatalism seems to be settling in on this city. Cairo does not want war and it is certainly not ready for war. But it has already accepted the possibility, even the likelihood of war, as if it had lost control of the situation.

From the whole tone of his piece, Reston was obviously persuaded that the men around Nasser were more reasonable than they sounded in their propaganda statements and that 'they say they do not want to "destroy" Israel, but they have a catalogue of complaints'. He said he got the impression that Cairo was not thinking so much about the legalities of maritime law in the Gulf of Aqaba 'but about the general settlement that would make a fundamental change in the relationships between the Arab states and Israel'.

They had also told him, he reported without direct attribution, that 'their actions there [at Sharm el-Sheikh] were forced by Secretary General Thant [of the UN] who had insisted on withdrawing all of UNEF from all its outposts including those overlooking the Straits of Tiran'. 'They have no intention, they say, of moving their troops [from] there,' Reston reported – evidently having failed to discover that the Egyptians had already seized the lot before officially communicating with U Thant.

All of the above seems to.support the contention that a climate of opinion was gathering in America – the *New York Times* being decidedly pacifist – where, had the Israelis not struck when they did, pro-Arabs would have-started exerting influence. This may well have been another factor in Tel Aviv's calculations.

❧ ❧ ❧

A considerable number of British and American correspondents spent a very unhappy and frustrating war in Cairo: they were eventually deported with insults and humiliation. In Cairo, by the third day of the war, there was still very little information. But High Command communiqués admitted two things: that UAR forces had fallen back on the second line of defence, and 'that the United Arab Forces at Sharm el-Sheikh have been withdrawn to rejoin the main body of United Arab Forces'. American pressmen had been ordered to the Nile Hotel where they were in effective detention. British journalists could still operate, but the mood of the town was becoming distinctly less friendly. Censorship was still comparatively sensible, since practically anything, if tactfully worded, would be allowed. But there was not any real information to be had. Air-raid warnings were being sounded but were not followed by raids. Nor was anything or anybody coming back from the front.

The Cairenes stayed near radios listening to the repeated newsflashes, interspersed with martial music. The newsflashes were pure propaganda. It was claimed on the Monday that 23, then 42, Israeli planes had been shot down. One of the difficulties for the propagandists was that they were receiving little information from military headquarters: in fact apart from these figures, only two directives were sent to them during the first day. The public was excited, but also relieved that the waiting was over; there was still no hostility towards Westerners. Meanwhile workers rushed to carry out the civil defence measures. The blackout, achieved partly by cutting off electricity but also by almost manic popular attention to the necessary precautions, was remarkably efficient. On Monday night Israel repeated her air attacks, but still only on the airfields. The Egyptians fired a few Russian SA2 missiles the first day and a larger number on the Tuesday and Wednesday nights. There seemed to be no shortage of missiles, particularly around Cairo-West, but they were ineffective at the heights flown by the Israeli planes.

Already, by the Monday morning, Egypt's Air Force had been virtually destroyed and the war was lost so far as Egypt was concerned. But the Egyptian public did not know this; nor, in the absence of precise news, did the Western world form this obvious conclusion. In fact, anyone sitting by his radio in England should have known by lunchtime on the first day that the Egyptian Air Force must have been destroyed for there had been no report of any bomb falling on Tel Aviv, an extremely vulnerable and exposed target. It can be said that Cairo was not bombed either but no one thought the Israelis capable of such an action.

Throughout the first four days of the fighting the Arab press and radio, particularly in Cairo, kept up its incessant propaganda. Muhammad Haikal, Editor-in-Chief of *Al Ahram,* who is close to President Nasser and the Egyptian High Command, said in a special article on June 6 that American and British aircraft had provided a protective 'umbrella' over Israel enabling Israeli aircraft to go on the offensive.

Another Egyptian newspaper, the *Egyptian Gazette,* on June 8, the fourth day of the war, when Israeli forces were already at the Canal, carried a banner headline: 'ARAB FORCES INFLICT LOSSES ON ISRAELIS'. It went on to say:

> Arab forces on all fronts inflicted heavy losses on the Israeli enemy yesterday. The UAR Armed Forces High Command said in

a communiqué last night that 'the UAR airforce inflicted heavy losses on an Israeli armoured brigade during an ammunition and fuel supply operation in the Khatmia area'....

The UAR Armed Forces also shot down 23 enemy aircraft over Sinai, Suez, and Sharm el-Sheikh, and annihilated a force of Israeli paratroopers dropped near the second line of defence in Sinai. . . .

Israeli President Shazar's home was hit yesterday during intensive shelling which was resumed from the few Jordanian positions in the Jerusalem area. Some damage to the building was reported.

It was not immediately known whether President Shazar was inside the building, but it was assumed he was in the air-raid shelter of the house.

These reports, needless to say, were untrue. In fact no Israeli paratroops were dropped during the six days' fighting. Instead on June 8, because of her heavy defeat both on land, sea and in the air, Egypt agreed to accept the cease-fire.

Even more remarkably the next day, Friday June 9, the *Egyptian Gazette* carried the splash banner headline 'ISRAELIS SUFFER MORE REVERSES ON ALL FRONTS – UAR SMASHES BACK'. Under the shoulder of this story in small type there was one truthful headline: 'CEASEFIRE ACCEPTED'. But the great mass of Egyptians, including the hundreds of thousands who were to rampage through Cairo demanding Nasser's return following his resignation, were kept utterly in the dark about what had happened at the front. As good Egyptian citizens they did not dream of asking precisely what Nasser was to call 'a setback'. Those who might have liked to would not have dared. The police, a force somewhat more effective than the Egyptian Army, saw to that. Telephone numbers, to which the public were urged to report at once any defeatist talk or 'suspicious behaviour', were published prominently in the newspapers. The UAR had all the apparatus of a police state.

The veiled and cautious communiqués put out by the Egyptian military command caused the Cairo crowds to realize the news was bad. Nonetheless, the majority of Egyptians, even to this day, probably have no idea of the crushing defeat inflicted on their forces.

Yet, in spite of the cynical manipulation of news and suppression of casualty figures, the cruel facts of war cannot be hidden from Egyptian families whose sons will never return from the field of battle. Peter Hopkirk of *The Times* was therefore right when he wrote, in an article on June 16, that 'Nasser will now stage a whole series of distractions, including new scapegoats, old ones resurrected, public trials, Arab summits, and every other trick he has learned over the years'.

Far from admitting defeat the Arab High Command now, at the end of the war, began to allege that 32 American aircraft had left Wheelus base in Libya for Israel and that British Canberras had taken part in bombing Egyptian positions in Sinai on the Monday afternoon.

Those in Britain who followed the war on radio and television may have wondered what was going on, for the BBC bent over backwards to be as neutral as McCloskey had stated that America would be. It was only possible to judge what was happening if, unlike the BBC, one assumed that the Israelis are naturally more veracious than the Arabs. Israel stated that it had destroyed 374 Arab aircraft on Monday June 5, and 15 – a significant decrease (obviously due to lack of targets) – on the Tuesday. These figures were in fact under-estimates. To those who were aware that the Israelis were vastly more capable of handling sophisticated weapons than were the Arabs, these Israeli figures seemed altogether credible.

The first man with the news of Israel's victory on the Monday was Michael Elkins, the BBC's Jerusalem correspondent. In the 10 pm news he was quoted as giving an unconfirmed report – and the word 'unconfirmed' was emphasized by the BBC:

> Less than 15 hours after fighting began Israel has already won the war. Egypt is no more a fighting factor. . . . it's the most instant victory the modern world has seen.

The BBC seemed sceptical. So did John Dodd, the television critic of the obfuscating *Sun*, who wrote unper-ceptively the next morning:

> I remained unconvinced. . . . Apart from the Elkins report, I thought the BBC were scrupulously fair. They almost busted themselves to get interviews with Arab students to balance Barnett Janner, MP, at a Zionist meeting, and photographed Arab ambassadors to level up with a brief interview with Jewish writers . . .
>
> By and large, it was the sort of night the BBC can be proud of.

Surely it is not the duty of the press, television and radio to be scrupulously fair in their allotment of space or time to either side? Their job is to get the truth and when their correspondents get it they ought to recognize it and back them up, even if it does make it a little bit harder for Mr Dodd to feel proud.

Some press reports too began to filter through disclosing the real situation. In *The Times* of June 7 Nicholas Herbert reported from Jerusalem:

Soon after dawn [on Tuesday] Israeli aircraft staged a massive raid on Jordanian positions near the Augusta Victoria hospital on Mount Scopus from which firing had been directed at the Israel-held Hadassah hospital. Mystère fighter bombers came in low, their bombs exploding only a few seconds after they swooped away above the Holy City and turned into the attack again.

Jordan anti-aircraft fire was sporadic and the Israeli aircraft flew over the entire area with impunity, swooping out of sight below the Jordan hills strafing and bombing Jordanian positions. At no time during the 24 hours after the battle began were any Jordanian aircraft seen. During the hours before dusk Israeli Mirage and Mystère aircraft flew dozens of sorties. One Mirage was hit by anti-aircraft fire and plunged into the Jordan valley.

Earlier youths had been asking sadly: 'Where are the one hundred million Arabs? Where is the Jordan Air Force?'

Amman airport was heavily damaged in yesterday's air attack by Israeli jets. The runway was put out of commission and three or four aircraft destroyed on the ground. They included a Jordanian Air Force Hawker Hunter, the British Air Attaché's twin-engined aircraft, and another belonging to General Odd Bull, the UN commander. Damage to the military side of the airport was not known, but blazing fuel dumps told their own tale in the sky.

And later the same day the *Evening News* correspondent reported : 'Israelis on the Canal. . . . Sharm el-Sheikh taken.'

⚜ ⚜ ⚜

Although the Egyptians launched no offensive on the field of battle, they took up the diplomatic war in earnest. The British consulates at Alexandria and Port Said were burnt. The collusion charge, so vividly detailed, served as justification for a severance of diplomatic relations with the United

States. Cairo had already broken off relations with London over Rhodesia. Now contact with Washington was summarily ended. These moves were backed by an announcement on June 6 that the Suez Canal was to be closed. Egypt acted with other Arab nations to cut off oil supplies to the West.

The alleged collusion between Israel, Britain and the US was the main topic of diplomatic discussion on Tuesday in the corridors of the United Nations. (The origin of this lie, the radio conversation between Nasser and Hussein, is referred to in Chapter 4. page 90.)

The Kremlin was showing signs of anger at Nasser's propaganda lie. The Egyptian ambassador in Moscow was coldly received by the Soviet Government. He was allowed to hold a press conference at which he repeated his allegations about British and US bombing. Significantly the Russian press failed to report this part of the press conference. One of the motives for this fiction was the hope that the Soviets would physically intervene. But after the charge was issued the Egyptian and other Arab ambassadors in Moscow were told by the Soviet Government that the story was a complete fabrication, in which the Russians wanted no part. The heads of Arab diplomatic missions in Moscow held a press conference where a tape-recording of the Cairo radio announcement was played to Russian journalists. Tass and Moscow Radio reported the press conference, but omitted all references to the allegation.

In Washington there was underlying tranquillity, until the Arab lie provoked anger. The State Department roused the Egyptian ambassador before dawn on June 6 to lodge a protest. Dean Rusk, leaving the White House Situations Room, went before the television cameras and angrily denied the charge. Meanwhile Pentagon analysts were making the reassuring prediction that Israel would win. Writing in the *New Statesman* on June 9, Andrew Kopkind said: 'Reports on the superiority of Israeli military force were not exaggerated. President Johnson knew he could afford to smile suggestively and leave the fighting to General Dayan.' According to William Beecher, of the *New York Times*, on June 7, several experts believed that Israel 'should be able to "punch through" Egyptian forces in one of two directions in Sinai in anywhere from one week to ten days'. The CIA too had given comfort to President Johnson.

It is probable that the Russians already understood the magnitude of the Israeli victory. This would explain why, after 36 hours of war, Kosygin sent a hot-line message to Johnson telling him that Russia would accept an unconditional cease-fire. Mr Federenko was instructed to vote for the first of the Security Council cease-fire resolutions, without insisting on a clause that the belligerents should withdraw to the 1956 armistice lines or that Israel should be condemned. President Johnson appeared on television that evening and said that the Russian attitude 'opens a very hopeful path away from danger in the Middle East'.

In the House of Commons on the Tuesday Harold Wilson dealt with the story that British aircraft-carriers were involved in the war. There were only two such vessels in the area, he said, and both, HMS *Victorious* at Malta and HMS *Hermes* at Aden, were over 1,000 miles from the scene of action. This in itself was a revelation of the lamentable weakness of the range of Britain's Fleet Air Arm; but doubtless it carried conviction. He announced a futile action – a 24-hour ban on British arms supplies to the Middle East to be continued if everyone else joined in: they didn't. He was not able to give the House of Commons a very illuminating picture of the war. If he had been reading the Foreign Office despatches with his usual assiduity he might have been able to give the House a more informative account of what was going on. 'The most serious operations on the ground,' he said, 'seem to have been on the United Arab Republic/Israel border, but information about them is unclear and disputed.'

That evening most observers were concluding, as Geoffrey Kemp, the Middle East specialist at the Institute of Strategic Studies, told BBC radio listeners to *Ten o'Clock,* that Egypt was fighting a rearguard action in Sinai, following 'an overwhelming Israeli victory in the air'. But Tom Little of the Regional News Service of the Middle East, just returned from a tour of the area, was still urging a cautious view: 'I have always presumed that President Nasser understood that the Gaza Strip was indefensible and that the Israelis would reach the sea, therefore in this report tonight that the Egyptians are launching an offensive towards the northern Negev, this would seem to me sound sense.'

On Wednesday, the third day of the fighting, as Israeli forces grasped the remainder of Sinai and conquered Jerusalem Egypt was putting out more 'evidence' of collusion. The Foreign Minister, Mahmoud Riad, claimed as proof a confession by an Israeli pilot Abraham Shelan. The story said that 17 British bombers, which arrived at Ajlun airport just before the attack, had been used to strafe military targets in Syria and Egypt. Ajlun is in fact a Jordanian radar station. According to *Al Ahram,* Jordanian radar had tracked waves of aircraft, taking off from two carriers off the Israeli coast. It was also said that Israeli pilots, when shot down, were found to be carrying maps prepared in Whitehall. Beyond Egypt there was a further round of diplomatic war, and four more oil-producing states, Saudi Arabia, Libya, Bahrein and Qatar, blocked supplies to Britain and the United States.

In New York the wagging of tongues continued as the Soviet representative, Federenko, hurried to put before the Security Council a resolution demanding that a cease-fire should take effect from 8 pm (GMT) on the evening of June 7. This was unanimously accepted. Abba Eban said that Israel would observe a cease-fire if the Arabs would do the same. The Russian Government, which had already warned Israel to observe a previous resolution, threatened to withdraw its envoys from Tel Aviv unless the Israelis complied. But the Israelis now felt sure enough of the outcome to reveal for the first time the full scale of their victory, including facts about the air-strike. General Rabin announced that Israel possessed Sinai, Sharm el-Sheikh, Jerusalem and the West Bank of Jordan.

As Jews flocked through the Mandelbaum Gate into the Old City of Jerusalem to see the Wailing Wall, the seeds of future controversy were sown when General Dayan said: 'We earnestly stretch our hands to our Arab brethren in peace, but we have returned to Jerusalem never to part from her again.'

Egypt, Syria and Iraq rejected requests for a cease-fire. Indeed, the Syrians claimed to be in hot pursuit of the Israelis, who were said to be fleeing towards Nazareth. King Hussein of Jordan broadcast a ringing declaration from the front: 'We will fight to the last breath, until we face God. We will wash this Holy Land with the last drop of our blood.' But half an hour later the Jordanian Prime Minister, Saad Juma, announced that his country had agreed to a cease-fire. The British Government was gravely worried about the vulnerability of Jordan, fearing that Hussein would be driven from power. That night there were false rumours that he had fled to Rome.

Following upon Nasser's statement that the Canal was closed, George Brown refused to be drawn into wrath by the Egyptian closure of the Suez Canal. Asked by Duncan Sandys in the House of Commons what the Government intended to do about reopening the waterway, Brown would only reply:

> The right honourable Gentleman has a passionate desire about opening the Canal ... I can only say that I envisage doing it by getting a cease-fire and proceeding to negotiate a settlement for the whole area.

As this book goes to press Mr Brown has not opened the Canal, nor is he being overly consulted about a settlement.

The Conservative politicians however were also raising the subject of the Canal outside the House. Edward Heath, addressing women party workers, said that Nasser's action was illegal, and should be raised by Britain at the Security Council.

⚜ ⚜ ⚜

Shortly after 10 am on Thursday, President Johnson received the startling news that the USS communications ship *Liberty* had been attacked off the Sinai coast by Israeli aircraft, killing 34 men and wounding about 75. Since US planes from the Sixth Fleet were dashing to the scene, Johnson thought it wise to inform Kosygin, over the hotline, of the reason for the aircraft taking off. As this message was being sent out, Israel sent word that the attack was accidental and made an apology. Johnson added the Israeli confession to the teletype communication.

In another Mediterranean incident, two Soviet warships, a destroyer and a small patrol craft, began to harass a carrier task force of the US Sixth Fleet. Possibly the Russians were bringing pressure on the Americans to abandon the tracking of a Soviet submarine they suspected was in the area.

In the House of Commons, Mr Heath asked the Prime Minister what had happened to the proposal for a 'hotline' between Moscow and London:

> Mr Wilson: 'It has not yet been installed but you will be happy to know that the communications between Mr Kosygin and myself on a personal basis have been continuing in a very intense way this week through the Ambassador.'

George Brown announced that as there had been no positive response from the Russians about arms supplies, Britain had lifted its embargo.

At the Security Council on the evening of June 8 delegates were inwardly preparing for a long polemic from Mr El Kony, when Mr Hans Tabor of Denmark, the President, announced that he would not, after all, be called to speak. U Thant then read a message from Mr El Kony announcing that Egypt would accept a cease-fire if Israel also complied. The other Arab delegates, and the Soviet representative, Mr Federenko, appeared to be taken completely by surprise. The news came in the middle of a conflict between the United States and the Soviet Union, which had put down contrasting draft resolutions for a cease-fire. Mr Federenko, making the best of a dismal situation for Russian diplomacy, lashed out at Israel:

> The extremist circles in Tel Aviv are obviously inebriated by their temporary successes. They are even laying down conditions for peace. . . . Israel shoulders the whole responsibility for the crises committed. 'It must', he said, 'be severely punished.'

This kind of talk, in varying shades from different delegates, typified the speeches made at the Security Council throughout the week and during the long aftermath of recrimination.

Chapter Nine
Sinai: The Jaws of Death

In the early hours of Wednesday morning, General Tal and General Yoffe met at Gebel Libni to plan the next stage of the Israeli campaign. The first Israeli troops, part of Tal's armoured task force that had been racing along the northern coastal road, were already on the Suez Canal – within less than 48 hours of the start of the war. That night [Tuesday/Wednesday] at Gebel Libni, Yoffe's troops had been able to grab a few hours sleep, their first of the war. Even Yoffe himself was able to get an hour's nap between 8 and 9 pm – the first sleep he had had since the Saturday night. As soon as night fell on the desert the air became chilly. Yoffe dozed off in the driver's seat of his tank which was still warm from the heat of the engine. But he could not sleep for long; soon he was awake again listening to the radio communications and going over the intelligence reports and other information that was coming in. He kept awake with relays of lemon tea every hour on the hour until at two o'clock in the morning Tal arrived. The, two generals paid particular attention to parcelling out the territory that lay ahead of them so as to obviate the danger of their own forces engaging each other. 'Tal and I were both in the British Army – we know how to behave,' Yoffe explained with a smile. They also had anguished memories of '56 when one whole Israeli company was virtually wiped out by another.

Brigadier-General Abraham Yoffe, a large jovial man, has described himself as 'built like a tank', which is perhaps appropriate for the commander of an armoured division. Three weeks before the outbreak of war, Yoffe was in the French Camargue engaged in his work of Nature Conservancy to which he had devoted himself since he retired from being a regular officer in the Israeli Army two years before.

At Gebel Libni it was decided that Tal's forces should take the more northerly route through Bir Gifgafa to block the road through the hills leading to Ismailia, while Yoffe's forces advanced on a more southerly route to the Mitla Pass, thereby closing the only escape routes to the Canal practical for vehicles.At the same time they agreed to make a co-ordinated attack at dawn that morning with Tal attacking the Egyptian positions at Bir Hama, ten miles to the west of Gebel Libni, and Yoffe's forces engaging the Egyptians in Bir Hassneh at the same time.

Tal's forces advanced before dawn and took Bir Hama, destroying a number of Egyptian SU-100 'Tank-killers', tanks that have especially heavy guns specifically designed for destroying other tanks. Then, with the reserve brigade in the lead, Tal's force sped westwards along the road towards Bir Gifgafa. On the way they ran into an ambush laid by a number of Egyptian T-55 tanks, the most modern on the battlefield. Only after losing several of their tanks were the Israelis able to break through the ambush and advance towards Bir Gifgafa.

Meanwhile at 0400 an advance force of Yoffe's armoured brigade had moved off in the direction of Bir Hassneh which it reached and succeeded in taking by 0900.

The next objective of Yoffe's forces has been described by their commander: 'We started running and racing into this opening called the Mitla Pass. The Mitla Pass is a famous name in Israel. Eleven years ago, the paratroopers took it, under the command of General Sharon. The Pass is about 23 kilometres long, and whoever commands the opening to the Pass is actually in command of all access to the Canal. Orders were to race there and strike, encircle and stop any enemy forces that tried to run into the Canal area.' From Bir Hassneh two battalions of Israeli tanks under Colonel Iska raced westwards to block the Egyptians' line of escape at Bir Thamada which commands the approach to the Mitla Pass as well as to a more northerly route through the mountains.

Meanwhile, further to the south, at Sharm el-Sheikh, Egyptian forces abandoned the promontory dominating the Straits of Tiran two hours before the Israeli heli-borne and naval assault force arrived from Eilat. By 1100 [Wednesday] the blue and white Star of David was flying over the Straits and an Israeli Navy MTB had sailed through the narrow channel, the first Israeli vessel to pass through the Straits since they had been closed by Nasser just over two weeks before.

Iska's forces reached the Mitla at about 1800 on the Wednesday evening, less than 60 hours after leaving Israeli territory. Many of his supply vehicles, including those carrying fuel, had been destroyed by the Egyptians along the way and 15 or 20 miles short of the Pass half his tanks ran out of fuel. Rather than abandon 7 of his 14 tanks, Iska had steel cables attached to them and towed them with the ones that still had fuel. Like this they made their way slowly, under heavy Egyptian fire, to the Pass where they took up positions. Even the tanks being towed kept firing as they went. At the Mitla, one of the tanks which still had fuel but had

had its turret jammed by a direct hit from an Egyptian shell, was able to line up its gun on the advancing Egyptian tanks by manoeuvring from side to side with its tracks. Disabled as it was, it usually hit its target after one or two ranging shots.

Meanwhile General Tal had established two battalions of tanks just north of Bir Gifgafa blocking the road from Bir Thamada to Ismailia, and had sent a battalion of light French AMX tanks into the hills ten miles to the west to guard against Egyptian reinforcements arriving from the Canal. Tal's main objective was to bring the Egyptian armour to battle. With their escape routes blocked by Israeli forces, the Egyptians would have no alternative but to fight. The three Israeli divisions were moving in for the kill: Tal and Yoffe had blocked the passes; Sharon was driving them into the trap.

⚜ ⚜ ⚜

By nightfall on the Wednesday Sharon's forces had advanced three-quarters of the way from Abu Agheila to Nakhl. Their progress had been laborious and slow, following the course of a wadi through the desert. Their average speed for much of the way had been no more than 3 mph. As they continued their advance by night they ran into a minefield and lost one of their armoured troop-carriers. Sharon abandoned any further advance that night and between 0200 and 0400 on Thursday morning, while the engineers cleared the way through the minefields, Sharon and his men 'slept like the dead'.

⚜ ⚜ ⚜

At dawn, as they continued their advance, they suddenly came upon a whole brigade of Stalin tanks – the heaviest tanks on the battlefield – facing them in the desert. Behind the tanks were several large self-propelled guns. The Israeli tanks raced forward to attack but the Egyptian tanks made no move at all. The Israelis could not believe their eyes: every tank was intact but deserted – there was no one there. Later, when the fighting was over, Sharon met the commander of this Egyptian tank brigade, Brigadier Ahmed Abd El-Naby, who had been taken prisoner and who arrived at General Sharon's command post at Bir Gifgafa and presented his visiting card.

He explained that he did not believe his armoured brigade could resist the Israeli attack (although he had no idea of the size of the Israeli force) so he had decided to escape with all his men without even stopping to blow up his tanks. 'You spoiled all my plans,' he told Sharon with great lamentation. The Egyptian commanders appear to be capable of acting only in accordance with a preconceived plan.

El-Naby said that he had been greatly alarmed on the Tuesday night when he heard the noise of a large body of tanks moving up near by. The tanks in fact turned out to be an Egyptian armoured brigade that was also moving up from the west about which he had not been told.

On the Wednesday night El-Naby once again heard tanks advancing upon him. By now he had had news of the Israeli advance through Abu Agheila and Bir Hassneh and, thinking he was about to be attacked, he decided to abandon all his tanks and artillery and withdraw his men in half-tracks westwards towards Bir Thamada which he believed was still in Egyptian hands. 'It wasn't,' Sharon commented with a grin. 'Our boys were already there.' After a skirmish with the Israelis, El-Naby abandoned his troops and, taking with him a lieutenant-colonel and a major, headed south-west on foot.

In an interview with Charles Mohr of the *New York Times*, published on June 20, El-Naby, when asked why he did not destroy his tanks, said: 'I had orders to withdraw.

My orders did not say to destroy my tanks. ... If I had blown up the tanks the Jews would have heard me. It makes a lot of noise to destroy a tank.'

El-Naby said that the first part of his withdrawal took place 'in very good order' with his troops still organized by unjts and responding to discipline. Trouble came at a road junction in the central desert when Brigadier El-Naby's men hit what he called an 'ambush' or an Israeli roadblock. 'Because of the ambush we had to take different roads and head for the Mitla Pass further south,' the Brigadier said.

Why didn't he try to fight his way through the roadblock?

'That was impossible,' he said. An Israeli captain who was monitoring the conversation broke in: 'Why? What kind of force and weapons do you suppose we had in that roadblock?' 'Well,' the Egyptian replied, 'I heard light machine guns and I think I heard .50-calibre heavy machine guns.'

The Israeli captain threw his hands and eyes upward and said, 'You had a whole brigade and we held the roadblock with light forces.'

'Yes,' said Brigadier El-Naby, 'but you must remember that I had left the tanks behind.'...

At the Mitla Pass the 125th Brigade fell to pieces, according to its commander's own account, although it was not in contact with enemy forces.

'I lost all my order at the Mitla,' the Egyptian said. 'Everyone wanted to flee for his own skin. All vehicles were abandoned and the men set off on foot to cross the mountains to the west.' Many of the Egyptians threw away their weapons, helmets and much of their personal equipment. 'I lost my luggage, which I bought in London a month before, and my transistor radio,' Brigadier El-Naby said wistfully.

He failed to take any water or food with him when he started his own trek, an oversight he could not now explain. He was asked whether he attempted to keep any men under his command with him. He answered:

'No, no. As I said, everyone wanted to save his own skin.'

The officer went three days without water as he walked to the area of [Ras] Sudr. ... He began to walk along a road and was lucky enough to be picked up by 'a very nice Israeli major and a patrol', as he put it. 'They were so kind to me,' he said. 'They got an ambulance and let me sleep in it. I was in very bad shape and they were so kind.' 'How would you have treated us?' the Israeli captain asked with a hard edge in his voice. Brigadier El-Naby, sensing an implication in the question, seemed offended and straightened up on the cot on which he was sitting. 'I had no orders to do anything bad to any Israeli prisoners,' he said with firmness.

In their meeting after the war Sharon asked El-Naby what discussions he had had with his men in the days of waiting that preceded the war. He replied that he would not dream of talking to his men. 'That is the difference between us,' said Sharon. 'I have had long talks with my men about the war and the fighting that was to come. I have great respect for my men while the Egyptian commanders despise their own troops. I think the Egyptian soldiers are very good. They are simple and ignorant but they are strong and they are disciplined. They are good gunners, good diggers and good shooters – but their officers are shit, they can fight only according to what they planned before. Once we had broken through, except for the minefield between Bir Hassneh and Nakhl, which was probably there before the war, the Egyptian officers placed no mines and laid no ambushes to block our line of advance. But some of the soldiers, particularly at the Mitla where we had blocked their line of retreat, fought to the death in an attempt to break westwards to the Canal. Just as they did at Faluja [30 miles due south of Tel Aviv] in 1948, where, incidentally, Nasser was fighting as a junior officer.'

Sharon continued: 'Even at Kusseima [one of the first Egyptian positions to fall] the Egyptian officers gave the order "every man for himself", jumping into the first jeep or transport that was available and abandoning their men. We came across one Egyptian soldier by the roadside crying, "They left me, they left me."

'No Israeli officer would ever behave like that. Our officers don't ever use the word "forward" – it is always "follow me". That is why officers form more than 20% of our casualties. [The figure for this war is more than 23% of the total.]

'Egyptian prisoners I have talked to,' Sharon added, 'said that they had been told that when they reached Israel they would kill the men and rape the women. This might be all right as a philosophy while you are advancing but it is not so good when you are in retreat. Then you're inclined to abandon your rape intentions for another day and wish you were back with your own wife on the banks of the Nile.'

⚜ ⚜ ⚜

Leaving the Egyptian tanks behind in the desert, Sharon's forces continued their advance towards Nakhl. Sharon went on: 'We had heard that our forces advancing from Kuntilla had captured Thamad and that the Egyptian brigade which had held it was withdrawing towards Nakhl. I decided to capture Nakhl as quickly as possible and make a tank ambush for the retreating Egyptian brigade. I sent one of my officers in a scout helicopter to see where the Egyptians had got to. He reported that their main body was only 3 miles short of Nakhl – a forward troop of the brigade having passed through the town before we reached it.

'I positioned two regiments of tanks on the eastern outskirts of Nakhl, one facing the Egyptians approaching from the east, the other [on the right flank of the Israeli armour] facing north. I instructed them to prepare an ambush as quickly as possible and ordered the tanks to open fire on the Egyptians at no more than 200 yards range. I wanted as many vehicles as possible in the ambush.

'Meanwhile I had remained 7 miles to the NE of Nakhl with a regiment of mechanized infantry and one tank, and now headed SE to reach the road behind the Egyptian convoy 10 miles east of Nakhl. As instructed, our tanks, lying in ambush, waited until the Egyptians were only 200 yards from them before opening fire – almost immediately destroying nine T-54 tanks. Our tanks manœuvred continuously throughout the fighting to get into the most advantageous positions.

'I reached the road with my mechanized infantry and ran into six Egyptian Centurion tanks which opened fire on us. I called an air-strike which destroyed three of the six tanks with napalm. Thereupon my infantry commander raised his hand and the whole battalion rushed forward with him to destroy the three remaining Centurions.

'We then advanced upon the Egyptians from the rear. Between 10 am and 2.30 in the afternoon we destroyed 50 enemy tanks – T-54s and Centurions – two regiments of artillery, anti-tank and anti-aircraft batteries and more than 300 vehicles. The enemy suffered more than 1,000 casualties.

'This was a Valley of Death. I came out of it like an old man. Hundreds were killed: there were burning tanks everywhere. One had the feeling that man was nothing. A sand-storm had been churned up by the tanks. The noise was tremendous. Above the din of the guns and of the tanks there was the roar of our heavy transport aircraft – Stratocruisers – dropping supplies of fuel, water and ammunition by parachute and of helicopters evacuating the wounded.

'Meanwhile the shooting and fighting continued and vehicles loaded with fuel and ammunition were exploding all along the line. The dead lay all around.'

⚜ ⚜ ⚜

The Egyptians, in an attempt to break through the Israeli trap and reach the road to Ismailia, advanced northwards with a mechanized brigade towards two battalions of Tal's reserve brigade positioned on the road a few miles to the north of Bir Gifgafa. This attack was co-ordinated with that of a number of T-54 tanks attacking from the west and with two or three air-strikes by remnants of the Egyptian Air Force. Tal's two battalions succeeded in holding their ground and destroyed the Egyptian force, although the battalion of light AMX tanks that he had positioned in the hills 10 miles to the west of Bir Gif gafa came close to being overwhelmed.

After nightfall 40 Egyptian T-54 tanks, advancing from the direction of Ismailia to help their encircled comrades, ran into the small Israeli blocking force of AMX tanks. Both the Egyptian and the Israeli forces were taken by surprise – they opened fire on each other at 20 yards' range. The Israelis had established themselves in a leaguer with their AMX tanks on the outside and their fuel, ammunition and supplies in half-track vehicles in the centre. A savage fight ensued. The armour-piercing shells from the small guns carried by the

Israeli AMX tanks ricocheted off the heavy armour of the Egyptian T-54s. Early in the battle the Egyptians scored a direct hit on a self-propelled mortar half-track loaded with ammunition. The vehicle exploded, blowing up seven other half-track vehicles and an AMX tank. Twenty Israelis were killed outright. Shortly afterwards two other AMXs were destroyed by direct Egyptian hits.

A 19-year-old paratrooper, who had only recently left school, takes up the story: 'About midnight we were woken up by a,groaning, clanking sound of tanks approaching. Then suddenly we saw more than 40 Egyptian tanks advancing on us with their head-lights blazing. The Egyptian tanks opened fire and almost immediately one of our ammunition trucks was hit and blew up. The fighting was bitter.

'I suddenly felt my right hand was wet and I was unable to fire my rifle any more – only then did I realize that I had been wounded. I tied it up as best I could and thereafter acted as a messenger. I managed to climb aboard a half-track that had come to collect the wounded and take us from the battlefield. But it was soon overcrowded with people more seriously wounded than I was. I got off and ran along beside it. It looked as if it was just covered in flesh. I found it safer running beside the half-track. There was still a lot of shooting going on all around but with the half-track beside me I had at least some protection.' After being passed through a couple of casualty collection centres the paratrooper reached the field hospital at El Arish at 10.30 in the morning, some 7½ hours after he had been wounded. There his wound was dressed and he was flown back to Tel Aviv where he spent the next three weeks in hospital.

After holding its ground for more than 2½ hours the battalion received orders to retreat one kilometre. Meanwhile, Tal sent a medium tank company to reinforce it. As soon as this reinforcement of heavier tanks arrived the battalion commander, without waiting for further instructions, immediately counter-attacked, regaining the one kilometre of ground that he had lost and destroying ten of the T-54 tanks.

When Tal heard that the Egyptians were forming up once again to the south of Bir Gifgafa in an attempt to break through with another mechanized brigade, he sent one of his armoured brigades, positioned at Gebel Houtmir, fifteen miles north-east of Bir Gifgafa, southwards to attack the Egyptian force from the rear while his reserve brigade to the north held fast in their positions and blocked the Egyptians' escape. In a short and bloody battle the Israelis succeeded in destroying the whole Egyptian brigade.

Meanwhile, there was a continuous stream of Egyptian troops, vehicles and armour rushing headlong from eastern and central Sinai towards the Mitla with no idea that the western end of the Pass had been blocked two days before by an Israeli air-strike that effectively prevented all but tracked vehicles from passing. As they converged from all directions the Israeli Air Force strafed them and bombarded them continuously with rockets, napalm and high explosives; and Yoffe's armoured brigade completed the slaughter.

Iska's men had been fighting now for three days and much of two nights with scarcely a break and were close to exhaustion. But once at the Mitla they had no time to reorganize themselves or rest. Almost immediately they found themselves under heavy attack from thousands of Egyptians trying to force their way, with their vehicles and armour, through the Pass towards the Canal and safety. At 2200 hours Iska radioed Divisional Headquarters to in- form them that he was almost completely surrounded and under heavy attack. At midnight Yoffe ordered his second brigade, which had caught up with him earlier the previous morning, to advance at 0300 (Thursday) and relieve Iska's forces at the Mitla. At one stage these forces, advancing westwards along the road in the darkness, found they were suddenly interlocked with a troop of Egyptian tanks heading in the same direction as themselves. In the darkness and the dust it was impossible to distinguish friend from foe. The Israeli commander ordered his men to continue to advance in line-ahead with the enemy for a number of minutes. Then, abruptly, he ordered his tank commanders: 'Move sharply to the right – shoot anything that remains on the road.' Thereupon the Israeli tanks right-wheeled off the road and shot up the Egyptian tanks that had remained on it.

Iska's men put up a gallant fight throughout the whole night. According to one of his soldiers, by morning the tanks had no more than 2 rounds of ammunition left for each gun and half a box of .50-calibre ammunition for their machine guns. By this time, following an air-strike (in which 2 Israeli tanks were hit by mistake), the enemy were abandoning their tanks and vehicles and taking to the hills on foot.

Yoffe has described the scene at the Mitla Pass: 'We were there for a day and a night and another day, in a defensive position, trying to take all the armour and all the columns rushing desperately towards the Canal area and finding the way blocked. Just imagine, the same brigade [Iska's] which started [from Israel on Monday] went all the way through and blocked the Pass. By Thursday morning they were at the end of their power; they had been fighting for 72 hours or more non-stop.

'So I had to do something in the middle of a battle, something which is not usually done. I put in a brigade to take over the job of the other brigade, while keeping the tanks firing. It was a very complicated business, but the boys did it, and did not fire on each other. The initiative and imagination, not only of the commanders but of the tank crews themselves, helped ensure that we did not have any mishaps.'

Yoffe said later that at one point in the Mitla Pass where the road passes through a narrow fissure there was a detachment of half a dozen brand-new T-55 tanks, not damaged in any way : 'They were blocked both in front and behind. They had no means of escape. You can see how they tried desperately to escape up the almost sheer rock face – they are there today like flies on a wall.'

With the greater part of seven Egyptian divisions broken in the desert behind them Tal and Yoffe ordered their forces to advance westwards to the Canal. Yoffe's second brigade relieved Iska's exhausted forces at noon on Thursday under heavy Egyptian fire. The bulk of this new brigade then battled through to the western end of the Pass. It took them nearly half a day, as the tanks had to make their way round the hundreds of Egyptian vehicles and tanks which had been shot up from the air and blocked the narrow way through the hills in several places. That evening, now on the western side of the hills and approaching the Canal, the Israeli tanks found their path blocked by two or three strong Egyptian positions supported from the rear by tanks. Unable to break through before dark, the Israelis decided to rush the Egyptian positions by night, advancing on them with the searchlights of their tanks blazing. At their approach the Egyptians abandoned their positions and fled. By 0200 on the Friday morning Yoffe's forces had reached the Canal opposite Shalufa, while another group also under his command was at Ras Sudr, having headed south-west from the eastern end of the Mitla. At the same time the less exhausted of Iska's troops who had been withdrawn from the Mitla to Bir Thamada had advanced along the Wadi Gidy road to the southern end of the small Bitter Lake and were also on the Canal.

Tal sent one of his armoured brigades to advance through the hills to Ismailia. The Israeli tanks had fierce battles at several points along the way with nearly 100 Egyptian tanks, half of them T-55s. The Egyptian tanks hid behind the crests of the dunes, which rose at intervals of 400 yards, in such a way that an Israeli tank advancing over the crest of a dune would be fully exposed to view but could see nothing of the Egyptian tanks except their gun barrels. Several of Tal's Centurions got three or four direct hits and were destroyed in this advance. The Israelis, therefore, took to shooting at the Egyptian tanks from a range of nearly two miles and succeeded in destroying several of them. The Egyptians thereupon moved 500 yards off the road and laid side-ambushes for the Israelis. Each time the Egyptians changed their tactics they succeeded in destroying more tanks. This forced the Israelis to alter their tactics; they continued their advance with two tank companies moving carefully forward across the dunes while a battalion of tanks went forward in column along the road, opening fire whenever the Egyptian gun-fire gave away their positions. In this way, Tal's armoured brigade succeeded in destroying 100 Egyptian tanks for the loss of only 10 by the time they reached the Canal opposite Ismailia.

The first Israeli forces to reach the Suez Canal had been the special task force that Tal had sent west along the coast road from El Arish. Already by the early hours of Wednesday morning – within 48 hours of the beginning of the war – they were at the Canal. However, as soon as Dayan heard of this, he ordered them to withdraw 20 miles to the east in order to minimize the risk of Israel becoming involved in any international controversy over the Canal. The next day, after being allowed back to the Canal, the force was strafed and bombed by MiGs in a couple of Egyptian air attacks. Two battalions of Egyptian artillery which opened fire from the far side of the Canal shortly afterwards were hit by an Israeli air-strike and destroyed. When, after the cease-fire had come into force, the Egyptian artillery once again began shelling Israeli positions along the Canal, Tal ordered his own guns to open fire on Ismailia, returning two shells for every one fired by the Egyptians. 'Now they have a taste of what our kibbutzim have been suffering for years along the Syrian border,' Tal remarked dryly.

According to General Yoffe, his division 'in just less than four days, finished something like 157 tanks – counted – and reached three points on the Canal.

'We had quite a lot of prisoners – Generals and Colonels who talked quite freely too. We helped many Egyptians by giving them water and showing them the direction to the Canal. We could not cope with so many prisoners, so we took some and others we helped to cross the Canal.'

'The first I knew of any of my forces on the Canal,' he said afterwards, 'was when one of the commanders asked for permission to wash his feet in the Canal. This was the first I knew that he was near there. I said: "No", and his feet are still unwashed.' However, unbeknown to General Yoffe, Colonel Iska did have a paddle in the Canal.

⚜ ⚜ ⚜

This was one of the swiftest and most decisive victories the world has ever seen. In less than 4 days the Israelis had broken Egypt's proud army of 100,000. Thousands of vehicles had been taken or destroyed, together with more than 700 Russian-made tanks, some of them the most modern in the world. Their victory was due largely to the superior quality of their manpower, in particular of their officers, also to the fact that they knew what they were fighting for – the existence of their country and the lives of their women and children. Their ruthless determination, their flexibility, their speed of decision and manœuvre, coupled with superior training was decisive. But such a rapid and dramatic result could never have been achieved but for the total air supremacy achieved by the Israeli Air Force throughout the skies of the Middle East. To have been an Egyptian sitting in a tank in the Sinai desert for 4 days without air cover, at the mercy of the Israeli jets, cannot have been a pleasant experience. Even the bravest and most resolute of armies might have been daunted by the ceaseless bombing and strafing from the air. 'We hacked them continuously,' declared General Hod, the Israeli Air Force commander. 'We didn't make the mistake we made in '56. Then we attacked them from the eastern end of Sinai and they got away with much of their equipment. This time we blocked the western end of the Mitla at the outset, blocking their escape route; then we hacked them from west to east.'

By the time the Egyptian Government agreed to a cease-fire late on Thursday night little remained of the seven whole Egyptian divisions in Sinai except thousands of soldiers, the tattered remnants of an army, making their way singly and in groups towards Egypt. The bulk of their equipment had been taken or destroyed. Many of them, 'fellaheen' (peasants) from the Delta and the banks of the Nile, unused to wearing shoes, discarded their boots and personal equipment as they headed westwards across the desert. The desert was not kind to them, nor were the bedouin. Such vehicles as had got away had been occupied to a large extent by officers. They, humble peasant people, lied to by their government, deceived and betrayed by the folly and ambition of Nasser, abandoned by their officers, at the mercy of their enemy and the desert, struggled hopelessly towards home. Some found water and food in the hundreds of vehicles that lay abandoned and wrecked beside the roads, and after several days' march in the tormenting heat of the desert reached the Canal. Here they either swam across or were taken prisoner by the Israelis and transferred to Egypt by boat at Qantara. However, many never reached the Canal. Flying by helicopter low over the desert in the week after the war, one saw them, slumped on the sand in a crumpled heap, lying where they had fallen. Some lay spread-eagled, their faces upwards, their skin blackened, almost charred by the sun.

Even for those who did survive, it was a terrible ordeal. One Egyptian pilot who was shot down by the Israelis over Sinai spent three days in the desert. On the Wednesday morning of the war he and two other pilots had received instructions from Field Marshal Amer himself, the Egyptian Commander-in-Chief, to take off with the only three MiG-17s remaining at the Fayid airbase and attack Israeli forces in Sinai. When his aircraft was shot down he bailed out over the desert and landed by parachute in the sand. He got out of his Russian-made G-suit which was too cumbersome and too hot for walking across the desert and shortly afterwards came across two other Egyptian soldiers with whom he joined forces. They had scarcely any water between them. However, the following day they saw an Egyptian officer in a jeep passing nearby. They gesticulated and shouted and the vehicle slowed down for a while but then went on its way. The next day they came across a bedouin leading a camel through the desert and asked him for water. He told them that there was a waterhole not far away and that he would be back within an hour. They waited all day but they never saw him again. Finally on the third day, by which time they had no water for 48 hours, and they were suffering from heat and exhaustion, they ran into an Israeli patrol which took them prisoner.

Along the roads of Sinai, Israeli vehicles stopped for the stragglers – provided they were unarmed and had their hands above their heads – to give them either water or a lift towards the Canal. Helicopters too and observer planes were told to keep a look out for them. When they saw them, which was rarely, they would drop them water.

The Israelis could not begin to take them all prisoners. Thus they helped them to the Canal where those that could swim were told to make their way across it at a point where it is no more than 100 yards wide. One group, as they were in mid-stream, were mown down by their own forces on the far side of the Canal with machine guns. This was observed by several Western newsmen. The reason is difficult to understand; it has been suggested that Nasser and the senior Egyptian Army officers did not want them back so that the true story of Egypt's defeat in Sinai would never be known. The transfer of prisoners was later established on a more regular basis. They were ferried by two small motor boats at Qantara to the Egyptian side of the Canal where they were put in compounds surrounded by barbed wire. The Israelis did, however, take prisoner a large number of Egyptian officers up to the rank of General. These numbered nearly 5,000 in all and the Israelis sought to exchange them for the Israeli prisoners held by Egypt who numbered fewer than a dozen. At the time of going to press the Egyptians are still haggling.

Chapter Ten
The Syrian Heights

It was not until Tuesday June 6 that Syria joined in the ground fighting against Israel. It came as a surprise to the Israelis that the Syrians, who had been of all the Arab states the most voluble and hostile, did not launch an attack on the Monday. Brigadier-General Elazar thought that this hesitation on the part of the Syrians was due to their pique at the agreement signed between Egypt and Jordan, the week before the outbreak of hostilities. The Syrians, therefore, waited to see what was happening in Sinai before risking their own fortunes in war. Evidently they – like the Jordanians the day before – were taken in by the lies from Cairo and on the Tuesday they began shelling from their positions along the ridge all the way from the southern end of the Sea of Galilee up to Banias at the foot of Mount Hermon.

Since the beginning of June, the Israelis had noticed a major Syrian troop concentration in the vicinity of the Customs House opposite the Israeli village of Mishmar Hayarden, which consisted of several infantry brigades together with one armoured and one mechanized brigade. A large number of Syrian armoured units were also concentrated on the road from Qnaitra to the Customs House near the border. The Israelis regarded this as a clear indication that the Syrians were planning offensive action against Israel. Syrian plans, found by the Israelis when they reached Qnaitra, would seem to indicate that their aim was to break through into Israel on three axes. The main attack was to be through Mishmar Hayarden, striking westwards towards Haifa. From this line of advance another force was to turn southwards towards Nazareth. The second line of advance was through Tel Qazir at the southern end of the Sea of Galilee by way of the Jordan valley and swinging north-westwards towards Afula. The third attack was to be directed against Acre through Lebanese territory.

As it turned out, only three ground attacks were made by the Syrians into Israel during the war and these were local, each consisting of no more than one infantry battalion with 15–20 tanks. They were directed against the Israeli settlements of Tel Dan, Kibbutz Dan and She'ar Yashuv in the extreme north-eastern corner of the country and they all took place on June 6. 'In my opinion,' General Elazar said later, 'these attacks were secondary feints intended to draw our forces to that area and perhaps to effect small territorial gains so that the enemy would be able to boast that they had been able to capture one or two settlements.'

The Israelis remained in a purely defensive deployment for the first part of the week and from the Tuesday onwards were under intense artillery bombardment from the guns along the Syrian Heights. According to General Elazar, in the first three days of shelling the Israelis never once initiated the artillery fire since this would immediately have revealed their own positions which were in full view of the Syrians on the ridge above. The Israelis, on the other hand, were unable to see (except from the air) the positions from which the Syrians were shelling.

On the Monday of the war, the Israeli Air Force was fully occupied with the destruction of the Egyptian, Jordanian and Syrian Air Forces. On the Tuesday and Wednesday it devoted its efforts to tank busting and to giving close support to Israeli ground troops in Sinai and the West Bank area. However, on the Thursday, Friday and Saturday it was able to turn its full attention on the Syrians.

Over a period of 19 years the Syrians had been at work establishing a great 'Maginot Line' of underground bunkers, tank-pits and gun emplacements along the ridge that runs northwards from the Sea of Galilee and dominates the low-lying plains of Israel beneath it to the west. General Peled, a divisional commander under General Elazar, has said, 'These defences were more than 10 miles deep. There were no first, second and third lines of defence as such: just row upon row of emplacements and guns.' According to General Elazar the Syrians were able to launch more than 10 tons of shells per minute from the 265 guns they had along the ridge. He excluded from this figure the Russian-made vehicle-launched *Katjusha* missiles. Each vehicle carries 12 rockets on a launcher and is capable of firing 24 rockets per minute. He remarked that the missiles, with a range of 10 miles and a 10–12-lb. warhead, were not particularly accurate but gave good area effect. Among the guns the Israelis later found on the Syrian Heights were a considerable number of brand new Russian 130 mm guns which have a range of 16 miles, with the date 1966 stamped on their casings. In addition to the artillery there were some 200 anti-aircraft guns deployed along the ridge.

On Thursday June 8 the Israeli Air Force turned its full attention to these emplacements. According to General Hod, commander of the Israeli Air Force: 'We used bombs with proximity fuses which exploded directly above the anti-aircraft emplacements; they had a devastating effect.' After knocking out the anti-aircraft batteries the IAF went on to deal with the artillery which had been pouring a merciless fire on the Israeli positions and settlements on the plain below. On the Friday and Saturday they pounded the Syrian bunkers incessantly. The concrete of these bunkers was so thick that the Israeli 500-lb and 1,000-lb bombs were unable to destroy them, nor was napalm any more effective since the bunkers had been.designed with overhanging lips to prevent the flaming liquid flowing inside. Nevertheless, wave upon wave of Israeli aircraft came in at 10-minute intervals to blast the bunkers throughout the day. 'We just pounded them continuously to break their morale,' remarked General Hod. 'Even at night we made sure they got no sleep.' By the Saturday morning the Syrians were running from their bunkers. Thereafter the IAF pursued them up to a self-imposed limit 25 miles short of Damascus.

General Elazar had wanted to attack the Syrian Heights since June 6, when the Syrians began shelling the Israeli settlements and positions along the border, and made the three minor ground attacks into Israeli territory previously mentioned. He was convinced that even without the reinforcements that were to come from the Jordanian front later in the week, he could with the forces at his disposal have achieved his objective. But the attack was postponed several times. The final postponement from the Thursday to the Friday would seem to have been Dayan's decision. The two main factors militating for postponement were the need to give the Israeli Air Force time to 'soften up' the Syrian positions and the need to allow time for the troops who had been switched from other fronts, where they had been fighting continuously since the Monday, to regain their strength. Undoubtedly, with more troops, the Israelis would be able to take the Heights more quickly. And time, as Dayan and the Government were keenly aware, was vital.

Perhaps there was also a third factor. The Israelis probably already knew in the early hours of the Thursday morning on which the attack had been planned to go in, that that night Syria would have to decide whether to accept or reject the United Nation's call for a cease-fire. If she was under heavy attack and losing ground – as was the case with Egypt – she would have been more likely to accept and observe a cease-fire. This could have proved embarrassing to the Israelis who were keen to finish the job. Maybe they felt it was better to postpone the operation twenty-four hours and carry it out with the maximum speed after the cease-fire had either been rejected or broken.

When the news reached the Israeli soldiers waiting along the Syrian front that Syria, shortly after Egypt, had agreed to a cease-fire at 0320 GMT in the early hours of Friday morning, they were bitterly disappointed. As one Israeli paratrooper put it:

> We all wanted to have a go at the Syrians. We didn't much mind about the Egyptians; we have a certain respect for the Jordanians, but our biggest score was with the Syrians – they have been shelling our kibbutzim for the past 19 years.

He had been one of the paratroopers scheduled to take part in the airborne assault on El Arish in Sinai on the Monday night. When this operation had been cancelled his unit was switched to the Jordanian front and from there on the Wednesday morning they were moved up to the hillside above Tiberias on the western shore of the Sea of Galilee in preparation for the attack on Syria. A large number of captured Jordanian vehicles had joined their convoy and many captured Jordanian flags were flying from their own jeeps and half-tracks. They were feted all the way by the inhabitants of the villages through which they passed, who threw them flowers, cigarettes and bottles of beer as they went by.

Just as Napoleon lined the main roads of France with trees so that his soldiers could march in the shade, so the Israelis, over the past 20 years, have planted double lines of trees on either side of their roads in order to provide effective cover from the air for their vehicles. On the west side of the Sea of Galilee Israeli tanks were hidden in this way. The same paratrooper remarked:

> First we were going to Egypt, then to Jordan and then to Syria. We even thought we might get a trip to the Lebanon – we paratroopers like taking sight-seeing tours. The country around Kinneret (Galilee) is very beautiful – some of it is just like Switzerland. We made camp on the hillside near an old Moshav (co-operative settlement). We had to wait here so we rigged up a shower from the irrigation system and just sat around. We became experts on orchards and mosquitoes. At the northern end of the lake we could see the fields of Almagor on fire from the Syrian shelling. At night the sky was a deep red in that direction.
>
> We listened to the news on our transistors. It was saying that the Syrians were shelling our kibbutzim – all we could see was our artillery and aircraft pounding the Syrians without letup. For two days the positions were bombarded. The sky was red the whole time. Every time our guns hit anything, we all cheered – just like anywhere else in the world I suppose. Nobody, from the mosquitoes upwards, paid any attention to the cease-fire.

0320 GMT, the hour appointed for the cease-fire, came and went. There was a brief lull in the artillery barrage and the Israelis called off their air-strikes; but in a short space of time everything was back to 'normal' again, the artillery resuming its fire and the Israeli Air Force, soon afterwards, resuming the air-strikes. Who broke the cease-fire, assuming there was one and this itself is in dispute, it is impossible to say. Undoubtedly the Israelis were itching to get at the Syrians and would have regarded it as a most unsatisfactory end to the campaign if they had been stopped by the bell, since it was the Syrians who were in a large measure responsible for the situation which had led to the outbreak of war. Equally the Syrian Army, still feeling secure in its lines of bunkers and gun emplacements, saw no reason why it should obey the call for a cease-fire from New York or even from its own Government in Damascus.

Later on the Friday morning, therefore, General Elazar received his orders to attack and at 11.30 the forces under his command began their lightning offensive. According to the General, the Syrian deployment was as follows: 3 regular brigades, the 11th, 8th and 19th which had manned the lines throughout the year: further to the rear, 2 infantry brigades, the 90th north of Qnaitra and the 32nd south of Qnaitra. Besides this each of the 5 Syrian infantry brigades had a battalion of T-34 and SU-100 tanks as well as the 30 tanks which were normally dug in along the ridge in peace time. In addition, there was a striking force composed of 2 armoured brigades and 2 mechanized brigades which were reinforced before June 5 with a further armoured and mechanized brigade. 'Since we estimated that our action would take place mainly on the "edges" (the northern and southern ends of the Israeli/ Syrian border), we engaged from June 5 in a deceptive action in the Korazim sector (at the northern end of the Sea of Galilee),' General Elazar remarked.

On the Thursday night a force of mechanized infantry, paratroopers and an armoured brigade, together with engineers and bulldozers, assembled under cover of darkness. At

11.30 on the Friday morning the Israelis began their attack against the Syrian defences above Kefar Szold. The Israelis chose one of the steepest points – hence one of the less heavily defended for their break through into Syria. A battle team, consisting of infantry heavily reinforced by armour, of more than brigade strength assaulted the ridge close to Ain Fite and Zaoura, 1,500 feet above the plain. First to advance were the bulldozers, whose task was to prepare a path for the armoured and mechanized units behind them. The bulldozers manned by the engineers were completely unprotected. As they zig-zagged up the steep hillside making a way for the tanks and the infantry in halftracks they came under heavy fire from the Syrians shelling the column from tanks buried in the ground. These tanks were almost invulnerable as only their guns and turrets were above ground level. The Israeli casualties were heavy. The battalion commander, Lieutenant Colonel Mosa Klein, was killed leading his troops into the attack. The second-in-command who took over was killed shortly afterwards. The command then went down the line as others were killed after them. The buried Syrian tanks were finally put out of action by the Israeli infantry who crawled up the hill, opened the hatches and dropped in hand grenades. Of the eight bulldozers that forced their way up this hillside only five returned. But few of their drivers came back with them. An infantry force then attacked the strong Syrian positions of Tel Azaziyat, Tel Faq'r and Bourj Bravil. Tel Faq'r, the strongest of these points, was the scene of a bitter fight. The first wave of infantry reached the barbed-wire defences, a few of the second wave got through the wire and the minefield, the third wave reached the entrenchments. After three hours of fighting, much of which according to Elazar was 'with fists, knives, teeth and rifle butts', the position was taken.

Meanwhile, the Syrian artillery, instead of directing their fire at the Israeli forces or at the road along which they were advancing, continued to shell the settlements – which they had got in the habit of doing over the years. Their artillery fire on the Israeli settlements seemed to be totally pointless for all the kibbutzim have well-constructed underground shelters for the women and children and all the men were in the trenches.

After the war was over, General Elazar catalogued the damage done by the Syrian artillery in these four days of ceaseless and intense shelling: '205 houses, 9 chicken coops, 2 tractor sheds, 3 clubs, 1 dining hall, 6 barns, 30 tractors and 15 motor cars were hit and some 175 acres of fruit orchards and 75 acres of grain and other fields were burnt down. Our losses in men were 2 killed and 16 wounded, in the main, superficially.' With such paltry results as these, the anger of the Syrians' Russian instructors is understandable. At one point in the fighting the Israelis intercepted a radio message in Russian ordering: 'Stop firing on the settlements – shoot at the troops.' And at a later stage in the battle the following rather cryptic statement was intercepted: 'The "black ones" are running away.' – 'Of course that could refer to sheep,' remarked General Yariv, Chief of Israeli Intelligence. General Elazar also confirmed the interception of radio signals in Russian, including instructions directly relating to the direction of artillery fire.

At the same time as the main Israeli attack went in, Elazar initiated two subsidiary attacks in the vicinity of Gonen and Ashmura further to the south in order to keep the Syrians guessing which was the main Israeli thrust. These penetrations were also used to secure an axis on which another Israeli armoured force advanced from Gonen by way of Rawiye on the Saturday morning to reinforce the attack. By nightfall the Israelis had two bridgeheads on the heights. Elazar said afterwards: 'We did not exploit our success any further that night for the breakthrough had been made along steep and narrow axes. We had encountered many serious difficulties in the scaling operations – difficulties in operating the tanks and in bringing up supplies. We needed the night in order to regroup to enable us to continue the following morning with our second blow.'

The following morning, with heavy air support, the Israelis embarked on the second stage of their attack and began advancing in the direction of Qnaitra. A new Israeli armoured force attacked at dawn in the direction of Tel Tamra, thereby helping the Golani brigade in the capture of Banias, and then cleared out the whole of the northern area along the Syrian/Lebanese border before turning back eastwards to take part in the attack on the town of Mass'ada.

Meanwhile, the main battle team, which had achieved the breakthrough on the previous day, was racing forward towards Qnaitra. The armoured force, which had broken through opposite Gonen, advanced rapidly towards Rawiye across the difficult mountainous terrain. It overcame numerous anti-tank gun emplacements before swinging south towards Qnaitra. Once the Golani brigade had finished in the Banias area, they too headed for Qnaitra to clear the Syrian forces out of the town.

By 1300 hours on Saturday Qnaitra was surrounded and at 1430 it was taken. The battle had lasted just 27 hours and in that time the Israelis believe that the only units of the Syrian Army left undamaged were two brigades, one armoured, and one mechanized, which had been in the Qnaitra area and which had retreated towards Damascus to defend the city following the entire collapse of the rest of the Syrian Army.

General Elazar said later: 'After we took Qnaitra we had nothing to do but put a few finishing touches to the borders of the territories we had taken. The road to Damascus was almost entirely open and I believe we could have been there within 36 hours.'

Elazar estimates that about 1,000 Syrians were killed and a further 5–600 were taken prisoner. Israeli losses were 115 killed and 306 wounded. According to Israeli estimates the Syrians lost about one-third of the 300 or so tanks they had before they started (about 40 of them were undamaged and taken over by the Israelis). Over 50 per cent of the guns of eight Syrian artillery regiments were destroyed. The other half are in Israeli hands.

Earlier that morning another Israeli force under the command of Brigadier-General Elad Peled had entered Syria from the southern end of the Sea of Galilee. It consisted of an infantry force which climbed up the cliffs of Tawafik, an armoured force which managed to find a way up the side of the Yarmouk Valley onto the high ground and a paratroop force flown in by helicopter to attack the Syrian positions from the rear, thereby cutting across their lines of communication. An additional armoured force that also entered Syria that morning, advanced through Dar Bashiyeh, mopping up the area, and later joined Peled's forces at Boutmiyé.

The paratrooper who has been quoted previously was in General Peled's force which was landed in Syria by helicopter. He gave the following description of the scene:

> The flight took six minutes. It was a beautiful trip – all that was missing was an air hostess. We passed over a Syrian anti-aircraft gun manned by four soldiers. They didn't fire a shot. You won't

find anything like this except in an Arab army. We landed in a wheat field and finished them off.

We captured an army camp just outside Fiq. All the soldiers had left and the camp was empty but they left a sentry on the gate – we dealt with him. Compared to the lordanian camps, where their former British training was evident, the Syrian camps were all filthy. We could find no food – nothing but chocolate and perfume, masses of eau de Cologne. Even in their tanks they had chocolate and eau de Cologne. They had very nasty cigarettes, much inferior to the Jordanian ones. But they had very good dates. We came to a dug-out which had obviously been occupied by a couple of officers as there were two mattresses in it. One of them stank so badly that we burnt it. It was a very difficult job, it kept on going out and smouldered for a long time – the smell was disgusting.

At Fiq we were joined by some naval commandos. They didn't have much to do at sea so they had come up looking for a fight.

An hour and a half after we had landed, the armoured column came up to support us. The tank commander shouted at us: 'Aren't there any tanks around here apart from donkeys?' There weren't.

That evening we listened to the weather forecast on the radio. Usually it just says what the weather will be like for Galilee, Tel Aviv and the Negev. But this time it included Gaza, Jordan West Bank, Qnaitra, Hebron, Sinai and Sharm el-Sheikh. We all cheered every time the announcer mentioned a new place. You could hear the excitement in his voice: it was very moving.

From where we were on the plateau we could see across the Sea of Galilee to the hills beyond. That night as soon as it was dark we could see all our kibbutzim lit up – more brightly than they had been for nineteen years – and beyond them we could see Mount Tabor and Mount Zefat. At the kibbutz of Tel Qazir, just below us on the plain, they had a party which went on until four in the morning.

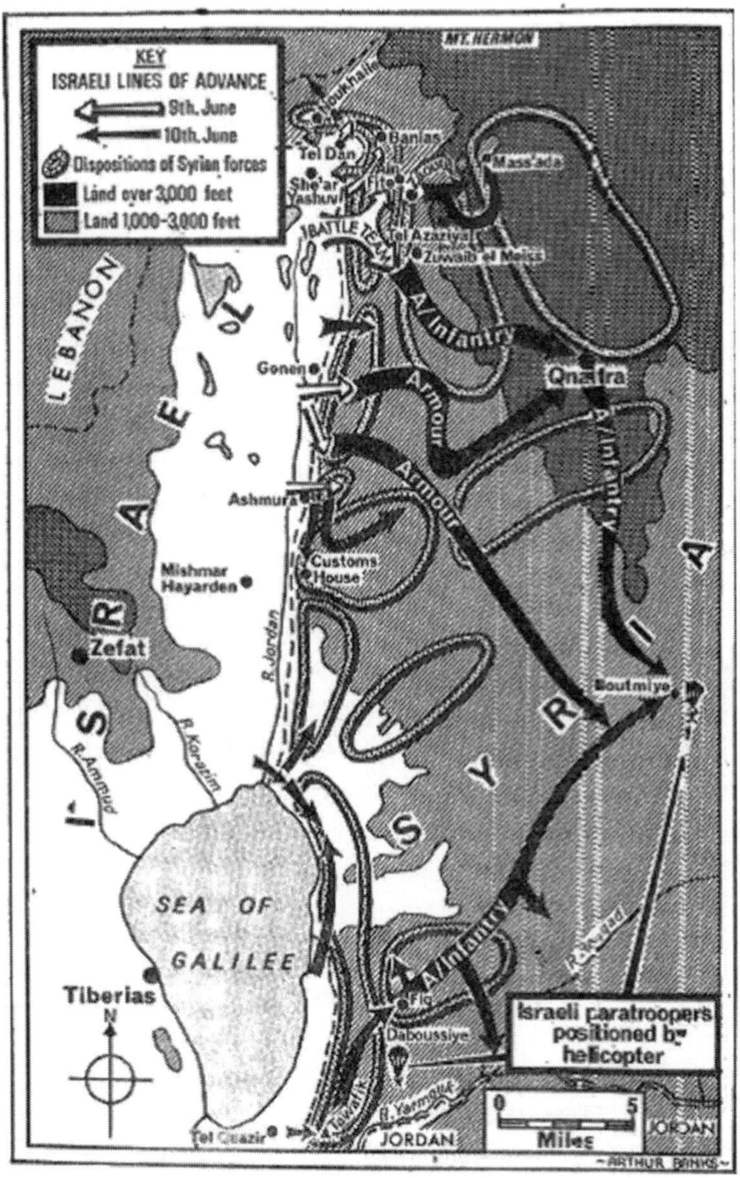

MT. HERMON
KEY
ISRAELI LINES OF ADVANCE
9th. June
10th. June
Dispositions of Syrian forces
Land over 3,000 feet
Land 1,000–3,000 feet
Banias
Tel Dan
Mass'ada
She'ar Yashuv
Tel Azaziyat
Zuwaiti el Mefis
LEBANON
ISRAEL
Gonen
Qnaitra
Armour
A/Infantry
Ashmura
Customs House
Mishmar Hayarden
Zefat
R. Jordan
R. Korazim
R. Ammud
Boutmiye
SYRIA
SEA OF GALILEE
Tiberias
N
Fiq
Daboussiye
Israeli paratroopers positioned by helicopter
R. Yarmuk
Tel Quazir
JORDAN
0 5
Miles
ARTHUR BANKS

By Saturday evening we had a lot of prisoners. We sat them down by the side of the road facing away from it so they couldn't see the transport that was moving on the road. They were sitting out in the sun – I am afraid we didn't supply them with any shade : there just wasn't any.

On the Sunday I joined a supply column as escort and we drove up to Boutmiyé. It is lovely up on the Syrian plateau. The wheat up there was ready for cutting and in places there were quite a few tomatoes and peppers growing. Our boys had been clearing out the Syrians all along the ridge and had cut them off from behind. There were a lot of bodies along the road – not a very pretty sight.

The official end to the six-day war came at 1930 hours on the Saturday evening when firing ceased after both the Syrians and the Israelis accepted the Security Council's repeated call to put an end to the hostilities.

By a feat of arms unparalleled in modern times, the Israelis, surrounded by enemies superior in quantity and quality of equipment and overwhelmingly superior in numbers, had fought a war on three fronts and not only survived but had won a resounding victory.

As the paratrooper put it:

This is an interesting country – there's never a dull moment. You have a war : in six days it's over and you have turned the whole world upside down.

Chapter Eleven
Aftermath

It took a little time after the cease-fire for the world to realize that Israel had become the strongest power in the Near and Middle East. Israel had shown that she had the most effective Air Force and Army in that area with perhaps the exception of Turkey. With a population of 2½ million, as against 40 million in the actively belligerent Arab nations, this was a staggering achievement. It is clear that Israeli supremacy will be the dominating factor in Middle Eastern politics for a long time to come. Only the overt intervention of Russia or the United States, the two super powers, could alter the balance.

Israel's victory represents a massive defeat not only for the Arab world but for the Soviet Union. For the past 20 years the Soviet Union has been playing politics in the Middle East with the unswerving objective of removing the military, political and economic influence of Britain, France and the United States and replacing it by her own. Ironically this was the reason why the Soviet Union had been one of the first countries to recognize the State of Israel. Since 1955, when the Soviet Union began the Middle East arms race with its arms deal with Nasser, she has made colossal economic, but principally military investments throughout the entire area, including in Algeria, Egypt, Syria, Iraq, Yemen and Somalia. In terms of time and resources wasted and in terms of damage to Soviet interests the Israeli victory represents a set-back to the Soviet Union far graver even than the Cuban missile crisis. The main question-mark hanging over the Middle East today is whether the Soviet Union will accept the situation or whether, like the United States three years before in Vietnam, she will feel that her vital interests are involved and will seek to reverse it.

After the cordial meeting between Mr Kosygin and President Johnson at Glassboro it would appear that the Soviet Union does not intend to challenge the decision of the battlefield and risk a showdown with the United States in the Middle East. Nevertheless, within two weeks of the end of the war some 500 Antonov long-range heavy transport aircraft landed in Cairo from the Soviet Union and Eastern-bloc countries. It is perhaps early days yet.

The campaign had been too short for much outside influence to make itself felt but, looking back over the nineteen years of Israel's history, it was abundantly plain that not only was Israel a more powerful state than her immediate Arab neighbours but the forces of world Jewry were immeasurably more effective in argument and finance than those of the Arab world. The unity of Arab nationalism had been exposed as a sham. The Holy War had led to a unholy mess. The state of topsidum turvey was exposed by the Israeli Foreign Minister, Abba Eban, on July 7. When passing through London on his way to Tel Aviv from New York, he said that it was the first war in history in which 'on the morrow the victors sued for peace and the vanquished called for unconditional surrender [of their enemies]'.

The cease-fire left Israel in possession of much of her enemies' territory – the Gaza Strip; Sharm el-Sheikh and the whole of the Sinai peninsula up to the Suez Canal; the Old City of Jerusalem, which was promptly reunited with the new; the West Bank of the Jordan; and finally, the Syrian Heights which dominate the northern part of Israel. Apart from Jerusalem and certain parts of the Holy Land which are of deep religious and historic significance to the Jewish people, the value to Israel of the territories she has gained is primarily strategic. The towns of Kalkilya and Tul Karm and other points along the border of Jordan's West Bank were used as bases by the Jordanians to shell Tel Aviv and the seaside town of Natanya further to the north as well as Lod international airport and several of the Israeli air bases. The Latrun enclave, jutting southwestwards into Israel, and the high ground held by the Jordanians dominating the road from Tel Aviv to Jerusalem could endanger access to the Israeli part of the Holy City. And, most seriously of all, a large concentration of hostile forces on the West Bank could threaten to cut Israel in two at a point where her territory was no more than 10 miles wide.

By taking the Syrian ridge above Galilee, the Israelis were able to lift the fear of the sniper's bullet and Syrian shelling that for years had hung over their farm-workers on the plain below: they were also able to guard against any further attempts by the Syrians to divert the head-waters of the Jordan or the Yarmouk rivers.

But perhaps more vital to the security of Israel than even the Syrian Heights or parts of Jordan's West Bank, is the Sinai Peninsula. In this age of jet aircraft and possible surprise attack minutes can be vital, as the Israelis themselves have proved. The Egyptian Air Force, from its Sinai base of El Arish, used to be within 7 minutes flying time of Tel Aviv. Today, from its Canal bases, it is more than 20. This fact will undoubtedly weigh heavily with Israel before she considers giving back what, on the face of it, would appear to be a worthless piece of desert. Nor is it so worthless. The oil production of the wells in the vicinity of Ras Sudr on the Gulf of Suez which is running at 150,200 barrels per day, is enough, if joined to Israel's small existing production, to make Israel self-sufficient in oil. By holding Sharm el-Sheikh she is in a position to guarantee the freedom of her shipping to and from Eilat. Israel is unlikely to place much faith in the ability of the United Nations to do this for her, by reason of her previous bad experience when the UN was withdrawn as soon as Nasser chose to challenge Israel's right of free passage.

Israel might well be prepared to give up virtually all her territorial gains in return for a thorough-going peace settlement with firm guarantees. But until such a settlement is arrived at there can be little doubt that Israel feels that territory is a greater guarantee of her security than a document signed under duress which may be torn up and stamped upon at a moment's notice.

As none of the Arab countries seemed any more disposed to recognize the State of Israel after the war than they had been before, it soon looked as if any final settlement would be long deferred. Obviously it is Israel's best hope that she should argue with her neighbours one by one. Nasser's best, hope lies in preserving at least a veneer of Arab unity. But after the disastrous war which he had provoked, veneer will no longer be enough. The wide differences in the interests of the Arab states, particularly between those that have oil and those that have none, were already evident during the war and were to become more so with every passing week.

In a perceptive series of three articles published after the war in *The Observer* Colin Legum wrote :

'Israel is still in a state of shock,' one of her leading soldier-politicians said in explaining the political climate after the miracle of arms in her six-day war against the Arabs.

'The only analogy I can think of,' he added, 'is if Britain had found herself in occupation of Berlin just three days after Dunkirk. The suddenness of the transformation from a situation of acute danger to unparalleled victory is too much for any people to absorb. It will take time to get over it.'

Three laws were passed through the Knesset on June 27 annexing the Old City of Jerusalem and reuniting it with the New on the next day. Whatever else Israel may be prepared to negotiate we may be sure Jerusalem is not included. The freeing of the city from the rule of Islam had long been the dream of Christians and Jews alike. It was ironic that the Christians who had led the Crusades and had liberated Jerusalem in 1918 under the command of General Allenby should, despite all Arab lies, have played no part in driving out Arab control. Of course, in Christian eyes, Jerusalem is still in the hands of the unbelievers but now that Pope Paul VI has formally freed the Jews from all guilt for the death of Jesus this may no longer be a matter of grievance to Christians, however ardent their belief. The Jews and the Christians were both there before the descendants of the Prophet and the Christians may be justly pleased that Jerusalem is united, as certainly are the Jews. Whatever way you value the disputed claims to Jerusalem, two-thirds of the ancient title-deeds devolve historically on the heirs of Jerusalem and Christianity. The Old and the New Testaments heavily outweigh the Koran. It would certainly be a general convenience to tourist and devotee alike to be rid of the non-sense of being smuggled through the Mandelbaum Gate. A unified control of the Old City is obviously preferable to its division. It may even be that some of the sacred manuscripts of the Armenian Church which have recently been hawked about the salerooms of London, the Dead Sea Scrolls and the like may benefit from the new arrangement.

⚜ ⚜ ⚜

On Friday June 9, while Syria was still fighting, the world was astonished to learn that Nasser had made a speech resigning all his positions. In a broadcast on radio and television, Nasser said:

> Brothers, we have been accustomed together in times of victory and in times of stress, in the sweet hours and in the bitter hours, to speak with open hearts and to tell each other the facts. ... We cannot hide from ourselves the fact that we have met with a grave setback in the last few days.... I tell you truthfully that I am willing to assume the entire responsibility. I have taken a decision with which I want you all to help me. I have decided to give up completely and finally every official post and every political role and to return to the ranks of the public to do my duty with them like every other citizen.

Few people knew what to say about this exciting development.

As early as Wednesday, the third day of the fighting, the *Evening Standard's* Middle East specialist, Jon Kimche, had alleged that Nasser was in grave domestic trouble. According to his account, Nasser was at loggerheads with his Army commanders. Reporting on June 7 that General Mortagi, the Egyptian commander in Sinai, had taken command of all Egyptian armed forces, Kimche had written that 'a full-scale military coup may have taken place in Cairo last night'. The next day he made this interesting prediction about the successor to Nasser:

> The solution of the governmental crisis which now seems to have most support among the insiders of the régime is the formation of a Civilian National Government in which the armed forces would, in fact, have control over military and foreign policy.
>
> The name most canvassed as head for such a government is the former Prime Minister and chief of secret police, Zakaria Mohieddin.

Kimche seemed to be proved correct when Nasser, at the end of his speech, nominated Mohieddin as his successor.

On Wednesday evening, Miles Copeland, who was connected with CIA's backing for Nasser in the early 'fifties, gave his views on the BBC-TV programme *24 Hours* He thought that Nasser was still 'very much in' but added:

> There had been some talk for some time of retiring him to some super position – say, to the head of the Arab Socialist Union, and I think that is probably what he'll do now.

He was warm in praise of Mohieddin:

> Zakaria is a person who is eminently acceptable to both the Americans and the Russians. We Americans like Zakaria very much. ... He is highly competent in dealing with purely Egyptian problems as such; and he is the man who is the logical one with which our government, the British Government or the Western powers, or the Western powers plus the Russians, can talk about what to do next.

However, Copeland's trend of thought was interrupted, for at that moment news came through that Nasser would, in view of the response of the Egyptian people, reconsider his decision the next day. On Saturday he announced that he would remain as President. That weekend, rumours that he was in the hands of the Army were scotched. On Sunday Nasser announced that he had 'accepted the resignations' of General Mortagi, the Sinai commander, Muhammed Mahmoud, the Air Force Chief of Staff, and Soliman Izzat, the head of the Navy. Nasser remained in supreme command of all Egyptian forces, though a new post of Commander-in-Chief was created for General Fawzi. His reputed successor, Mohieddin, was taken on as one of the deputy prime ministers together with Aly Sabry, former Secretary of the Arab Socialist Union.

When Nasser 'returned' to power, Egyptians still knew little if anything of the scale of defeat. At a press conference in Tel Aviv on June 11, General Gavish announced that between 7,000 and 10,000 Egyptian soldiers had been killed and several thousand wounded. Over 700 tanks had been captured or destroyed. In Sinai, the remaining Egyptian troops tried to make their way back on foot, without food, water, or shelter from the desert sun. Over four days elapsed before the Egyptians decided to restore the flow of fresh water through the pipeline running from Egypt under the Suez Canal into Sinai. The Israelis and the International Red Cross scoured the desert to recover survivors from the furnace. As the stragglers returned, Egyptians caught glimmerings of the truth. Many survivors did not reach home, but were kept in cantonments to prevent the spread of despondency among the civil population. Others were shot by their own soldiers as they swam to the Egyptian side of the Canal.

Within a week of the war, wild rumours were spreading in Cairo. One was that the Army, or what was left of it, was seething with disillusionment and anger against the Air Force for being caught on the ground, and that a coup was imminent. Another story said the coup had already taken place and that Nasser had resigned at gunpoint. However, the rumour said, when the mutineers saw how the crowds reacted, they were alarmed and decided to keep him in power, but as a puppet. In one account, he had left the country. Those who accepted this pointed out that Nasser had not been seen in public since his resignation speech on television. Such stories mainly circulated among professional people, who were the first to realize that things had gone wrong.

For the recovery of his fortunes, Nasser depended heavily upon Soviet aid. On June 25, following President Podgorny's visit, Cairo International Airport was closed to commercial airlines at one hour's notice. It was the beginning of a huge Russian air-lift. It is still impossible to judge to what extent Egyptian losses will be replaced; but even if all that was lost is made good it will still take a long time to train an effective and courageous Egyptian Army and Air Force.

⚜ ⚜ ⚜

On June 29 Mr David Ben-Gurion, the elder statesman of Israel and the man who had conducted the Suez War 11 years before, gave an interview to the younger author of this book. This interview was broadcast in *The World at One* BBC radio programme on July 12.

In his interview, Ben-Gurion declared that not only the Straits of Tiran but the Suez Canal should be free for Jewish navigation, according to international law; and Jerusalem, he said, must remain a Jewish city. As to the rest, he indicated that Israel should take nothing if this were the means to make peace. He thought however that Hebron should go to Israel since 'it is more Jewish even than Jerusalem'. Jerusalem became Jewish three thousand years ago under King David but Hebron became Jewish four thousand years ago under Abraham and included a number of settlements that were destroyed two days before Israel was established. Otherwise, said Ben-Gurion, the people of the West Bank of the Jordan should receive autonomy and lead their own life as a free people but tied to Israel. And finally Ben-Gurion was asked : 'Do you see this great victory that Israel has achieved as being a turning-point in your history?' He replied : 'In a way, yes, but if I had the choice, I would prefer to go back if possible. You cannot change the past, but if I could prevent this war, I would prefer to remain as we are, without any conquests, because we've paid a very high price for that; the best of our youth was killed, something like seven hundred people ... I prefer peace to any war, even if the war is a beneficent one, it's too high a price.' Ben-Gurion insisted that two factors were prior conditions to Israel surrendering any captured territory. One, that the Arabs should recognize the State of Israel and two, that a genuine peace treaty be signed.

It is hard to tell how far these views represent the ideas of other political leaders in Israel. Probably most of them would go the whole way with Ben-Gurion.

Apart from the annexation of Jerusalem, the Israeli Government made no specific rectification of frontiers, and remained uncommitted to any particular settlement. That there would be no return to the armistice lines of 1948 was certain, and they still made it plain that they would remain where they stood until a satisfactory settlement had been reached. Israel's fundamental demand was voiced by Abba Eban, in a private interview a few days after the fighting:

> We shall make the peace not on the basis of territorial claims but on the necessities of our security.

Yigal Allon, also speaking in private, speculated in greater detail. He thought it might be advisable to demilitarize the Sinai Peninsula while retaining the Gaza Strip, the West Bank of the Jordan, Jerusalem, and the Syrian Heights. The boundaries of Israel, he felt, should at least be those of the former Palestine mandate. Gaza had never been a part of Egypt, nor the West Bank a part of Trans-Jordan.

In public talk about the peace, there was some difference of emphasis among Israeli politicians. Neither Eshkol nor Eban would go beyond general principles. However, General Dayan had recorded his opinions even before the fighting in Syria was ended, in an interview filmed on June 9 and broadcast in the US two days later. He gave a list of terms:

(1) Neither the Gaza Strip nor the west bank would be returned;

(2) Jerusalem would be retained, and all religions in the city would have their freedom guaranteed;

(3) Israeli forces would stay at Sharm el-Sheikh until there were firm guarantees of free passage for Eilat-bound shipping;

(4) Passage through the Suez Canal would be secured;

(5) All problems between Israel and the Arabs would be settled by direct contacts between them.

Meanwhile, in an interview with the *Sunday Times* published on June 11, Premier Levi Eshkol would say no more than this:

> The threat of destruction, that hung over Israel since its establishment and which was about to be implemented, has been removed. Never again shall we permit this threat to be renewed.

Dayan's outspokenness at times embarrassed the Government. On July 5, after visiting Gaza, Dayan was quoted by the Israeli Radio as saying: 'The Gaza Strip will have to become part of the body of Israel.' But the following day a Government spokesman made a categorical denial that Dayan had spoken 'about the annexation of the Gaza Strip or any other area, or hinted at any intention of this sort'.

The gulf was reopening between Eshkol and Dayan, and there were rumours that Dayan would be forced out of the Government. Eshkol hinted that, as Prime Minister, he would soon once more combine with this office Dayan's post of Minister of Defence. On July 8 he even went so far as to suggest that Dayan had been irrelevant to Israel's war effort:

> The old government could have carried on but some Cabinet Ministers became panicky and pressed for Dayan's inclusion to boost morale before the outbreak of hostilities.

Israeli politics were turbulent as ever: Dayan and the Rafi party seeking to exploit their credit as the men of action and victory, the other ruling parties trying to maintain their ground. Already politicians had set their sights on the next General Election, though it was more than two years ahead.

Both Eshkol and Eban appealed to the Arab nations to join in talks for a permanent settlement. There was no indication of any positive response. Speaking at the United Nations on June 19, Abba Eban emphasized the extent to which Israel wished to help the Arab states. They would be offered co-operation in the development of agriculture, industry and communications. The arms race should be curtailed and the great powers should 'remove our tormented region from the scope of global rivalries'.

Israel was already dealing directly with more than a million Arabs, inhabitants of the conquered territories. From the start, the Israeli Government planned a serious assault on the problem of the Arab refugees encamped around her former frontiers. On the West Bank of the Jordan were about 300,000 refugees from the war of 1948; and, living in enforced squalor in the Gaza Strip, were 315,000 others. There were sound reasons for the priority attached to the refugee problem. Since 1948 the Arab states had sought to exploit the refugees as a political instrument against Israel and had made no effort to solve the problem – only an effort to maintain hatred and terrorism along the frontiers in order to remind the world of Arab claims to Palestine. By tackling the refugee question the Israeli Government would be able to deal a political blow to hostile Arab states, while also showing a conciliatory spirit towards the Arab people, justifying to the world their retention of the conquered lands should there be no settlement.

Gaza and the West Bank were contrasting problems. Egyptian Governments had treated the Gaza refugees more or less as inmates of a concentration camp, while Jordan, with one-tenth the population of Egypt had at least made some attempt to rehabilitate the unfortunate victims of war and integrate them into the economy of the country. The Gaza refugees had been prevented from maintaining contact with Egypt or enjoying even the strictly limited liberties of the Egyptian people. Travel to Cairo was by permit only; and permits were difficult to obtain. These 315,000 people were effectively prevented from taking employment or moving on. They depended for their existence upon UNWRA, and so indirectly upon the US, by far the largest contributor to UN funds. The Gaza refugees were forbidden to emigrate, unlike their fellows in Jordan, to other countries in spite of the need for manpower in for example, Iraq. They were maintained as a depressed political class for the use that could be made of them.

On the West Bank of the Jordan, the refugees were comparatively fortunate. Because Jordan allowed them to emigrate, about 100,000 had moved out of the camps, some to find work in the Gulf states and particularly in Saudi Arabia. They sent back every year considerable remittances to their relatives. General Herzog, who was called out of military retirement after the war to become Governor of the West Bank, described the refugee camps there as

> more or less normal Arab villages, with stone and cement buildings, roads, schools, and vocational centres.

When 100,000 Arabs fled during and after the fighting to the east bank, and flooded into Amman, there were stories of heinous acts by the invading Israelis. But Colin Legum, writing in *The Observer* on July 9, commented :

> Despite a certain amount of looting – by Arabs as well as Jews – few armies of occupation have behaved as well or with more friendliness than Israel's. This tribute comes from every [Arab] mayor I talked to on the West Bank.

The Arabs had fled partly to be out of the way of the fighting, partly from fears of a harsh occupation instilled by Arab propaganda from Amman and Cairo, and in many cases to ensure that they still received their remittances from the Jordanian Government and from other Arab states.

On July 2 the Israeli Cabinet announced that refugees who had crossed into the Kingdom of Jordan would be allowed to return. There was some disappointment when the Israelis insisted that they must first of all register themselves and make applications, so delaying the date of return until August 10. But the announcement rebutted those who argued that Israel welcomed the flight of Arabs and wanted to colonize the West Bank with Jews.

To ease the refugee problem, the Israeli Government decided to allow those of 315,000 Gaza refugees who so wished to move to the West Bank, where many of them had relations. David Ben-Gurion's proposal for an autonomous Arab state on the West Bank, under Israeli protection, won favour as the other main approach to the problem. In Jordan there was anxiety when stories circulated that Israeli officials had taken Arabs from the West Bank to see their former homelands, seductively displaying to them the new wealth of the land since the Israelis took it over.

Israel now has for the first time a practical control over the refugee problem. If she can further divide the Arab world by establishing friendly Arab neighbours, under Israeli protection, she will doubtless do so. But the initial financial strain will be immense. Though UNWRA continues to sustain the refugees, Israeli Government experts estimate that it will cost Israel about £2 million a month to maintain living standards on the West Bank; however, in a matter of a few years, with irrigation, mechanization and Israeli know-how, the West Bank area could be self-supporting.

⚜ ⚜ ⚜

The Arab world, in the aftermath of the war, managed for a time to achieve unity on two issues. One was the denial of oil supplies to Britain and the United States; and the other was an adamant refusal to make any step towards negotiating with Israel. As time passed, hopes of a settlement faded;

and sporadic skirmishing broke out along Israel's cease-fire lines.

As we have seen, Britain was somewhat less dependent than in 1956 upon the Suez Canal for her oil supplies. But the Canal was still important. A report in *The Times* on July 12 gave precise details for the first time of the obstructions laid by the Egyptians. There were two Egyptian pilgrim ships blocking the north entrance, south of Port Said; two floating docks filled with cement between Ismailia and the Great Bitter Lake; and a small tanker at the southern entrance. With the lifting gear they have in Port Said and Ismailia, the Egyptians could probably reopen the Canal within 48 hours, if Nasser were to show willing. In any case vessels other than the largest could still use the Canal if they were not barred by Nasser. The Canal's importance to Britain is demonstrated by the fact that at least 20 per cent of British imports and exports are shipped through it. However, the Canal was no longer the major supply route for British oil, only 25 per cent of which passes through it. But the blocking of the Canal indirectly has had a considerable effect on Britain's supplies. There is a world shortage of tanker capacity. With the Canal blocked Europe has to be supplied around the Cape: a distance of 10,710 miles instead of 6,270 miles. The result is a huge demand on tanker capacity, with higher charter rates and freight costs damaging the balance of payments, and a reduction of supplies to Europe below the amount required. Apart from the higher import costs, Britain also faced the problem of arranging for alternative oil supplies. For, on the second day of the war, Arab states began to cut off supplies to Britain and the United States, as a reprisal for alleged Anglo-American air intervention. The states nominally co-operating in the embargo could have stopped 67 per cent of Britain's supplies. Kuwait, Saudi

Arabia, Libya, Iraq, Algeria, and Abu Dhabi, and Qatar enforced the blockade.

The boycott was a double-edged weapon. If Britain found it hard to arrange alternative supplies, the Arabs could not easily find alternative markets. Saudi Arabia, which supplies 20 per cent of Britain's oil, cut off supplies on June 6 to Britain and the US but resumed them on June 14. Mecca Radio announced that there was no basis for the ban, now that it was established that British and US aircraft had not helped Israel during the fighting. But indignation against the West was running high among the Arabs. If Saudi Arabia had attempted to restore supplies during the war, it might have provoked action by pro-Nasser oil workers.

Britain was simultaneously hit by events in Nigeria, where the Federal Government, in an attempt to strangle the rebel state of Biafra, blockaded the oil terminal of Bonny. The British Government remained optimistic, placing its faith in heavy stocks, other sources of supply, and the weakening of the Arab embargo. Nevertheless on July 4 a Bill was passed through the House of Commons to authorize, if need be, petrol rationing and the control of oil supplies. The United States sought to aid Europe by releasing oil supplies for export. But the French Government co-operated with the Arabs by ensuring that supplies purchased by France were not re-sold to Britain or the United States. Some commentators suggested that, while Britain might be forced on to rationing, France would infiltrate the Arab oil industry, perhaps taking advantage of any expropriation of British and American companies. But so far no expropriation has been attempted, and there are signs that oil will soon be flowing again from at least some Arab sources. Once again it looks as if Arab unity will prove a sham.

⚜ ⚜ ⚜

While keeping up pressure against Britain and the United States, Egypt also tried to establish footholds on the eastern side of the Suez Canal in Sinai so that the Canal should not become the final cease-fire line. President Boumédienne of Algeria and President Nasser maintained close contacts with Moscow. Boumédienne, whose country stubbornly refused to accept a cease-fire, saw Kosygin in Moscow on June 12. On June 20 the Soviet Chief of Staff arrived in Cairo with a strong military delegation to discuss rearmament and to discover the reasons for the Arab defeat; and, while Kosygin was in the United States, President Podgorny spent three days (June 21–24) in Cairo.

Following Podgorny's visit to Belgrade, *en route* for Cairo, the Yugoslav newspaper *Borba* reported that the Russians would adopt a very realistic position. They had concluded that there was no way of liquidating Israel's territorial gains unless the Arabs could be induced to negotiate, recognize Israel's existence, and make some concessions about her maritime rights. The muted tone of the communiqué which marked Podgorny's departure from Cairo seemed to reinforce this evidence. The Egyptians were also putting out feelers for resumed American aid. The night before the Glassboro summit, the Egyptian Foreign Minister, Dr Mohammed Fawzy, requested a secret session with Dean Rusk at the Waldorf Astoria, and *Al Ahram* later released the story.

King Hussein of Jordan set out on a mission to Western capitals in an effort to restore his country's fortunes. After speaking at the United Nations on June 26, and calling for the withdrawal of Israeli forces, he visited President Johnson, Harold Wilson, General de Gaulle, and Pope Paul VI. By July 10 he was back in Cairo, where Nasser greeted him with another and perhaps equally ominous kiss.

During the following week, five Arab heads of state conferred in Cairo. As if to provide a martial backcloth, a Russian naval force of 13 ships, including missile-carriers, arrived on a one week's visit to Alexandria and Port Said. The Russian commander, Admiral Molotsov, announced that his ships were ready 'to repel any aggression'. When the Arab leaders began their discussions in Cairo, it was with the aim of convening a full summit meeting of all Arab states, and determining its agenda. That is what King Hussein had urged from the start. But, apart from King Hussein of Jordan and President el Azhari of Sudan, the participants were drawn from the pro-Soviet and extremist camp of the Arab states. There were two rounds of talks. Nasser, the Algerian Premier Boumédienne and Hussein took part in the first. When President Aref of Iraq and President Atassi of Syria arrived later in the week, King Hussein, perhaps disturbed at this gathering of extremists, flew his own Caravelle back to Amman. Nor was it agreed to hold a full summit meeting. For the *Guardian,* Harold Jackson reported on July 17 that Hussein was discomfited by the Cairo talks.

> The series of foothill discussions which has been going on not only does not satisfy him but is bound to create the suspicion that the revolutionaries of Egypt, Syria, Iraq and Algeria are plotting behind his back.

Of all Israel's immediate neighbours, Jordan had the greatest interest in a settlement with the Israelis. King Abdullah, Hussein's grandfather, had been assassinated because of the suspicion that he was dealing with the Jews. Now Hussein, sovereign of a ruined country, with his remaining territory for a while occupied by 15,000 Iraqi troops who might or might not be his friends, was the sole representative of realism among the vanquished. The spirit of Egyptian politics was caught by *Al Ahram*'s declarations: 'The battle is still going on. Victory is ours.' When the Cairo talks ended the Arab leaders were said to have agreed one point: that negotiations with Israel were forever ruled out. On July 15 a new Cabinet took office in Amman, and skirmishing broke out between Jordan and Israel for the first time since the cease-fire.

While Hussein sought a settlement, Egypt stepped up the propaganda war against Israel, and a series of incidents occurred along the Suez Canal, the cease-fire line between the two countries. The first major clash was on July 1 when a company of Egyptian troops crossed the Canal at noon about ten miles south of Port Said. The purpose, according to the Israelis, was to 'establish a *fait accompli*'. A second attack followed at about 7 pm when the Egyptians opened fire with mortars on Israeli troops near Qantara. The fighting continued the following day, and Egyptian attempts to cross the Canal were beaten back. A week later, on July 8, an air battle developed, the first since the cease-fire. Four Egyptian MiGs engaged two Israeli Mirages near Qantara and one of the Egyptian aircraft later crashed. The Israeli Air Force also went into action to silence Egyptian artillery at several points close to Port Said, at the northern entrance to the Canal. A gun duel across the Canal and a minor engagement at sea off the Sinai coast followed on July 12. In the first, eight Israeli soldiers were wounded. The naval skirmish resulted in the sinking of two Egyptian MTBs by the destroyer *Eilat* and Israeli MTBs off the Northern coast of Sinai under the nose of a Russian fleet only 15 miles away. Still as imaginative as during the war, the Egyptians were claiming on July 14 to have shot down four Israeli planes near the town of Suez, and a fifth near Port Tewfik. The Israelis said their planes were all safe.

Within 24 hours, fighting had extended to new stretches of the Canal. A fresh issue had ignited the conflict : rights of passage along the waterway. As the UN observers prepared to take up their positions, General Dayan informed General Odd Bull of the Israeli view. The cease-fire line, according to the Israelis, ran down the centre of the Canal. Dayan insisted that the arrangement should be that both countries could sail their boats along their respective sides. On July 15 at Kabrit on the Bitter Lake and at El Firdan, between Qantara and Ismailia, the Egyptians opened fire with tanks and artillery. The Israeli Air Force bombed Egyptian batteries at both places, and one Israeli jet was shot down by anti-aircraft fire, the pilot parachuting to safety over Sinai. Seven Israelis were killed, and 22 wounded in the day's battles.

⚜ ⚜ ⚜

On June 17 Mr Kosygin had arrived in the United States for the meeting of the United Nations General Assembly. He stopped in Paris on the way to see General de Gaulle and did the same on his way back. He did not think it necessary to stop in London on either journey, although he did have the pleasure of meeting the British Foreign Secretary, Mr George Brown, in New York during the meeting of the General Assembly. At the General Assembly Kosygin tried to secure the acceptance of a resolution which, in addition to condemning Israel and ordering her to withdraw her forces, appealed to the Security Council to 'undertake immediate effective measures in order to eliminate all consequence of the aggression committed by Israel'. This is what Russia had tried and failed to achieve in the Security Council during the war. Kosygin said that the actions of the Israeli invaders in the territories they had overrun brought to mind the heinous crimes of Hitler's Germany. When Eban, speaking next, rebutted the Soviet charges, Kosygin and Gromyko walked out of the meeting. But this Soviet resolution, along with every other proposal for a settlement put down before the General Assembly, was rejected.

Kosygin's more serious work was accomplished in two long *tête-à-têtes* with President Johnson, on June 23 and 25. The 'summit' at the small town of Glassboro, midway between Washington and New York, appeared to be an afterthought of Kosygin's sword-rattling at the General Assembly. But it is more likely that his appearance at the United Nations was designed to provide the Russian premier with both the opportunity and the excuse for talks with Johnson. This might lay him open to criticism not only in Cuba and China, but in the Arab world; however, he and his associates obviously thought it right to run this risk.

Johnson, for his part, was definitely not pleased when the news first reached him that Kosygin was coming. It is believed he only allowed himself to be persuaded to a summit after great hesitation. He accepted on the ground that the public expected it of him: and after reminders of his first State of the Union message in 1964, when he sought to pursue a *détente* in the Kennedy style, saying : 'I hope the new Soviet leaders can visit America so that they can learn about this country at first-hand.'

The first meeting between Kosygin and Johnson was certainly a greater success, at least on a personal plane, than most Americans, including White House officials, had dared to hope. There was relief that after a week of diplomatic haggling about when and where the meeting should take place, the two men had agreed the details at last. Their promise to meet again on the Sunday also raised expectations.

But that said, a momentary euphoria engendered by the 'grandfathers' summit', at which both men could readily agree that they fervently hoped their heirs would live in peace, was swiftly succeeded by a mood of caution. Immediately after his five and a half hours' talk on Friday with Kosygin, Johnson flew to a Democratic Party banquet where he said: 'We reached no new agreements – that doesn't happen in'a single conversation – but I think we understand one another better.' In their discussions, three hours of which were spent alone except for interpreters, the two men touched on Vietnam and the Nuclear Non-Proliferation Treaty, as well as the Middle East. They seemed to make most progress on agreement to limit the spread of nuclear weapons. It was, of course, the least contentious of the three items.

While they talked, Rusk and Gromyko, with McNamara and McGeorge Bundy, were conferring in the next room. The subject of defence against ballistic missiles loomed large. McNamara was anxious to avoid the enormous expense – £14,000 million over ten years – of installing an anti-missile system for American defence. It had been known for a long time that the Russians were establishing such a system for themselves.

There was nothing to suggest that Kosygin and Johnson did more than state their respective positions on Vietnam and the Middle East. It was scarcely an advance for them to have reached consensus, as White House spokesman George Christian expressed it, that 'Israel does exist as a nation'. Moscow has never held otherwise.

However, Kosygin, following his talks with Johnson at Glassboro, accepted an invitation to Expo '67 in Montreal and flew on to Goose Bay, Labrador, before returning home by way of Cuba and Paris. At Goose Bay Kosygin told Premier

Smallwood of Newfoundland that the Soviet Union had never had any desire to see Israel destroyed. He also told the same thing to Cyrus Eaton, the American millionaire financier of Cleveland, whom he arranged to meet during the same occasion, Mr Eaton being the noted promoter of Russo-American understanding at his Pugwash conference.

Kosygin and Johnson obviously hit it off well as human beings and fellow professionals. They made a good deal of their common bond as grandfathers, the Russians bringing a golden cup as a present for the newest addition to Johnson's family, Luci Nugent's firstborn. Kosygin played up to the crowd as he had done earlier in the year in England. As he was leaving the brownstone Hollybush House, he stopped his car and scrambled down a grassy bank, smiling and waving, to make a short speech to a crowd of about a thousand : 'I want to thank you for having us to this beautiful place. I want to assure you of only one thing: that the Soviet people want to live in peace with you. We want war everywhere to be stopped. There are so many wonderful and beautiful things to be done.'

On the Sunday, Johnson and Kosygin met again for four and three-quarter hours, as affably as before, but with little concrete result. Most American observers, looking back on Glassboro, felt that Johnson emerged from the affair as decidedly top dog. The White House believed that it cost Kosygin more 'face' than it did Johnson to have the meeting take place. Glassboro did very well for Johnson's personal political standing in the Gallup and Harris polls. Gallup showed him leaping from 42 per cent approval in March to 58 per cent in June. For British commentators, the summit was a sobering revelation of the relative insignificance of Britain's role in world politics. When George Brown was entertained to lunch on the day before the summit, 130 in all sat down at table, which precluded a fashionable 'working' meal. With Brown as Johnson's guests were the Danish and Italian premiers.

At the United Nations, on July 4, the US representative, Arthur Goldberg, put before the Assembly the 'ten essential elements of peace' which President Johnson had proposed to Mr Kosygin at Glassboro. They were:

1. The withdrawal of all armed forces and the end of a state of war.
2. An agreement by all members to a declaration of respect for the rights of every member to maintain 'an independent national State of its own'.
3. An assurance of the territorial integrity and political independence of all Middle Eastern States.
4. Guaranteed protection for the vital security interests of all States in the area.
5. The abandonment of force in relations between States in the Middle East.
6. The rights of all nations to free and innocent passage through international waterways.
7. A just and permanent settlement of the refugee problem.
8. An agreement that the improvement of national economies and living standards should take precedence over an arms race.
9. The safeguarding of the holy places and an international guarantee of freedom of access for all.
10. An international system, to include help from the United Nations, should be set up to help the States concerned achieve the aims outlined above.

Once again the United Nations proved more of a sounding-board for conflicting national policies than a forum of international decision. Three contrasting resolutions were before the General Assembly on July 4, and all failed that night to win the two-thirds support necessary for them to be carried. The Russian resolution, originally introduced by Kosygin, branded Israel as the aggressor and demanded the withdrawal of her troops. The voting was 22 in favour and 71 against with 27 abstentions. A Yugoslav resolution, for which both the French and Russians lobbied with vigour, called on Israel to return to the 1948 armistice lines and join with the Arabs in ending the state of war. It won too feeble a majority: the vote was 53 in favour and 46 against, with 30 abstentions: less than the requisite two-thirds majority. Britain and the United States gave their support to a Latin-American formula, which linked an Israeli withdrawal to the conclusion of a Middle East settlement. In what seemed to many a mournful count, this too was narrowly voted down by 57 votes to 43, with 20 abstentions.

The Israelis were pleased that the two resolutions calling for their unilateral withdrawal had failed, while most people deplored the futility of the General Assembly. Mr Abba Eban with his usual sagacity said that in the Israeli view the General Assembly had shown itself to be in 'a mood which was healthy, sceptical and wise'. The Middle East situation would now be referred back to the Security Council, which was the proper place for dealing with it. It was through the Security Council that the UN was able to make a contribution to the peace. On July 10, after urgent discussions arising from clashes along the Suez Canal, the Security Council agreed to the stationing of observers along both sides of the waterway. They were due to take up their positions at noon on July 16; but the Israelis insisted on a clarification of the conditions under which they would operate. Finally, at 4 pm GMT on July 17, eight UN observers took up their posts on either side of the Canal, the first guardians of the new and uneasy cease-fire line. The same day, and fresh from their decision to liquidate Israel's gains, President Boumédienne of Algeria and President Aref of Iraq arrived in Moscow.

According to Jon Kimche, writing in the *Evening Standard* of July 20, King Feisal had recently sent King Hussein a cheque for £5M; a similar sum was said to have been sent from Kuwait. If this report had been correct this generosity might be construed as an attempt by Saudi Arabia to put off possible annexation by Iraq of what is left of Jordan. And reports were soon coming in that the Iraqi Army was being withdrawn from Jordan. Perhaps the money did the trick.

Whatever signs could be detected in the weeks following the cease-fire, President Nasser made it plain that he was as intransigent as ever. While implying that he and the old guard must fade away, he insisted in a speech in Cairo on July 23 that the United Arab Republic's defeated armed forces were being reconstructed and reorganized to continue fighting against Israel. He reiterated the Arabs' determination to crush Israel : 'There is only one solution : We haven't given in and the struggle goes on'. He went on: 'We have to struggle everywhere in order to mobilize the Arab people. We are not the first to lose a battle.'

This as least was some advance. It was his first admission that Egypt had been beaten. Later he repeated the Russian lie that the war was started by Israel's intention to invade Syria. He also said that Cairo had been first informed by Damascus that 18 Israeli brigades were massed on the Syrian frontier. The Egyptian Government checked these reports and were wrongly informed that there were 13 brigades. As has already been stated, the Israeli force there amounted to a company of only 120 men.

⚜ ⚜ ⚜

And so, finally, we must ask ourselves what is the best hope for the future of Jew and Arab in the Near and Middle East. More than once in this short book it has been indicated that the authors believe that the best interests of the area and of the world would be served by the big powers ceasing to play politics there. It would be fatal if a final settlement merely represented a compromise between the Soviet Union and the United States with Britain and France chipping in unhelpfully from time to time. Such a solution might possibly receive the accord and blessing of the United Nations but it would certainly not be a guarantee of a just and lasting peace.

Having said this, it may seem impertinent for outsiders to offer any advice. But in general terms it can do no harm to suggest what is in the interests of all the parties concerned. Israel should be careful: magnanimity should be her guiding star and any rectifications of frontiers she may seek should be in the general interests of peace. The best interests of the Arab world, on the other hand, lie in the recognition of the facts of life. Israel is in the Middle East to stay. No amount of huffing and puffing will get her out. Recognition of Israel as a state is the prerequisite of any tranquillity or prosperity in the area. Good relations might follow and even eventually friendship.

'Ah,' will cry the defeatists throwing up their hands aghast, 'you can never reconcile Jew and Arab.' The authors do not accept this so melancholy a conclusion. Remarkable things have happened in the world before now. Who would have believed half a century ago that Ireland could be partitioned and divided from the British and within a decade you could travel from Ireland to Britain without a passport?

Who would have believed still more that the partition of Northern and Southern Ireland would come to be, with union of Ireland merely regarded as a distant goal to be achieved one day by comprehension of mutual interests and a still further melting of human hearts?

All that is needed to procure such blessed results are time and stability. When, and it may take a long time, the Arabs have come to a settlement with the Jews, one by one each agreement should be ratified and guaranteed by the United Nations. And the intransigent Arabs, meanwhile, would find that these would ensure peace with Israel and the Western world and would prosper while those who chatter savagely in the corner will smoulder in their barbaric poverty. Israel has much to offer to the Arab world. Her tiny bit of desert she has turned into a garden.

By her adoption of modern agricultural methods Israel has broken the bondage of centuries which condemned a man to get no more from the earth than was needed for himself and his family to survive. The visitor passing from Israel, with its irrigation, giant bulldozers and combine harvesters, to the West Bank of Jordan goes back 2,000 years. There the harvest is still reaped with sickles and the grain thrashed by donkeys or camels walking round a tether. Israel could show her Arab neighbours how to revolutionize this basic industry and would gladly help them in the task. With peace established in the area on firm foundations, western capital would flow into the area and immense strides could be made to alleviate poverty and bringing the Arab world forward into the twentieth century.

An imaginative idea for improving conditions in the Middle East was put forward in a letter to *The Times* of June 28 by Mr Edmund de Rothschild. He suggested that atomic desalting plants capable of producing 100 million gallons of fresh water per day should be set up; one in Israel, one in Jordan and possibly a third of half that capacity in the Gaza Strip. The cost of the larger ones was estimated by Mr de Rothschild at $170M to $210M each. The turnover article in *The Times* the next day by Mr Michael Ionides, author of *Water Resources of Trans-Jordan and their development,* seemed to think that this project was feasible and it was later commended by Sir Alec Douglas-Home in the House of Commons on July 6. Such a scheme is timely and might help remove at least one of the major causes of dispute between Israel and her neighbour states. What is being spent through the United Nations, largely by the United States, to feed the Palestinian refugees could well be used to provide them with water to grow their own food. This might prove no more costly and certainly the results would be more satisfactory. If the Soviet Union were to join with Britain and the United States in establishing such plants it would be a major step towards a lasting peace in the Middle East.

All this must be the aim of all men and nations–the desire for a just and honourable peace. The peace may be precarious but after so decisive a victory as Israel has gained it would seem certain that her existence and security could not be threatened for many years to come. Given 20 years, much could happen. Given 50, practically all that is needed. So the great powers should hold the ring and encourage in every possible way every Jew and Arab whose path seems bent on peace. And let them avert their beneficence from those who cry for conquest and revenge.

Appendix 1
The BBC Coverage

It was originally the intention to survey and compare the way in which British television and radio covered the six-day war. Most of the BBC's news and current affairs programmes were monitored when they were on the air. And the BBC's Library and Audience Research Service generously made available all the transcripts and other information requested to enable us to complete the investigation. Thanks are due to the Honourable Kenneth Lamb, the Secretary of the BBC, who authorized these facilities and everyone else at Broadcasting House and BBC Television who gave their help.

Since the author who stayed at home does not normally watch ITN, we had hoped to base our study of independent television coverage on similar transcripts of the relevant programmes. However, on the ground that studying the transcripts without actually looking at the programmes would lead to a distorted account, Sir Geoffrey Cox of ITN declined to co-operate in the venture. We regret that we are thus prevented from making the comparison which we had intended. Nevertheless the study has not been without its useful lessons.

First a word must be said about the cheeseparing tactics of the British Government which rendered the free world an ill service during the Sinai war. In the bazaars of the East the BBC is listened to with considerable respect. And when stories are exchanged it is always a bull point, except among paid agitators, if the teller of the story can say he has heard it on the BBC. This being so, it was unfortunate that on April 1 the Government compelled the BBC to reduce its normal transmission time in Arabic from 12 hours to 10 hours per day.

On June 5, when the war started, the Foreign Office asked that the Arabic service be stepped up by an additional 1½ hours. As staff had been dispersed it was only possible to add an extra 3 hours on June 6 but between June 7 and 14 the Arabic service was on the air for 171/4 hours every day. The strain on the BBC's staff was so great that on June 14 the service was reduced to 12 hours and by June 171/4 it was back to 10 hours daily.

Of course, it was very easy for Arab propagandists to write off these extra hours as fabrications put on for the war and as part of Britain's attempt to help Israel. Services, such as the Arabic service, can only be of value if they are maintained at an even tempo in peace and war.

⚜ ⚜ ⚜

Wars and crises always increase the circulation of newspapers particularly in the evening field where several editions may be bought. Thus the London *Evening News* put on 20% in the week of the war, while its smaller rival the *Evening Standard* put on no less than 27%. The serious morning papers also increased their sales.

The BBC Audience Research figures tell an interesting story. Both the BBC and ITN broadcast a news programme at 5.55 pm. In the week before the war, of the potential audience aged 5 years and over in the United Kingdom, the figures show :

11.7% watched BBC
6.2% watched ITN

In the week of the war the figures altered dramatically:

BBC 16.2% ITN 9-5%

Both rose in very much the same proportion. A different story emerges, though, with the news programmes which they both broadcast shortly before 9 pm. There the figures read, for the week before the war :

BBC 18-7% ITN 13-6%

And the week of the war:

BBC 17-9% ITN 16-7% 22

At this time of the evening, the ITN's share of the audience went up while that of the BBC went down.

The authors suspected, before enquiries were made, that some people might share their own habit of listening to BBC radio when they really want to get the news. (After all, you get much more news in the given space of time and you do not have to look at the announcer's sometimes smirking face.) The authors' guess was right buf the change was not so significant as one might have expected :

BBC Home Service	Average weekday audience as a percentage of population aged 5 and above	
Times	*May 29-June 2*	*June 5-9*
7 am	5.9	6.1
8 am	10.2	11.2
1 pm	7.7	9.6
World at One	5.5	6.3
6 pm	2.8	3.7
Radio Newsreel	1.9	2.6

The statistics are one measure of the value of the BBC's coverage. What these figures cannot convey, however, is the extent to which viewers and listeners were satisfied with what was given to them. The television coverage of the war was, in a fundamental sense, unsatisfactory. There was too much talk in London and Washington, and not enough film from the battle areas. The BBC cannot be wholly blamed for this. But there must remain a suspicion that had money not been so lavishly spent on the attempt to exploit the voyage of Sir Francis Chichester (or on the inanities of *Jeux Sans Frontières*) there might have been more cash to cover the Middle East. The £100,000 spent on vainly trying to beat ITN on the final rendezvous with Chichester might well have brought surprising results in Sinai and Jordan.

On reflection, the six-day war demonstrated one of the inherent and so far ineradicable weaknesses of television as a news medium. It is usually impossible in the present state of technical development to present live visual coverage of world events. Old film is no substitute for actuality. And by leaving pictures to the imagination, radio can often have the edge of immediacy.

The best war film the BBC was able to show was provided by courtesy of the Columbia Broadcasting System of America. It showed Mr Charles Collingwood with a powerful team of assistants going in from old Jerusalem to new Jerusalem. They proceeded to film everything in sight. Columbia must have spent as much money on the war as the BBC had spent on the Chichester project. Mr Collingwood had at his disposal a staff of 39 people and a Lear jet for flying out the film. They had not spent all their money on chasing yachtsmen.

⚜ ⚜ ⚜

The problem was not so much getting men to the news as getting the news out. Censorship, crowded telephone and radio circuits, and interrupted flying schedules made it impossible to use normal procedures. Flights from Tel Aviv were unpredictable. As BBC Foreign Editor Arthur Hutchinson put it: 'It's been a glorified treasure hunt. . . The men on the spot can only say they've handed the film in to El Al. From then on it is pot luck. We scoop it up wherever we can.' To get voice reports back to London it was often found easier to relay from Geneva, Moscow and Paris. For film, a film editor was sent to Rome to pass anything sent from Cairo and Tel Aviv through the Eurovision link.

There were unavoidable delays. The first piece of war film was sent by John Bierman from the Gaza Strip. It appeared on the evening of June 6. Israel supplied some official film but not a foot of official or unofficial film emerged from Egypt after the fighting began. An attempt was made to send some film by courier across the desert from Cairo to Benghazi, but the courier was intercepted and the film confiscated.

On May 17, *24 Hours,* sensing war in the offing, interviewed John Morgan of *Panorama* who had returned from Israel the day before. Tousled, tired, and angry at the cynicism of the great powers which had sold arms indiscriminately in the Middle East, Morgan assessed the situation with remarkable penetration.

Throughout the crisis, *24 Hours* used Early Bird to bring news and interviews from New York and Washington. Charles Wheeler and Gerald Priestland reported on the futilities in the Security Council. On May 24, for example, Wheeler noted that 'the debate so far has really concentrated on an argument about whether there should be a debate or not....'.

With elementary wall maps and movable symbols, *24 Hours* allowed military experts to size up the opposing forces and later to analyse the course of the fighting. On May 25, for example, Desmond Wettern of the *Sunday Telegraph* expressed a professional scepticism about the existence of the alleged Egyptian minefield in the Straits of Tiran.

The war introduced viewers to a new personality: Brigadier Peter Young, sometime officer in the Jordanian Army, now teacher of history at Sandhurst. With unerring precision, Young plotted and analysed the course of the campaign. His knowledge of the terrain and the troops gave him an air of authority which, mixed with a genial humour, made him the most effective expert brought to the studio.

24 Hours on May 18 offered a detailed breakdown of Arab/Israel military capability and called in Brigadier W. F. Gray Thompson for an expert assessment. Thompson went straight to the heart of the matter, asserting that Israel must attack first if she felt certain she was going to be attacked. Egypt would be the prime target; Jordan would be left alone if possible.

Jon Kimche, interviewed by Michael Barrett on *24 Hours* (May 19), explained that it was not the UN force which had kept the peace but Israeli and Egyptian policy. The UN force was created as a face-saver for the British and French after Suez. Barrett, turning to Christopher Mayhew, invited him to comment, 'looking at it perhaps through Arab eyes' – a practice which was soon to involve Mayhew in a minor political controversy. Mayhew spoke of a secret agreement between Hammarskjöld and Nasser in 1957 in which Hammarskjöld agreed that the UNEF would leave whenever Nasser asked. Neither Mayhew nor Kimche expected war. Nor did Elkins when he reported the next day (May 20). According to Gordon Waterfield (*BBC World Service* May 20) Egypt and Syria had shown no desire to coordinate military effort with Saudi Arabia and Jordan. 'If it were thought in Cairo that war was really imminent with Israel, would it not be natural for Arabs to close their ranks however bitter their political differences?' It is true that only Egypt, Jordan and Syria took any effective part in the fighting, but all the Arab countries beat the war drums against Israel and made gestures of varying hostility. The event proved that it was largely bluff: it was all over before the more distant ones like Algeria could act.

On May 22, Mr George Brown faced Robin Day on *Panorama*. The Foreign Secretary was unhappy about how precipitately U Thant had moved but remained a 'very strong pro-United Nations man'. Brown belted the critics who had queried the wisdom of his delaying his trip to Moscow. 'Absolute rubbish!'

A brief interview with Ben-Gurion was followed by a report from Israel by John Morgan. The principal domestic quarrel, it seems, was about compulsory autopsies and the transplantation of eyes from the newly dead to the living.

The subject was soon to have an unexpectedly macabre relevance.

In the days before the fighting, British attitudes were melodramatically, though probably accurately, crystallized in the Prime Minister's phrase, 'Israel has a right to live.'

News stories were pegged on the real threat to Israel's existence. Ian Trethowan (*24 Hours* May 31) caught the mood in his report of opinion in the House of Commons: '. . . the most potent danger, which seemed to build up palpably before our eyes during this debate is the threat to the very life of Israel.' Was Nasser planning to wipe Israel off the map? Anthony Nutting thought not:

'People are awfully inclined to get hysterical directly Nasser does anything, or even opens his mouth, but what Nasser has done has been to reverse the gain which Israel made as a result of Israel's aggression, sponsored by Britain and France, in 1956.... I don't think you can call it an act of aggression on Nasser's part.' *(World at One* May 24.)

Two days later on the same programme Selwyn Lloyd had a predictably different view. What had happened recently showed simply that 'leopards [like Nasser] don't change their spots'.

⚜ ⚜ ⚜

News of the outbreak of war first broke during Jack de Manio's breakfast programme, *Today*, at 7.30 am on Monday June 5. For the second edition of *Today*, a telephone conversation with the BBC's former Middle East correspondent Peter Flinn had been taped. Flinn, who had covered the Suez war in 1956, was heard frequently during the week analysing the situation on the basis of reports as they came in, and his grasp of Middle East affairs was always impressive.

The World at One was the first BBC programme to have a chance to assess the situation. The reports were fragmentary, confused, and occasionally trivial. Charles Wheeler in Washington informed us that President Johnson had been woken up at 4.30 am with the first news. Michael Elkins was drawn into a curiously protracted conversation about whether Tel Aviv airport was closed to civilian traffic. Winston Churchill, briefly back from Israel, was also interviewed on this programme : *Interviewer:* Winston Churchill, you're just back from the Middle East, and I believe last Tuesday you had a meeting with a famous man. Can you tell me something about it?

Churchill: I was with Mr Ben-Gurion at the King David Hotel in Jerusalem, Tuesday before last, when the news came over the radio at 7.30 in the morning that the Straits of Tiran had been closed by the Egyptians, and this old man – he is, I think, eighty now – he shook his great head and said, 'I'm frightened, not for Israel for she will survive, but for our youth, for the best people of this country, because this war, if it comes to war, will be far more terrible than '48 or '56, and many people will die on both sides. Our officers don't lead from behind, and they're by and large our best people. And,' he added, 'one thing you've got to understand is that for the Arabs, what is military defeat? It's the loss of an army. In ten years they'll have another army. For us, military defeat means probably death for every single one of us.'

Panorama attempted global coverage. Richard Kershaw reported from Cairo; Michael Parkinson from Tel Aviv; Ivor Jones from Beirut; Michael Charlton interviewed George Ball in the USA. Christopher Mayhew's much-advertised interview with President Nasser was followed by Parkinson's interview with Abba Eban. In London James Mossman quizzed Alistair Buchan; and Robin Day chaired a discussion between Jeremy Thorpe, Christopher Mayhew and Duncan Sandys.

The news was thin and speculation often based on false assumptions. Robin Day repeated without comment the Arab claim to have destroyed over 160 Israeli planes, and despite Michael Parkinson's report that the Israeli Ministry of Information spokesmen were 'wearing huge smiles' much of the subsequent discussion hinged on the fear that Israel would be defeated.

Ivor Jones from Beirut partially confirmed stories that most of Israeli Jerusalem had fallen to the Jordanian Army. Michael Elkins, who might have corrected this, could not be contacted. Jeremy Thorpe insisted with firm jaw that Britain ought not to 'wash our hands and allow a small nation to be exterminated'.

None of the commentators realized the speed of the Israeli victory. Alistair Buchan, Director of the Institute of Strategic Studies, thought it would take two or three days before the result of the air battle would be known. In answer to James Mossman's question, Buchan argued that, if the Israelis lost the air battle disastrously, then they could be swept into the sea. The Mossman/Buchan dialogue ended with a pessimistic exchange. *Mossman:* Since the major powers of the world have armed and sold arms to both sides in this disgusting conflict, are they in a position if they wished to stop it? *Buchan:* They're not in a position to stop it, I don't think, because both sides have a great deal of armaments. It took three to four weeks to stop the India-Pakistan conflict two years ago when the great powers had much greater control over armament. But as you say, having casually armed both sides, the great powers appear to be disassociating themselves from the consequences. It makes me sick.

Everything was rush and flurry on *Panorama*. Robin Day fluffed his introduction, saying that *Izvestia* had sided with Israel instead of Egypt. And Ian Trethowan, who described the feeling at Westminster as one of 'uneasy impotence', prompted at least one gathering of Oxford dons to delighted speculation on the symptoms of '*easy* impotence'.

Christopher Mayhew's interview with Nasser, filmed before the outbreak of hostilities, was notable for two reasons: Nasser's poignant declaration 'we have no intention to attack Israel', and Mayhew's pro-Arab tone.

The charge that Mayhew was too sympathetic to Nasser is difficult to sustain from a careful reading of the transcript. Mayhew at once went on to examine Nasser's declared aim of eliminating Israel, concluding 'aren't you giving the Israelis a choice between either sort of beating you in war, or losing their state altogether? Aren't you, so to speak, goading them into taking action against you?' A question which Nasser could only evade.

It must be admitted, however, that Mayhew's sympathies (or the stern rationality of his position) were exposed in his live confrontation with Jeremy Thorpe later in the same programme:

Thorpe: Could I ask Mr Mayhew one question . . . Would he then stand aside and watch this nation exterminated?

Mayhew: If you mean – would we declare war on the Arab world when Israel is beaten and not declare war on the Arab world when Israel is strong, I see no logic in that at all.

It was in this same discussion that Mayhew branded the Israelis as the aggressors as far as the actual outbreak of war was concerned.

Mayhew's views brought upon him a small shower of protest from a section of the Parliamentary Labour Party. Ted Rowlands, MP for Cardiff North, and 25 other Labour

MPs wrote to the Government Chief Whip complaining about the selection of Mayhew as the Labour representative in a panel discussion. Mayhew, said the protesters, was pro-Arab and his opinions were not those of the Government as expressed by George Brown, the Foreign Secretary.

Instead of consulting Mayhew and calling for a copy of the transcript of the programme, John Silkin, the Chief Whip, passed on the complaint to the BBC. Mayhew responded by releasing to the press a copy of a letter he had sent to Rowlands. Mayhew denied that his statements were at odds with those of the Foreign Secretary, and added: 'But even if my statement had diverged from party policy, your public protest would still be deplorable, giving, as it inevitably does, a strong impression of wishing to stifle one side of the Arab-Israeli argument.'

The lesson of the affair was something in a way much more important than whether Mayhew's brand of neutrality was more hypocritical than George Brown's. (The Foreign Secretary, under pressure in the House of Commons, had made a transparently veiled reference to the special interest in the fate of Israel which honourable members should have credited to the husband of a Jewess.) The wider issue was the freedom of the BBC to select politicians to participate in current affairs programmes. As Mayhew concluded, 'this kind of fuss inevitably influences junior producers in their choice of politicians'.

There is certainly a case for someone influencing junior (and senior) producers in their choice of politicians. It was understandable that, with little film to show, television men had to rely on studio interviews. But what is not so clear is why they relied on the same faces day after day. Mr Rowlands and his colleagues were wrong to complain about Mayhew's views being aired. It would have been more to the point had they complained about their *repeated* appearance to the exclusion of other competent commentators.

The TV personality of the previous week had been the itinerant Mr Eban. He again provided the most rhetorical phrases of the day. 'We are the victims of outrageous aggression. All this with the proclaimed intention of destroying this great and dramatic reality of a resurgent Israel. . . . Our cause is just . . .' etc.

A few hours later, the *24 Hours* team presented a capsule history of Arab/Jewish relations and a survey of the opposing forces. Neville Brown, the Defence Correspondent of the *New Statesman,* ventured the unfortunate opinion that the Israeli claims of successful air-strikes were wildly exaggerated. 'If they have destroyed fifty or sixty [planes] they have done rather well.' On the Home Service at about the same time, Geoffrey Kemp of the Institute for Strategic Studies was making similarly unfortunate predictions: 'it's completely wrong to assume that the Egyptians are going to repeat the *débâcle* of 1956 ...'

Perhaps the most interesting guest was Oleg Orestov, London correspondent of *Pravda.* The Soviet view, which is not normally given space in the mass circulation newspapers, was here cogently expounded to millions of viewers. Orestov slated the British press for ignoring Israel's planned moves against Syria.

Orestov: But what is important in my opinion is that war began about a month ago, when Israel was preparing attack on Syrian Republic.

Michelmore: Earlier tonight I heard President Nasser on *Panorama* saying that it began in 1956 – or even in 1949.
Orestov: Well that is referring . . .

Michelmore: No, no, he put this point you see. And this is precisely what he said. You can't say it began a fortnight ago. You can't say it began in 1956, what you could say is it began in 1949.

Orestov: But I believe that actual war operations began in the beginning of May because that was the time when Israel was really preparing an attack on the Syrian Government and when now some people say well let us stop war today – tomorrow – why did not these people try to prevent this Israel attack on Syria a month ago?

Michelmore: But wouldn't that have been prevented in many ways if the actions of May 17th hadn't happened? If the United Arab Republic had not asked for the withdrawal of United Nations forces, if the United Nations Forces had actually been left in position at the time then you would have had some kind of a cushion, some kind of [buffer?] between one and the other.

Orestov: But Mr Michelmore, you again trying to put, as the whole British press does, you know, to put the United Arab Republic as aggressor as a country which attacks ...
Michelmore: No, I wasn't doing this. I was talking about the United Nations force at this point, that if it had been left there it would have been a buffer between Israel and the United Arab Republic, both ways round, to have stopped ... going anywhere.

Orestov: Oh, it was illegally stationed in Egypt first of all, so the Egyptians had all the right in order to ask for a withdrawal. But now the question is that there was aggression – aggression which began a month ago, and nobody stopped it. Nobody in the West wanted to stop it, look at the British press, it was absolutely silent when Israel was preparing this attack. They began to shout only when United Arab Republic, as defensive measure, mobilized its forces.

The Russian was followed by US Senators Hartke and Macarthy.

Hotfoot from the *Panorama* studio, Christopher Mayhew turned up on *Ten O'Clock* on the Home Service with Quintín Hogg. Mayhew repeated his view that Israel had taken the initiative that morning. Hogg at once was moved to heated expostulation: 'I am bound to say I was filled with a feeling of nausea at Christopher Mayhew's visit to Nasser . . . it's absolutely disgusting that anyone as innocent of Middle East affairs, and as wholly unable to study the objective realities of the case, should go and visit these dictators and give them an opportunity of putting forward their own rather tendentious points of view.'

In some ways, the most informative and best balanced of all BBC programmes on the first day of the war was probably not heard by most British listeners: the World Service's *The World Today*. By far the most penetrating brief analysis of the Egyptian armed forces was given by David Wood of the Institute for Strategic Studies; David Holden of the *Sunday Times* made the best sense of the Arab case, and there was a thoughtful discussion of the diplomatic implications of the day's events.

There were, of course, some defects in the BBC's coverage of that first hectic day. But at least one television critic, John Dodd of the *Sun*, found that learning about the war from the comfort of his armchair was an exhilarating experience.

WHY WE TURN TO THE BBC IN A CRISIS

By John Dodd

... The BBC have hardly ever displayed their resources so well as they did on 'Panorama'....

Occasionally, connexions went wrong and the reporters' voices were lost in the crackle of telephone interference, the sound of propaganda blaring from street microphones, or the cheers of the crowd hailing successes.

Then there was John Bierman from near the battle being constantly cut off by the censor, his voice returning for the odd phrase, then finally falling silent.

It was riveting, dramatic, and historic.

But we did not know which way the war was going, which diametrically-opposed claim to believe.

Then, in the news, came an unconfirmed report from an American-voiced Michael Elkins in Jerusalem – the BBC newsreader emphasized the word 'unconfirmed'. It was very un-BBC-like.

'Less than 15 hours after fighting began Israel has already won the war,' he said.

'Egypt is no more a fighting factor . . . It's the most instant victory the modern world has seen.'

I remained unconvinced. Normally, a BBC man would have said 'claimed' half a dozen times and added many words of caution.

That's why, when it is a thing like a war, we tend to turn to them. But true, untrue, or partially true, Michael Elkins must have put the newsroom into a fair old tizzy as to whether his report should have been used. ... Apart from the Elkins report, I thought the BBC were scrupulously fair. They almost busted themselves to get interviews with Arab students to balance Barnett Janner, MP, at a Zionist meeting, and photographed Arab ambassadors to level up with a brief interview with Jewish writers.

By and large, it was the sort of night the BBC can be proud of.

Had Mr Dodd been fortunate enough to hear the portion of Elkins' report which the BBC thought fit to suppress, his view might have been different.

The suppressed passage reads: 'Radio Damascus and Radio Cairo monitored here have reported heavy air raids on Tel Aviv. At the moment I broadcast, these reports are not true. Tel Aviv is under an air alert and planes, unidentifiable from the streets, have appeared over the city but there has been no air raid. There is also a report, unconfirmed as yet, that Israeli air-strikes have virtually wiped out the Egyptian Air Force. The Israeli Army is reported to have gone over to the attack and the Israeli people seem to be totally confident, reflecting the mood of their Defence Minister Major-General Moshe Dayan, who broadcast to the armed forces after the Egyptian attack started, saying "They are more numerous than we, but we shall beat them." '

Tuesday June 6

On the second day of war the BBC's correspondents and experts were pondering the outcome. Without committing himself to the belief that the war was already over-, Peter Flinn, the former BBC Middle East correspondent, reflected on a disturbing possibility : if Israel won, what would she do to make use of the breathing space?

'Could she use the interval to develop enough atomic weapons to discount the balance of [Arab] power? ... For with atomic bombs, no matter how small her manpower, Israel could easily destroy half a dozen Arab capitals even though she were obliterated herself. The threat alone might secure an awful stalemate.'

Geoffrey Kemp threw out the same idea, almost casually, on *Ten O'Clock* that same evening:

'I really do feel that the only thing that's going to solve the problem in the immediate future is a direct balance of power between Israel and the Arab states, possibly with nuclear weapons.'

By lunch-time, Michael Elkins was free to substantiate what he had already said the previous evening: that the

Israelis appeared to have achieved major successes, indeed that 'the war has virtually been won'. News of how the air-strikes had been carried out was still hard to get.'I cannot tell you except that the general assumption that I would go on, an assumption based on conversation with people who might very well know, would be that a fair proportion of the Egyptian planes was caught on the ground.'

24 Hours brought Brigadier Young back for a return engagement. 'It looks to me,' concluded the jolly Brigadier, 'as if the pattern of 1956 is being followed with an unhistorical repetitiousness – what an awful word!'

Oddly enough, it was listeners to the BBC's African Service who were given the fullest and frankest admission of how little was really known about the first day's fighting. Swahili speakers were informed that the despatches in the morning newspapers carried many signs of censorship, as did the reports of radio correspondents, which had arrived with considerable censored gaps.

The nearest thing to a lapse from the BBC's normally emasculated objectivity came in the World Service's Asian topical talk by Burnard Selby. After rebuking the Soviet Government for not showing itself willing to scale down its arms shipments to the Arab States, he turned his displeasure towards Nasser :

'President Nasser's announcement that the Suez Canal is to be closed because of British and American help for Israel is the kind of impetuous action which can harm the chance of a genuine settlement. It is based on a complete untruth....'

Wednesday June 7

The World Today first hit the air on the World Service at 5.45 am; but the programme had been recorded the previous day. Later editions of the programme carried a significant revision. Nicholas Carroll of the *Sunday Times* had originally summarized the attitude of the British Press as follows :

'Press comment in Britain has been limited in its impact because the actual battle picture has been so unclear; but the most interesting feature of their newspapers' comments so far has been their concern for the fate of Israel should the combined Arab forces overwhelm her. Most papers, while agreeing with the Government's policy of not taking sides, believe that it would be wrong for Britain to stand aside and see Israel destroyed....'

By the time Wednesday morning's newspapers had been assimilated, this passage was replaced by :

'Press comment in Britain, only a day ago worried about what would happen if the Arabs pushed the Israelis into the sea, is now voicing very different anxieties in the light of Israel's phenomenal successes. The feeling is that Israel should not push her luck too far by demanding too much as a price for shipping rights and thereby risk forfeiting sympathy in the Security Council; it is there that Press attention is now concentrated; getting the cease-fire resolution implemented will be a very much harder problem. As for public opinion, I sense a distinct gratification that Israel, in a numerical sense very much the underdog, has won such unexpected victories; there is also a sense of relief that the likelihood of Big Power military involvement seems to have lessened.'

Although, as Dennis Blakely confirmed from Moscow, not everyone was treating the Israeli victory as an Arab rout, the burden of the day's discussions on the BBC proceeded from that assumption.

On the *The World at One,* Lord Lambton and Jon Kimche vied for the silly prophecy prize. Kimche, claiming information from unique Egyptian sources, asserted that 'Nasser's authority over the armed forces seems to have been largely removed in one form or another'. This reading of the situation prompted Lord Lambton to the fantastic prediction that Nasser might be spirited to Moscow and installed as a Middle East trouble-maker in exile.

The question of the moment was Israel's objectives. From the immediate military point of view, Brigadier Young predicted that the Israeli field commanders might remain deaf for a day or two until various missile bases had been put out of action. Diplomatically, no one envisaged that Israelis and Arabs could sit round the conference table to settle their affairs. Terence Prittie of the *Guardian* (*World Service* 2309 GMT) optimistically announced that Israel 'will not tackle this problem in any mood of vainglorious over-confidence, but in a sober spirit of seeking a worthwhile and lasting peace'. But everyone was groping and guessing.

Thursday June 8

Anticipating all possibilities, the *World Service* produced (but did not use) obituaries of both Nasser and King Hussein. According to Mr George Barrell, the author of both these pieces, Nasser's aims were those 'of a visionary rather than a would-be emperor'.

On *The World at One,* William Hardcastle looked for even more scalps. Speaking to Adrian Porter in Tel Aviv, he inquired :

'Is Eshkol very much in command of events inside Israel?' Porter was not drawn. 'He may be, but I should say that Dayan is the popular hero.'

The analysis of possible peace terms was not much further advanced by the day's pundits.

The evening brought the first worthwhile piece of Israeli war film, the first glimpses of the actual battle-scenes. The films were brief but enough to demonstrate what General Dayan said a few minutes later at his press conference about Nasser being a 'paper tiger'.

24 Hours repeated the film, seen earlier in the news, of U Thant announcing the UAR's acceptance of the cease-fire. The Secretary General was followed by Abba Eban, speaking with his customary fluency. Later the plight of the refugees was analysed with some old film and some rather vague guesses at the extent of the problem.

As if to underline that the crisis was off the boil, the programme closed with a report on the aquanautical experiments of Miss Mary Margaret Revell.

Friday June 9

Is Nasser in or out? That was the question of the day. It was really a non-question for there were very few who doubted that he was still in control. Miles Copeland, probably the frankest commentator of the week, made it clear that 'the National Assembly will do what it is jolly well told to do'. *(24 Hours)*

The *24 Hours* team scored some easy points at King Hussein's expense, rolling some old film of the anti-Nasser Hussein. And then it was Christopher Mayhew again with the policeman's friend, Eldon Griffiths. Griffiths was in a tough and realistic mood : 'If Nasser stays and retains the sort of policies that he has pursued before, then he will remain non-negotiable and it will be very difficult for us to have relations with Cairo at all.'

With the war virtually over, the first reports from Cairo trickled in. Ronald Robson spent much of his time explaining that US pressmen had been confined to their hotel; and that all scripts had to be supplied for vetting several hours before transmission.

⚜ ⚜ ⚜

In the days immediately following the end of the fighting there was further speculation about the significance of Nasser's resignation gesture. Donald Watt (*World Service*, 10 June) argued that Nasser had demonstrated that even in defeat he is 'unshakeably resilient'. On the same day, in a Hausa language broadcast, Peter Niesewand summarized the views of the leading English daily papers. The *Guardian* was not sure that Nasser's resignation was a good thing. It felt that there 'were nastier men than Nasser': they did not specify who they had in mind. *The Times* also had some sympathetic words for him in its 'independent and influential' columns.

Discussion and comment on the Middle East continued to dominate the news bulletins. After the 6 pm news on Saturday June 10, for example, the only item in the newsreel which did not deal with the war was an obituary of Spencer Tracy.

The most interesting news item of the evening was Tom Mangold's report on the Israeli attack on USS *Liberty* – an excellent though inevitably incomplete summary of this strange event.

It was not only the usual news and current affairs programmes which dealt with the Middle East. The first question in *Any Questions?* was 'What are the team's reactions to the resignation of President Nasser?' All four speakers – Lord Robens (and to think he was once shadow Foreign Secretary!), Bernard Levin, Lady Barnett and the Bishop of Chichester – assumed that Nasser was out beyond recall, which gave an added dimension of comicality to their remarks when they were rebroadcast after lunch on Sunday June 11.

For the first time since the war began, breakfast listeners on Monday June 12 heard something other than the Middle East crisis at the beginning of the news. Was it Vietnam? Nigeria? No. The big news was the reorganization of ITV.

In *Panorama,* Richard Kershaw had a censored dispatch from Cairo; but there were no pictures. All one saw was a tape machine revolving. On the Israeli side Mr Robin Day produced an excellent interview with General Dayan but it was not the BBC's own interview. It was an American film shot by Mr Charles Collingwood of the Columbia Broadcasting System.

As he spoke to the American interviewers, General Dayan was relaxed and confident. Hostile observers might have described his demeanour as cocky, perhaps irresponsible. For example, when asked whether there was an absolute necessity for the Arab leaders to discuss terms with the Israelis, he replied:

'No. I should say that they can ignore it. There is no practical pressure on any Arab leader now. That is to say that there is nothing which will not let him go on and in a way ignore us. But then there will be a new map, not of the Middle East, but of Israel. If they don't want to talk to us, to sit down to us [*sic*], then we shall stay where we are, and there will be an absolutely new Israel in the Middle East.'

In the news that followed there were some shots of the fighting in Syria. It was honourably indicated that they were seven days old. In the excitement of having some film, however inadequate, no one noticed John Bierman's clanger. The Israeli troops, we were told, were advancing towards Damascus, along the same road on which Saint Peter (rather than Saint Paul) experienced his revelation and conversion.

The BBC was never able to present much of a case on the Arab side. Arab censors were perhaps most to blame for this (Richard Kershaw in Cairo was unable to leave or to send out film). But even in London, apart from Russian newsmen and private individuals like Musa Mazzawi, the Palestinian lawyer, the Arab case lacked spokesmen. In *Panorama* (June 12), after Dayan's appearance, James Mossman made the pointed admission: 'this has been a pretty Israeli-oriented programme.' Mazzawi was then given an opportunity to seize on some of the weaknesses of the Israeli position :

'... the Arabs are not going to negotiate when their nose is being rubbed in the mud, they're not going to negotiate while General Dayan and people like him say, "Well these million people on the West Bank of Jordan are a nuisance to me, and I want the Gulf of Aqaba and I want Gaza Strip and I want this and that." Why? "Because my aircraft got up a bit early on Monday morning and they struck the Egyptian airfields and they blew them to smithereens and now we can dictate to these people." Well you can only do that for a short time. You can't do it for ever.'

On Saturday June 10, the astringent Mr Kenneth Robinson, in his weekly dose of mildly malicious pleasure at the expense of viewers (*Points of View*), cited complaints that Robin Day was pro-Israeli – and pro-Arab. Robinson also quoted, with pride, John Dodd's eulogy of the BBC's coverage of the first day of the war.

It was a measure of how dramatically the war was over that *24 Hours* on Monday 12 ignored the Middle East. After a week of virtually nothing but the Sinai campaign, Jordan, Syria and Egypt it was back to Miss Sarah Churchill, the Russian Venus probe, Biafra and the new commercial television arrangements.

From defeat, only King Hussein emerged sympathetically on television. His strained face under a dashing beret, then his quiet dignified manner with reporters after the war was over, must have appealed to many Western women if not to his former allies and enemy. *Panorama* (June 26) offered a particularly moving interview. He was bitter, he said, not so much about East or West, as about his own mistakes, 'that were numerous'. Almost in tears, he concluded that aid was needed and would be accepted 'from all our friends – if we still have any, and I believe we do'.

In the week after the war, film from both Egypt and Israel began to arrive. Such had been the impact of the previous week's events that the film when it finally appeared seemed almost antique.

The most disturbing report came in *24 Hours* on Wednesday June 14. It was a 'Stars for Israel Evening' in New York, with an excruciating parade of tasteless jokes, crass speeches and aborted lyrics. The *mot* of the evening was Mayor John Lindsay's 'Israelis stand for the same principles that New York has stood for for 300 years'.

Edgar Lustgarten's weekly *Focus* was taken over by David Holden and James Mossman on June 13. A feature of the programme was a studio discussion with journalists from Israel and Egypt, and Professor Vatikiotis of London University. It was a depressing talk : the principal conclusion being that peace negotiations should not and could not be rushed. Mr Eshed for Israel thought weeks, perhaps months might have to pass. Mr Zagloul from Cairo put things in a longer perspective : one million years.

Ivor Jones in Beirut reported that it was virtually impossible for journalists to get into Damascus.

Focus gave more opportunity than usual for the airing of the Arab case. Talib El Shibib, the Arab League

Representative in London (and former Iraqi Foreign Minister), explained why the Arab world could not accept Britain's professed neutrality :

'The newspapers their broadcastings, their television and all the news media and all the statements which were issued from this capital have been completely biased in favour of Israel and destroyed completely any effect of neutrality or any claim for neutrality.'

⚜ ⚜ ⚜

The excellent reporting of Michael Elkins in Israel was perhaps the outstanding feature of the BBC effort. Elkins is an American Jew, who speaks Hebrew and English with a detectable American accent. He is well known in Israel as the chairman of controversial discussion programmes on current affairs. As we have seen, his reports were not always given credence in London.

For all the limitations on their work, the various BBC teams produced film and voice reports which were used all over the world.

In this brief war, one small event, not revealed until ten days after it occurred, demonstrated how intense had been the emotional involvement of some of the reporters on the ground. On the first day of the war, Israeli officials were quiet about the progress of operations. In the previous week there had been much talk of the danger of Israel being swept into the sea. When a press conference was called on the Wednesday evening, it was, therefore, natural that there should be some apprehension among journalists. It was immediately dispelled. The announcement of the figures of Egyptian planes destroyed prompted the remarkable spectacle of the assembled corps of pressmen applauding.

It was perhaps only a moment of relief and admiration, a moment shared by millions throughout the world, before the enormity of the problem of peace-making was realized.

Looking back on the whole coverage of the war it must be admitted that television was a flop, there was too much talk and too few pictures. Radio failed to make the best use of its gifted reporters, particularly in the case of Mr Michael Elkins.

APPENDIX 2

ISRAEL'S POLITICAL PARTIES, TAKEN FROM THE OFFICIAL GUIDE TO THE KNESSET 1966

Name of Party	*First Knesset Feb. 1949*	*Second Knesset Aug. 1951*	*Third Knesset Aug. 1955*	*Fourth Knesset Aug. 1959*	*Fifth Knesse Aug. 1961*
Mapai (Israel Workers' Party)	46	45	40	47	42
Herut (Freedom Party)	14	8	15	17	17
Progressives { now Liberal Party	5	4	5	6	{ 17
General Zionists { now Liberal Party	7	20	13	8	
United Religious Front (comprising the Hapoel Hamizrachi, Hamizrachi, Agudat Israel and Poalei Agudat Israel)	16	—	—	—	
Hapoel Hamizrachi { (now Religious National Party)	—	8	{ 11	{ 12	12
Hamizrachi { (now Religious National Party)	—	2			
United Religious Front Agudat Israel	—	3	{ 6	3	4
United Religious Front Poalei Agudat Israel	—	2		3	2
Ahdut Ha'avoda—Poalei Zion		{	{ 10	7	8
Mapam (United Workers' Party)	10	15	9	9	9
Communists	4	5	6	3	5
Arab Parties	2	5	5	5	4
Yemenite Union	1	1	—	—	
Sepharadim	4	3	—	—	
Wizo (Women's International Zionist Organization)	1	—	—	—	
Fighters (Lechi—Lohamei Israel)	1	—	—	—	
	120	120	120	120	120

THE COMPOSITION OF THE SIXTH KNESSET

November 1965

Alignment M'Arakh (Mapai and Achdut Ha'avoda)	45
Gahal—Herut-Liberal Bloc	26
National Religious Party	11
Rafi—Israel Labour list	10
Mapam—United Workers' Party	8
Independent Liberals	5
Agudat Israel	4
Arab Lists	4
New Communist List	3
Poalei Agudat Israel	2
Ha'olam Hazeh—New Force	1
Israel Communist Party	1

ELECTION STATISTICS

	Number of registered Electors	*Votes required for one seat*	*Percentage of Voters*
The First Knesset	506,567	3,592	86.8%
The Second Knesset	924,885	5,692	75%
The Third Knesset	1,057,609	6,938	82.8%
The Fourth Knesset	1,218,724	7,800	81.5%
The Fifth Knesset	1,274,280	8,332	81.3%
The Sixth Knesset	1,499,988	9,881	82.98%